T0302191

Theory of Constraints, Lean, and Six Sigma Improvement Methodology

Making the Case for Integration

Theory of Constraints, Lean, and Six Sigma Improvement Methodology

Making the Case for Integration

By
Bob Sproull

Routledge
Taylor & Francis Group

A PRODUCTIVITY PRESS BOOK

First edition published in 2019
by Routledge/Productivity Press
52 Vanderbilt Avenue, 11th Floor New York, NY 10017
2 Park Square, Milton Park, Abingdon, Oxon OX14 4RN, UK

© 2019 by Taylor & Francis Group, LLC
Routledge/Productivity Press is an imprint of Taylor & Francis Group, an Informa business

---

Library of Congress Cataloging-in-Publication Data

Names: Sproull, Robert, author.
Title: Theory of constraints, lean, and six sigma improvement methodology :
making the case for integration / Bob Sproull.
Description: 1 Edition. | New York : Taylor & Francis, [2019] | Includes
bibliographical references and index. |
Identifiers: LCCN 2019005326 (print) | LCCN 2019008965 (ebook) | ISBN
9780429284007 (e-Book) | ISBN 9780367247096 (hardback : alk. paper)
Subjects: LCSH: Theory of constraints (Management) | Lean manufacturing. |
Six sigma (Quality control standard)
Classification: LCC HD69.T46 (ebook) | LCC HD69.T46 S674 2019 (print) | DDC
658.4/013--dc23
LC record available at https://lccn.loc.gov/2019005326

Visit the Taylor & Francis Web site at
http://www.taylorandfrancis.com

As we go through life, the people we meet along the way typically have an impact on our lives. While some people influence our lives more than others, there's usually only several that have a dramatic effect on how we live our lives. Such was the case with my brother Jim, who passed away on February 6, 2019. Jim and I grew up together in a small city in western Pennsylvania on a four-acre lot. Actually, this city, Parker, has been designated as "the smallest city in the entire United States." Back in the "oil boom days," Parker had roughly 50,000 residents, but I've been told that due to poor oil extraction methods and a series of massive fires, Parker now has fewer than 1,000 residents. However, throughout all of its problems, it has maintained its city charter to this day.

Jim and I lost our father in a freak hunting accident back when I was only ten years old. From that day forward, I looked at my brother as a father figure, seeking advice from him at every turn. Jim had a prestigious career in the United States Army, with 21 years of service before retiring as a Major. Jim was a decorated Airborne Ranger with three Bronze Stars, a Purple Heart, and numerous other military awards. Jim loved his country and always went out of his way to do great things for his beloved country.

One of Jim's hobbies was to collect books with author signatures, and he had hundreds of them when he passed away. I dedicate this book to my beloved brother Jim who will be sadly missed by all who knew him.

Bob Sproull

Contents

Preface

For quite a few years, I have been involved in improvement initiatives in a wide variety of different industry sectors. Back in the day when I started my improvement journey, I truly believed I had all of the tools in my improvement backpack that I needed in order to make significant improvements to processes and systems. After all, I had become somewhat of an expert in improvement efforts using approaches like Total Quality Management, Total Preventive Maintenance, Statistical Process Control, Failure Mode and Effects Analysis, Design of Experiments, and the list goes on and on. And by using the tools from my backpack, I was able to make considerable improvements to many different kinds of processes in a wide array of industry segments. I was living the proverbial dream, so to speak.

As I continued learning, I began to realize that some of the things I had taken as being gospel were in fact, pretty much bogus! I realized that maximizing the efficiency and utilization of each process step did not result in optimization of the total system at all. In fact, I learned that maximizing the efficiency of all operations only served to create mountains of needless Work-in-Process inventory. I learned that inventory was not an asset at all because it actually had a carrying cost associated with it. But more importantly, excess inventory increased the effective cycle time of the process which decreased an organization's ability to ship product on time. I also learned that inventory tends to hide other problems.

I learned that cutting the cost of each individual operation did not result in the system cost being minimized. In fact, many times in an attempt to minimize the cost of individual operations, companies made drastic cuts in operating expense and labor that were too deep, causing motivational, quality, and delivery problems! I also learned that in every organization there are only a few (and most of the time only one) operations that control the rate of revenue generation and subsequent profits. All processes are comprised of constraining and non-constraining resources, so the key improvement consideration must always be to pinpoint and focus improvements on the operation that is constraining throughput. Attempts to improve non-constraining resources generally result in very little improvement at all from a system perspective.

I continued learning and discovered that variability is clearly the root of all evil in a manufacturing process. Variability in things like product characteristics or variability in process parameters or variability in processing times all degrade the performance of a process, an organization, and ultimately, the total company. Variability negatively impacts things like a company's ability to effectively plan and execute its scheduled production plan. It also increases operational expense and decreases the chances of producing and delivering product to customers when they want them, and at the cost they are willing to pay. Because variability is so devastating, every effort must be made to reduce it and then control it. Six Sigma is the backbone of this part of the improvement effort.

I also discovered that excessive waste exists in every process and unless and until it is identified and removed, real process improvement will not happen. But having said this, companies should not attack waste in every area within their systems. The fact is, the focal point for waste reduction activities should be on that part of the system that is constraining throughput. While there are many forms of waste, the most obvious and perhaps the two most debilitating types are the waste associated with waiting and over-producing. Waiting and overproduction both work to lengthen the overall cycle time. Just like Six Sigma is at the heart of variation reduction and control, Lean is at the heart of waste reduction.

Another important learning point is that how people and organizations are measured will significantly affect their behaviors. For example, if a company measures operator efficiency and values high efficiency in every step in the operation, then predictably the organization can have very high levels of work-in-process inventory, low levels of quality, and a high incidence of late or missed shipments. As a corollary to this, maximizing the efficiency of an operation that is limiting throughput is mandatory for maximizing on-time deliveries, revenue, and profits!

Another conclusion I reached is that many companies don't have a clue as to where to focus and leverage their improvement efforts. While many companies have embraced both Lean or Six Sigma or a combination of the two, in doing so they have essentially attempted to solve world hunger by struggling to improve every operation. When this occurs, the improvement efforts become prolonged and many times end in frustration. Don't misunderstand, I am a huge proponent of both Lean and Six Sigma, but they are only one-third of the improvement pie.

My final thought is that organizations that fail to involve their workforce, typically do not succeed in the long run. Everyone within a company must know the goals of the company and how its individual and collective performance might be impacting these goals. After all of these years, it is apparent to me that the shop floor workers have a vast array of information and ideas, both of which must be sought out, implemented, and harvested.

Unfortunately, many of the companies in the business world of today, don't practice what I learned throughout my years. Many companies still use unproductive performance metrics and outdated accounting systems. Many companies don't understand, recognize, and capitalize on the constraining operation that exists within their systems. Add to this, many companies still don't appreciate that waste and variability encumber their processes and that active involvement of the general workforce is required if they are to successfully identify and reduce it.

During my earlier years, I had held positions in Healthcare, Manufacturing, Maintenance, Quality, Engineering, and others, and in every position, I was able to take the existing processes and make what I thought were significant improvements to practically all of them. Back then, I truly believed that the sum total of individual process improvements would translate into improvement to the system I was working in. As time progressed, I continued my learning and eventually became a Six Sigma Black Belt and then a Lean Sensei, and my improvement effort results kept getting better and better. I was on top of the world back then, but then a personal epiphany happened for me.

One day, one of my old bosses called me and asked me to come work for him at his new venture where he had assumed the role of the new CEO of a manufacturing company. When I asked him what my role would be, he simply told me that he had a manufacturing plant in Kentucky that he wanted me to manage. I was very excited because I had never been in a position where I was the "top dog" in a manufacturing facility. I had worked for other general managers in different manufacturing companies, but never had I had full responsibility for the facility's success. I immediately said yes to his request and agreed to meet him at this new location.

When I arrived at this new company, we had a closed-door meeting discussing things like this company's product line, its customer and supplier base, and its sorted history. Things seemed to be going well until I asked him if he had a specific way that he wanted me to manage the facility. He simply smiled, looked me in the eye and told me that all he wanted me to do was to shut the place down! I was shocked, to say the least, and at first, I thought he was joking. But to my disappointment and displeasure, he was dead serious about closing the doors of this manufacturing plant.

When I asked him why he wanted to close this facility, he just smiled again and told me that it was losing way too much money to keep it open.

I immediately pushed back on him and told him that if he wanted me to stay at his company, then he would have to give me a chance to turn this facility around and make it profitable, rather than closing it down. He just laughed and told me that they had already put the company's best plant manager in charge of this plant and that he was unable to make a difference, so he doubted that I could make change happen for the better. Because I insisted on trying to turn the plant around, he reluctantly agreed to let me at least make an effort, with one caveat. This facility had to be profitable after only three months and if it wasn't, then I had no choice but to close the doors. In Chapter 7, I will present a case study of what was done and what the ultimate outcome ended up being for this manufacturing plant.

As time passed, I felt like there was some kind of missing link in my arsenal of improvement tools, and then it happened. Eventually, in addition to my basic Lean and Six Sigma training, I studied hard and eventually became a Lean Six Sigma Master Black Belt. But then the epiphany happened when I learned about the Theory of Constraints (TOC). I studied hard and eventually became what is referred to as a TOC Jonah. I had discovered what this missing link was and that something was TOC. Once I learned the details of TOC, my ability to make fast, major improvements jettisoned upward to levels I had not experienced before. I must say that I was shocked in that I couldn't imagine why I had not come across this missing link before. And as the title of this book suggests, the Theory of Constraints played a pivotal role in how I approach improvement. As you will see, an integrated TOC, Lean, and Six Sigma is the common denominator in all of my case studies presented in this book.

Prior to learning about the Theory of Constraints, it was not uncommon for me to focus on individual parts of processes and improve them. I assumed that the sum total of these isolated improvements would result in system-wide improvements. After all, when you improve any part of a process, the system automatically improves. Right? But as I discovered, after learning about the Theory of Constraints, my assumptions were clearly erroneous! The sum total of improvements to isolated parts of a system does not translate into system-wide improvement. This fact dramatically changed my entire approach to improvement. The fact is, the only way the system will be improved is by focusing your improvement efforts on that part of the system that is limiting it!

Years later, the same CEO who wanted me to close the plant in Kentucky, called me and asked me to join him at another manufacturing company which produced truck bodies. This time, my role was to be in charge of the continuous improvement effort. Needless to say, I accepted his offer, but soon after I arrived, he fired the VP of Engineering and asked me to absorb Engineering into my span of control. I reluctantly agreed, and to my dismay, I found the Engineering group was in serious trouble. In trouble because of the length of time in which they completed their engineering work so as to be able to bid on new jobs. And to make matters worse, the morale in Engineering was in the tank. In one of the later chapters, I will present what happened at this facility in a case study format.

For those of you who have not yet had the opportunity to learn about TOC, I will open this book with a chapter on what it is and why it will work so well in your own improvement efforts. In addition, I will explain in detail, the method I use to teach newcomers what TOC is and what it will do for any company. TOC is clearly the "missing link" in most improvement initiatives.

In the second chapter, I will lay out the important points related to Lean Manufacturing and demonstrate how to identify and remove waste to make value flow. In Chapter 3, I will introduce the reader to Six Sigma and present key points related to variability and the significant impact it has on systems. In Chapter 4, I will demonstrate how I have effectively merged the Theory of Constraints with Lean and Six Sigma to achieve maximum improvement to your company's profitability. As you will see, while TOC works well in isolation, its full power is not realized until it is combined with Lean and Six Sigma. The same is true for Lean and Six Sigma in that their full value is not achieved until they are combined with the Theory of Constraints.

From that point forward, I will present various case studies where I have used this integrated improvement methodology, which I refer to as The Ultimate Improvement Cycle [1]. The case studies will clearly demonstrate how this methodology applies to seemingly every industry type. In one of the case studies, I will explain how it works in a manufacturing environment, while in another case study, I will demonstrate how well this same methodology works in a maintenance, repair, and overhaul facility. And in yet another case study, I will demonstrate how it also applies to a healthcare environment.

In the final chapter in this book, I will present something referred to as a *mafia offer*, which is an offer to potential and existing customers that is so good, they couldn't possibly refuse it. Closely related to this mafia offer is something referred to as a *viable vision*, which if used correctly will take your future profits to the level of sales that you have today.

The Ultimate Improvement Cycle [1] has served me well throughout my years in continuous improvement consulting, as well as my time spent in roles as a General Manager of a manufacturing facility and as a VP of Engineering. I consider myself very "lucky" to have come across the Theory of Constraints as the "missing link" throughout my improvement journey. But as I always say in my books, I wish you much luck in your improvement journey. But my definition of luck is Laboring Under Correct Knowledge ... you make your own LUCK!

REFERENCE

1. Bob Sproull, *The Ultimate Improvement Cycle – Maximizing Profits Through the Integration of Lean, Six Sigma and the Theory of Constraints*, CRC Press, Taylor and Francis Group, Boca Raton, FL, 2009.

About the Author

**Bob Sproull** is an Independent Consultant and the owner of Focus and Leverage Consulting. Bob is a certified Lean Six Sigma Master Black Belt and a Theory of Constraints Jonah. Bob has served as a Vice President of Quality, Engineering, and Continuous Improvement for two different manufacturing companies, was General Manager for a manufacturing company, has an extensive consulting background in Healthcare, Manufacturing, and Maintenance, Repair, and Overhaul (MRO), and focuses on teaching companies how to maximize their profitability through an integrated Lean, Six Sigma, and Constraints Management improvement methodology. Bob is an internationally known speaker and author of numerous white papers and articles on continuous improvement. Bob's background also includes 9 years with the Presbyterian University Hospital complex in Pittsburgh, Pennsylvania, where he ran the Biochemistry Department at Children's Hospital, performed extensive research in breakthrough testing methods and assisted with the development of organ transplant procedures. Bob completed his undergraduate work at the University of Pittsburgh and University of Rochester with a dual Math/Physics major. A results-driven Performance Improvement Professional with a diverse healthcare, manufacturing, MRO and technical background, he has significant experience appraising under-performing companies, developing and executing highly successful improvement strategies based upon the integration of Lean, Six Sigma, and Constraints Management methodology. Bob is the author of four books, including, *The Focus and Leverage Improvement Book,* CRC Press, Taylor and Francis, 2018; *The Problem-Solving, Problem-Prevention, and Decision-Making Guide - Organized and Systematic Roadmaps for Managers,* CRC Press, Taylor and Francis, 2018; *The Ultimate Improvement Cycle: Maximizing Profits Through the Integration of Lean, Six Sigma and the Theory of Constraints,* Productivity Press, 2009; and *Process Problem-Solving: A Guide for Maintenance and Operation's Teams,* Productivity Press, 2001; and co-author of *Epiphanized: Intergrading Theory of*

Constraints, Lean and Six Sigma, North River Press, 2012; *Epiphanized: A Novel on Unifying Theory of Constraints, Lean and Six Sigma, 2nd Edition,* and *Focus and Leverage: The Critical Methodology for Theory of Constraints, Lean, and Six Sigma (TLS).*

Degrees, Certifications, and Memberships:

- Bachelor of Science Equivalent in Math and Physics, University of Rochester
- Certified Lean Six Sigma Master Black Belt, Kent State University
- Certified Six Sigma Black Belt, Sigma Breakthrough Technologies, Inc.
- TOCICO Strategic Thinking Process Program Certificate
- TOC Thinking Processes (Jonah Course) L-3 Communications
- Critical Chain Expert Certificate, Realization Technologies
- Lean MRO Operations Certificate, University of Tennessee

Bob resides in Prattville, Alabama.

1

What Is This Thing Called the Theory of Constraints?

In the 1980s, Dr. Eliyahu M. Goldratt and Jeff Cox introduced us to their Theory of Constraints (TOC) improvement methodology through their highly successful and widely read business novel, *The Goal* [1]. Goldratt and Cox explained to us that systems are comprised of interdependent processes and functions which they equated to a chain. They explained that every chain has a weakest link, and in order to strengthen the total chain, you must first identify this weakest link and then focus your improvements on it until it is "broken." And when it does break, a new constraint will appear immediately. They further explained that any attempts to strengthen the other links in the chain will not result in a stronger chain because it will still break at the weakest link.

Goldratt and Cox analogized the concept of a chain to organizations and explained that failing to identify and strengthen the organization's weakest link, or system constraint, will not strengthen the global system. Similarly, attempts to improve non-constraint operations will not necessarily translate into significant organizational improvement resulting in profitability improvement. It's kind of like a professional baseball team signing free-agent sluggers when the real constraint is relief or starting pitching. They can score lots of runs, but in the end, if they can't hold the other team to fewer runs than they score, they'll never win a pennant.

According to Dettmer [2] and Goldratt and Cox [1], the Theory of Constraints is based upon the fact that there is a common cause for many effects we observe at the systemic or organizational level. TOC envisions a company as a system, or a set of interdependent relationships, with each relationship being dependent on others in some way. The global system performance is dependent upon the combined efforts of all of the relationships within the organization. In addition, there are disruptions and statistical fluctuations (i.e. variability) that interfere with the production and delivery of products to the next process step that ultimately impact delivery to the customer. It's important to understand that every for-profit organization has the same two goals, to make money *now* and to make money in the *future*. Therefore, every action or decision taken by an organization should be judged by its impact on "the organization's goals." This, of course, implies that before we can do this, we must first define the goal and, second, determine how we are going to measure or judge our decisions and actions.

While Goldratt and Cox used a chain analogy to define what a constraint is, I use a different approach when explaining TOC to people who aren't familiar with what it is. As I present this different approach, remember that the Theory of Constraints is a methodology for identifying the most important limiting factor (i.e. constraint) that stands in the way of achieving your goals and then systematically improving that constraint until it is no longer the limiting factor. So, let's look at a different way of describing TOC.

THE CONCEPT OF THE SYSTEM CONSTRAINT

Figure 1.1 is a simple piping system used to transport water. Water enters into Section A of this piping system, then flows into Section B and continues downward through all of the pipes until it collects in the receptacle at the base of the system. In this piping system, water flows via gravity, meaning that if you wanted more water, you could not increase the pressure to get more. In every system, there is a point that limits throughput and this piping system is no different. Think for a minute what you would have to do to achieve an increase in the flow of water through this system? Because Section E's diameter is the smallest, does it make sense to you that if you wanted to increase the flow of water through this system, the only way you could achieve this would be to increase the diameter of this limiting point? In other words, Section E is limiting the flow of water (i.e. throughput) through this piping system and because of this, it is designated as the system constraint (aka the bottleneck). Now ask yourself what would determine how much larger Section E's diameter must be? The answer to this basic question is that it depends upon how

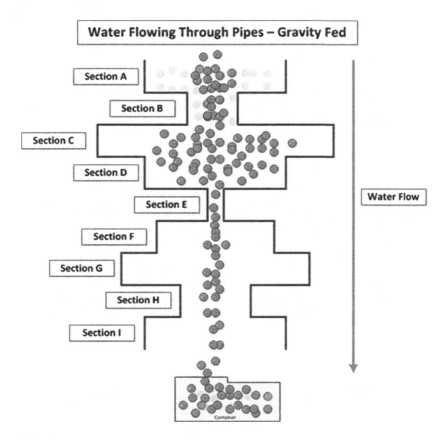

FIGURE 1.1
Piping system used to transport water.

much more water is needed. In other words, it's dependent upon the new demand requirement.

In Figure 1.2, we have now opened-up Section E's diameter and as you can see, more water is now flowing through the system. When Section E's diameter was increased, three distinct changes took place. First, the system constraint moved from Section E to Section B because it is now the smallest diameter pipe. Second, the throughput of water increased to the limit of the new constraint (Section B), and finally, water has now begun to accumulate in front of Section B.

Ask yourself, "Would increasing the diameter of any other section have resulted in any more throughput of water?" The answer is a resounding no! Only increasing the diameter of Section E would have resulted in more water flowing through this system. The inevitable conclusion is that the system constraint controls the system throughput and focusing

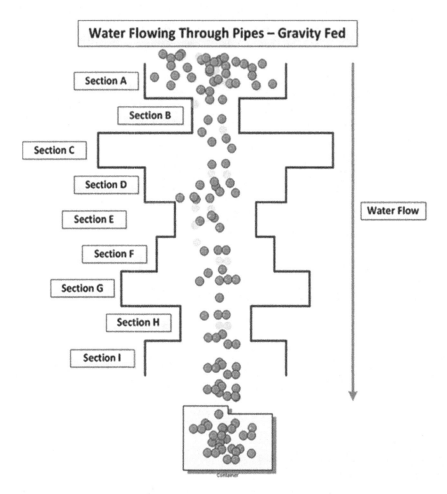

FIGURE 1.2
Piping system with Section E enlarged.

improvement efforts anywhere else is typically wasted effort. Let's now look at how this might apply to a simple manufacturing process.

Figure 1.3 is a simple four-step diagram of a manufacturing process used to produce some kind of product. Based upon what you have learned from seeing the piping system, ask yourself which step is limiting the production of this product through this process and why it is the limiting process step. Let's look at some different scenarios to help answer this question in more depth.

The first question we should ask is, based upon the processing times of each step, how long does it take to process a single part through this process? For the first part of this process, the processing time for one

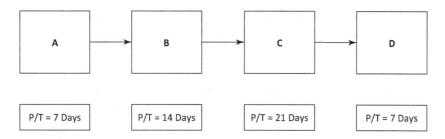

FIGURE 1.3
Basic four-step process.

part would be the sum total of each of the individual processing times as follows:

$$7 \, \text{Days} + 14 \, \text{Days} + 21 \, \text{Days} + 7 \, \text{Days} = 49 \, \text{Days}$$

The next question to answer is, once the production line is full, what is the output rate of this simple process? The answer to this question is that because Step C, at 21 days, limits the output rate, then the rate of this process, as it currently exists, is one part every 21 days. Figure 1.4 summarizes this process with the constraint highlighted. Let's now look at some additional scenarios that will have an impact on this manufacturing process.

Suppose that Step A has problems and goes down for 7 days, what would happen to the output rate of this process? The simple answer is, nothing changes because it only takes 7 days to complete, so there are still 7 days of buffer time left over to supply Step B. Now suppose Step B goes down for 7 days. Again, nothing changes, because it only takes 14 days to complete, so it should still be able to supply Step C in time before it is starved. Finally, if Step D goes down for 7 days, throughput remains the same because it has a time buffer of 14 days due to Step C's extended processing time.

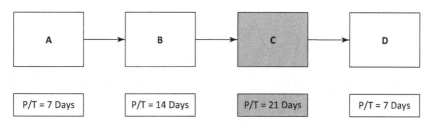

FIGURE 1.4
Basic four-step process with constraint highlighted.

Unfortunately, if Step C goes down for 7 days, you will have lost 7 days of throughput that is lost forever! Now let's look at how to increase the throughput of this process.

If you are able to reduce the processing time on Step A from 7 days to 4 days, what would happen to the output of the process? The simple fact is that if you reduce the processing time on Step A from 7 days to 4 days, throughput remains the same because of Step C's longer processing time. Likewise, if you reduce the processing time on Step B from 14 days to 7 days, what happens to the output of this process? If you reduce the processing time on Step B from 14 days to 7 days, no throughput improvement will occur, again because of Step C's longer processing time. If you reduce the processing time on Step D from 7 days to 4 days, what happens to the output of the process?

Just like the other examples, if you reduce the processing time on Step D from 7 days to 4 days, not much happens, again because of Step C's longer processing time. So, based on all of this, what is the only way to increase the throughput of this process? The simple answer to this question is that if you want to increase the throughput of this process, you must focus all improvements on the constraint operation and reduce its processing time!

For example, what happens to the throughput of this process if you reduce the processing time in the constraint from 21 days to 18 days as in Figure 1.5? The immediate effect of this time reduction is that you improve the throughput of the process from one part every 21 Days to one part every 18 Days, or a 17-percent increase! Because of the impact of your constraining step on the output, doesn't it make sense to focus most of your improvement efforts on the constraint? Exceptions to this would be if there are quality issues causing scrap or excessive rework with Step D or prolonged delays within Step B. This, of course, assumes that the demand for your product is high enough to be able to sell the additional product.

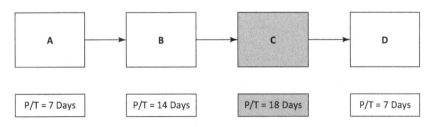

FIGURE 1.5
Basic four-step process with constraint time reduced.

The next, most obvious question you might ask is, how do you reduce the processing time in the constraint? The answer to this question is the essence of this book. By reducing waste (through Lean tools and techniques) and variation (through Six Sigma tools and techniques), focusing primarily on the system constraint. In other words, by doing things like off-loading work from the constraint to non-constraints, or by eliminating scrap or rework conditions in the constraint and non-constraint process steps after the constraint. The key factor to remember is that if you want to maximize the output of your manufacturing process, you should never allow the constraining operation to sit idle because every minute lost on your constraining operation is lost forever! In Chapter 5, we will look at a better way of measuring success.

PROBLEM-SOLVING AND THE THEORY OF CONSTRAINTS

In recent years, there has been much written about TOC and how it can be used to solve systemic problems. And although it is not my intention to go into a detailed clarification of this side of the Theory of Constraints, it certainly deserves some level of discussion, simply because of its usefulness as related to complex systems type problems.

The Theory of Constraints is a management philosophy developed by Dr. Eliyahu Goldratt and Jeff Cox, and made famous in their blockbuster business novel, *The Goal* [1]. In Goldratt's sequel to *The Goal*, *It's Not Luck*, he introduces problem-solving methodologies referred to as The Thinking Process Tools (TP). According to Goldratt, the most important tool, in terms of problem identification, is referred to as the Current Reality Tree (CRT).

While it's relatively easy to identify or locate physical constraints, constraints related to systems and policies can be somewhat difficult or maybe even frustrating. It's difficult because there are three things that conspire to work against breaking it. First of all, most people have trouble identifying and finding exactly what policy might be the root cause of a system constraint. Second, many times policy constraints are located outside your own area of responsibility, or span of control, and many times require someone else to change the existing policy. It's probably normal for this last reason simply because nobody likes to admit that something they are doing is the cause of poor system performance. Because of this, the person responsible for changing an existing policy seems to be in denial and therefore requires some form of proof as to the need to change the constraining policy. The final barrier is normal human resistance to change. Changing the status quo can be difficult, unless there is a strong and compelling argument made where the conclusion is obvious.

It's clear that the Theory of Constraints is systemic in nature and strives to identify those few constraints that limit the organization's success in terms of moving in the direction of its goal. It's important to understand that organizations function as systems, rather than as a collection of individual process steps. Goldratt introduced the world to his five focusing steps which we will discuss in more detail later:

1. Identify the system constraint.
2. Decide how to exploit the system constraint.
3. Subordinate everything else to the system constraint.
4. If necessary, elevate the system constraint.
5. When the constraint is broken, return to Step 1, but don't let inertia become a new system constraint.

Goldratt then teaches us that good managers must answer three vital questions in order to be successful:

1. What to change?
2. To what to change to?
3. How to make the change happen?

As part of the logical thinking process, Goldratt introduced a set of tools used to identify the root causes of negative symptoms, or Undesirable Effects (UDEs), that exist within all organizations. Goldratt believed that there are commonly only a few core problems that create most of the UDEs within a system, and if we can identify these core problems (i.e. What to change?), find their root causes, and then eliminate them, most of the UDEs will disappear. Let's talk a bit more about UDEs and how we can identify and understand them by looking at something called a Current Reality Tree (CRT). While you would think that we should now discuss CRTs, I want to take a different direction before we discuss this tool.

INTERMEDIATE OBJECTIVES MAP

Bill Dettmer, in his classic book, *The Logical Thinking Process – A Systems Approach to Complex Problem Solving* [2] has changed my entire approach to TOC's Logical Thinking Process (LTP). TOC's LTP has always begun by constructing a CRT, but for me, Dettmer changed the game. He begins by constructing something referred to as an Intermediate Objectives Map (IO Map). Dettmer's definition of an IO Map is, "A graphical representation of a system's goal, critical success factors (CSFs), and necessary conditions (NC) for achieving them" [2]. Dettmer further explains that "these elements are arrayed in a logically connected hierarchy, with the goal at the top, the CSFs immediately below it, and the supporting NCs below them." "Each of the entities in the IO Map exists in a necessity-based relationship with the entities below it." Necessity-based relationships use the syntax, "In order to have 'x,' I must have 'y.'" Dettmer explains, "The CSFs could be considered major milestones, or terminal outcomes, on the journey to the goal. NCs represent the conclusion of significant activities required to complete the CSFs."

So, what's the purpose of the IO Map? The IO Map's intention is to establish a firm baseline in terms of space and time, the system's goal, critical success factors, and necessary conditions, in order to achieve system success. In other words, it represents the system's benchmark for desired performance. Or as Dettmer explains, "Before you decide how well you are doing, you must have a clear understanding of what you should be doing."

Dettmer lists seven assumptions related to the IO Map as follows [2]:

1. All systems have a goal and critical success factors that must be satisfied if the goal is to be achieved.
2. The goal and CSFs exist in an interdependent, hierarchical structure.
3. The goal will be unique to each system.
4. Critical success factors and their relationships will be unique to each system and the environment in which the system functions or competes.
5. CSFs and NCs are related to each other in a necessity-based configuration that reflects the rule set governing the system's competitive/functional environment.

6. The Goal, CSFs, and NCs can be determined by people within or outside of a system.
7. A robust IO Map will present an accurate picture of a system's goal, CSFs, and supporting NCs.

I think the simplest way to describe how to construct an IO Map is to present an actual example of one being constructed. Incidentally, Dettmer later changed the name of the IO Map to a Goal Tree, so I will interchange both names going further.

IO MAP/GOAL TREE

Many people who have gone through training on the Theory of Constraint's LTP tools have come away from the training somewhat overwhelmed and somewhat speechless to a degree. Some "get it," and some just don't. Let's face it, the LTP tools are pretty intimidating, and after receiving the training, I have seen many people simply walk away feeling like they were ill-prepared to apply whatever it is they had supposedly just learned. Even for myself, when I completed my first iteration of this training, I had this same feeling. And in talking with others, there was a general confusion about how to get started. For the average person, the LTP tools are just not easy to grasp, so they end up kind of putting them on the back burner rather than taking a chance on making a mistake using them.

The other complaint I have heard many times is that a full LTP analysis typically takes many days to complete, and let's face it, an executive team typically doesn't have that kind of time to spend on this activity, or at least they feel like they don't. Well, for everyone who feels the same way, or maybe have gone through the same Jonah training as I did and feels somewhat hopeless or confused, I have hope for you. That hope for you is the IO Map or Goal Tree. As I explained, Bill Dettmer originally referred to this tool as an Intermediate Objectives Map (IO Map) but has elected to change its name in recent years [2].

Before going any further, I want to make sure everyone understands that I am a huge proponent of TOC's Logical Thinking Processes! But having said that, I am an even bigger fan of the IO Map/Goal Tree. Why? Because most people grasp what the Goal Tree will do for them and how simple it is to learn and apply. Many of the people I have trained on the Goal Tree have emailed me telling me they wished they had learned this tool many years ago. They learn it and apply it right away!

Bill Dettmer tells us of his first exposure to IO Maps was back in 1995 during a management skills workshop conducted by another TOC guru named Oded Cohen at the Goldratt Institute [2]. In recent years, Dettmer has written much about the IO Map, now referred to as a Goal Tree and now uses it as the first step in a full Thinking Process analysis. Bill is passionate about this tool and believes that it defines the standard for goal attainment and its prerequisites in a much more simple and efficient way. I happen to agree with Bill and believe that the Goal Tree is a great focusing tool to better demonstrate why an organization is not meeting its goal. And because of its simplicity, it is easy not only learn, but it's also much easier to teach others in your organization how to use it rather than the full LTP analysis.

There are other advantages of learning and using the Goal Tree, including a better integration of the rest of the LTP tools that will accelerate the completion of Current Reality Trees, Conflict Resolution Diagrams, and Future Reality Trees if you choose to use them. But what I really like about the Goal Tree is that they can be used as stand-alone tools resulting in a much faster analysis of the organization's weak points, and then a rapid development of an improvement plan for your organization. I have been teaching the Goal Tree for quite a few years, and I state unequivocally that the Goal Tree has been the favorite of most of my classes and workshops.

One of the lessons I always encourage my students to do is that they should always learn a new tool and then make it their own. That message simply means that even though the "inventor" of a tool typically has a specific use in mind, tools should be continually evolving, and such was the case for me with the Goal Tree for me. Personally, I have attempted to transform this tool into one that most people grasp and understand in very short order, and then see its usefulness in a matter of minutes or hours, rather than days.

When using any of TOC's LTP tools, there are two distinctly different types of logic at play, *sufficiency-* and *necessity-based*. Sufficiency-based logic tools use a series of if-then statements that connect cause-and-effect relationships between most of the system's UDEs. Necessity-based logic uses the syntax, in order to have x, I must have y or multiple ys. The Goal Tree falls into the category of necessity-based logic and can be used to develop and lay out your company's strategic and tactical actions that result in successful improvement efforts.

As mentioned earlier, the Goal Tree dates back to at least 1995 when it was casually mentioned during a Management Skills Workshop conducted by Oded Cohen at the A.Y. Goldratt Institute. It was not part of that workshop nor did it ever find its way into common usage as part of LTP. It was described as a kind of Prerequisite Tree without any obstacles.

Dettmer tells us that he never thought much about it for the next 7 years, until in late 2002, when he began grappling with the use of LTP for developing and deploying strategy. At that time, Dettmer had been teaching the LTP to a wide variety of clients for more than 6 years and had been dismayed by the number of students who had substantial difficulty constructing CRTs and Conflict Resolution Diagrams (CRDs) of sufficient quality. According to Dettmer, they always seemed to take a very long time to build a CRT, and their CRDs were not always what he would characterize as "robust." He claimed they lacked reference to a "should-be" view of the system—what ought to be happening. It occurred to Dettmer that the Goal Tree he'd seen in 1995 could be modified and applied to improve the initial quality of CRTs. As time went on, Dettmer began to realize that the Goal Tree could serve a similar purpose with CRDs. In 2007, Dettmer published his wonderful book, *The Logical Thinking Process: A Systems Approach to Complex Problem Solving* that introduced the world to this wonderful tool, and I highly recommend this book [2].

Dettmer tells us that one of the first things we need to do is determine the *system boundaries* that we are trying to improve as well as *our span of control and sphere of influence.* Our span of control means that we have unilateral change authority, while our sphere of influence means that at best, we can only influence change decisions. Dettmer explains that if we don't define our boundaries of the system, we risk "wandering in the wilderness for forty years."

The hierarchical structure of the Goal Tree consists of a single Goal and several entities referred to as Critical Success Factors (CSFs). CSFs must be in place and functioning if we are ever going to achieve our stated goal. The final piece of the Goal Tree are entities referred to as Necessary Conditions (NCs) which must be completed to realize each of the CSFs. The Goal and CSFs are worded terminal outcomes as though they were already in place while the NCs are stated more as activities that must be completed.

Figure 1.6 is a graphic representation of the structure of the Goal Tree with each structural level identified accordingly. The Goal, which is defined by the owners of the organization, sits at the top of the Goal Tree

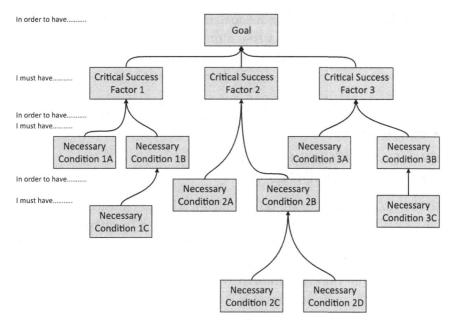

In order to have...........

I must have...........

In order to have...........
I must have...........

In order to have...........

I must have...........

FIGURE 1.6
Goal Tree/IO Map structure.

with three to five Critical Success Factors directly beneath it. The CSFs are those critical entities that must be in place if the Goal is to be achieved. For example, if your Goal was to create a fire, then the three CSFs which must be in place are (1) a combustible fuel source, (2) a spark to ignite the combustible fuel source, and (3) air with a sufficient level of oxygen. If you were to remove any of these CSFs, there would not be a fire. So, let's look at each of these components in a bit more detail.

THE GOAL

Steven Covey suggests that to identify our goal we should, "Begin with the end in mind," or where we want to be when we've completed our improvement efforts, which is the ultimate purpose of the Goal. A Goal is an end to which a system's collective efforts are directed. It's actually a sort of destination, which implies a journey from where we are to where we want to be.

Dettmer also makes it very clear that the system's owner determines what the goal of the system should be. If your company is privately owned, maybe the owner is a single individual. If there's a board of directors, they have a chairman of the board who is ultimately responsible for establishing the goal. Regardless of whether the owner is a single person or a collective group, the system's owner(s) ultimately establishes the goal of the system.

CRITICAL SUCCESS FACTORS AND NECESSARY CONDITIONS

In the Goal Tree, there are certain high-level requirements which must be solidly in place and if these requirements aren't achieved, then we simply will never realize our goal. These requirements are referred to as Critical Success Factors (CSFs) and Necessary Conditions (NCs). Dettmer recommends no more than three to five CSFs should be identified [2]. Each of the CSFs has some number of NCs that are considered prerequisites to each of the CSFs being achieved. Dettmer recommends no more than two to three levels of NCs, but in my experience, I have seen as many as five levels working well. While the Goal and the CSFs are written primarily as terminal outcomes that are already in place, the NCs are worded more as detailed actions that must be completed to accomplish each of the CSFs and upper-level NCs.

The relationship among the Goal, CSFs, and the supporting NCs in this cascading structure of requirements, represents what must be happening if we are to reach our ultimate destination. For ease of understanding, when I am in the process of constructing my Goal Trees, the connecting arrows are facing downward to demonstrate the natural flow of ideas. But when my structure is completed, I reverse the direction of the arrows to reveal the flow of results. In keeping with the thought of learning a tool and making it my own, I have found this works well for training purposes, even though this is the complete opposite of Dettmer's recommendations for construction of a Goal Tree.

As we proceed, it's important to understand that the real value of a Goal Tree is its capability to keep the analysis focused on what's really important to system success. Dettmer [2] tells us that a "Goal Tree will be unique to that system and the environment in which it operates." This is an extremely important concept because "one size does not fit all." Dettmer explains that even two manufacturing companies, producing the same kind of part, will probably have very dissimilar Goal Trees.

CONSTRUCTING A GOAL TREE/
INTERMEDIATE OBJECTIVES MAP

A Goal Tree could very quickly and easily be constructed by a single person, but if the system it represents is larger than the span of control of the individual person, then using a group setting is always better. So, with this in mind, the first step in constructing a Goal Tree/IO Map is to clearly define the system in which it operates and its associated boundaries. The second consideration is whether or not it falls within your span of control or your sphere of influence. Defining your span of control and sphere of influence lets you know the level of assistance you might need from others if you are to successfully change and improve your current reality.

Once you have defined the boundaries of the system and your span of control and sphere of influence you are attempting to improve, your next step is to define the goal of the system. Remember, we said that the true owner(s) of the system is/are responsible for defining the goal. If the true owner or owners aren't available, it is possible to articulate it by way of a "straw man," but even then, you need to get concurrence on the goal from the owner(s) before beginning to construct your Goal Tree. Don't lose sight of the fact that the purpose of the Goal Tree is to identify the ultimate destination you are trying to reach.

Dettmer tells us that the Goal Tree's most important function, from a problem-solving perspective, is that it constitutes a standard of system performance that allows problem-solvers to decide how far off-course their system truly is [2]. So, with this in mind, your goal statement must reflect the final outcome and not the activities to get you there. In other words, the goal is specified as an outcome of activities and not the activity itself.

Once the goal has been defined and fully agreed upon, your next order of business is to develop three to five CSFs that must be firmly in place before your goal can be achieved. As I explained earlier, the CSFs are high-level milestones that result from specific, detailed actions. The important point to remember is that if you don't achieve every one of the CSFs, you will not accomplish your goal.

Finally, once our CSFs have been clearly defined, your next step is to develop your NCs which are the simple building blocks for your Goal Tree. The NCs are specific to the CSF they support, but because they are hierarchical in nature, there are typically multiple layers of them below each of the CSFs. As already stated, Dettmer recommends no more than three layers for the NCs, but on numerous occasions I have observed as many as five layers working quite well. With the three components in view, you are now ready to construct your Goal Tree. Let's demonstrate this through a case study where a company constructed their own Goal Tree.

THE CASE STUDY EXAMPLE

The company in question here is one that manufactures a variety of different products for diverse industry segments. Some orders are build-to-order, while others would be considered orders for mass production parts. This company had plenty of orders to fill, but unfortunately, they were having trouble not only filling them but filling them on time. As a result, this company's profitability was fluctuating between making money one month and losing money the next. Because of this, the board of directors decided to make a leadership change and hired a new CEO to effectively "right the ship."

The new CEO had a diverse manufacturing background, meaning that in his career he had split his time between job shop environments and high-volume manufacturing companies. When the new CEO arrived, he called a meeting of his direct reports to not only meet them but to assess their proficiencies and capabilities. He soon realized that most of the existing management team had been working for this company for many years and that their skills appeared to be limited. Before arriving, the new CEO had concluded that the best approach to turning this company's profitability around and stabilizing it would be to use the Theory of Constraint's LTPs. But after meeting his new team and evaluating their capabilities, and since time was of the essence, he decided instead to use the Goal Tree to assess his new company and lay out an improvement strategy.

THE FIRST MEETING

The CEO's first order of business was to provide a brief training session on how to construct a Goal Tree for his new staff. The first step was to define the boundaries of their system which included receipt of raw materials from suppliers to shipping of their products to their customers. Within these boundaries, the team concluded that they clearly had defined their span of control because they had unilateral change authority. They also decided that they could influence their suppliers and somewhat the same with their customers, so their sphere of influence was also defined.

In advance of this first meeting with his staff, the CEO had met with the board of directors to determine what the goal of this company actually was. After all, he concluded, it's the owner or owner's responsibility to define the goal of the system which was "Maximum Profitability." After discussing his meeting with the board of directors to his team and the goal they had decided upon, the CEO posted the goal on the top of a flip chart as shown in Figure 1.7.

The CEO knew that the board of directors wanted maximum profitability, both now and in the future, so he added the future reference to the Goal box. But before moving on to CSFs, the CEO decided that it would be helpful if he explained the basic principles of both the concept of the system constraint and Throughput Accounting. His staff needed to understand why focusing on the constraint would result in maximum throughput, but equally important, his staff needed to understand how the three components of profitability, Throughput (T), Operating Expense (OE), and Investment/Inventory (I) worked together to maximize profitability. So, with this in mind, the CEO began training his new team on the Theory of Constraints.

"Before we discuss Throughput Accounting, we need to learn about something called the Theory of Constraints." The CEO continued, "Consider this simple piping system (Figure 1.8) used to transport water. The system is gravity fed whereby water flows into Section A, then flows through Section B, then Section C and so forth until ultimately, the water collects in a receptacle immediately below Section I. It has been determined that the rate of water flow is insufficient to satisfy current demand and you

> **Maximum Profitability Now and in the Future**

FIGURE 1.7
Goal statement.

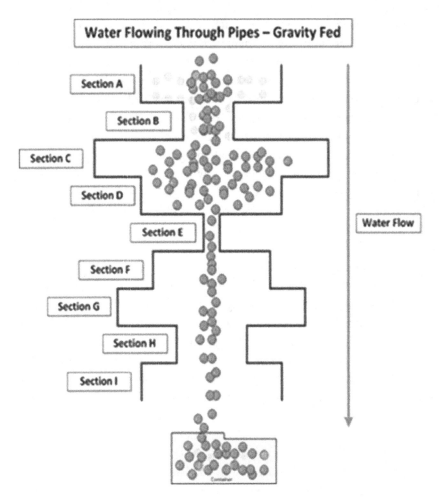

FIGURE 1.8
Piping system.

have been called in to fix this problem." He then asked the group, "What would you do and why would you do it?"

After examining the diagram, the Operations Manager spoke up and said, "Because water is backing up in front of Section E, then Section E's diameter must be enlarged." The CEO smiled and asked, "Would enlarging the diameter of any other section of the piping system result in more flow of water through this system?" Everyone shook their heads from side to side meaning that they all understood that only enlarging Section E's diameter would result in a higher flow rate of water. The CEO then asked, "What factor determines how large Section E's diameter must be?" The Quality Manager raised his hand and said, "That would depend upon how

much more water was needed. In other words, what the demand was."
Again, the CEO smiled, flashed a new slide (Figure 1.9) on the screen and
said, "So let's see what happens when we enlarge the diameter of Section E
of our piping system based upon the new demand requirement."

"As you can see, Section E's diameter has been changed and water flow
has increased. If you selected your new diameter based upon the new
demand requirements, you will have 'fixed' this problem," he explained.
"But what if there is another surge in water demand? What would you
do?" he asked. The Junior Accountant said, "You'd have to enlarge Section
B's diameter and again its new diameter would be based upon the new
demand requirement." The CEO then explained that Section E and now

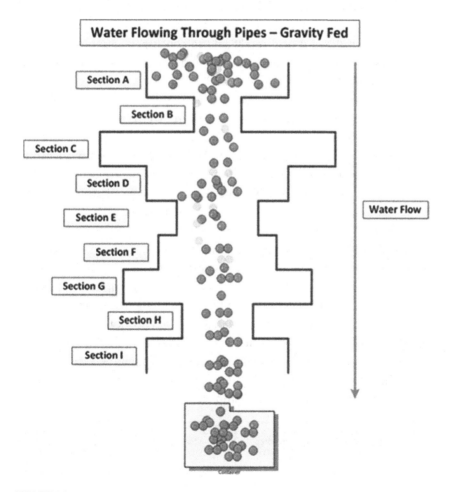

FIGURE 1.9
Piping system with diameter E enlarged.

Section B are referred to as system constraints (a.k.a. bottlenecks). The inevitable conclusion in any business the system constraints control the flow and throughput within any system. He then asked, "So how might this apply to our business?" and flashed another slide (Figure 1.10) on the screen.

He continued, "For any type of business, there is a process that is at least similar to this figure. Materials, SKUs, or parts are delivered to our business and enter into our manufacturing system. Step-by-step things happen to change the materials until you have a finished product." The CEO continued, "Parts or raw materials enter Step 1, are processed for 30 minutes and then passed on to Step 2. Step 2 processes what it has received from Step 1 for 45 minutes and then passes it on to Step 3. Steps 3 and 4 complete the processing and the finished product is either shipped to the company that ordered it or directly sold to consumers. Suppose that you wanted to sell more parts. What would you do to increase the throughput of parts through this four-step process?"

The CFO spoke up and said, "Because Step 3 takes the longest amount of time to complete, it is the system constraint, so the bottom line is that the only way to increase the throughput of this process is to reduce the time required in Step 3 (i.e. 90 minutes)." "You're right and what would determine how much to reduce Step 3's processing time?" asked the CEO. The CFO replied, "Just like the piping diagram, it would depend on the demand requirements." The CEO then asked, "Would reducing the processing time of any other step result in increased output or sales?" Once again, the Junior Accountant raised her hand and said, "Absolutely not because only the system constraint controls the output of any process!"

The CEO continued, "Many businesses are using manpower efficiency or equipment utilization to measure the performance of their processes, and as a result of these performance metrics, they work to increase these two metrics? Since increasing efficiency is only achieved by running close to the maximum capacity of every step, what happens when this takes place? That is, Step 1 makes 1 part every 30 minutes and passes it on to Step 2 which takes 45 minutes to complete, etc."

FIGURE 1.10
Simple manufacturing process.

The CEO explained, "After the first 8 hours, this is what this process looks like (Figure 1.11). Work-In-Process (WIP) begins to accumulate—total processing time increases—on-time delivery deteriorates—customers get frustrated. Frustrated because of our company's inability to ship product on time which negatively impacts our ability to ship products on time. And as time passes, after three eight-hour days, WIP levels continue to grow, negatively impacting flow, and unless something changes, the system becomes overwhelmed with WIP (Figure 1.12). This increase in WIP extends processing time even further which negatively impacts on-time delivery and customers end up threatening to take their business elsewhere. So, what is the answer?"

The CEO continued, "As you have just witnessed, the performance metrics efficiency or equipment utilization both have negative consequences, so maybe they're not such good metrics for us to use after all, at least not in non-constraints? They are both excellent metrics to use to drive constraint's output, but not in non-constraints. So, in order to avoid an explosion of WIP, doesn't it make sense that Steps 1 and 2

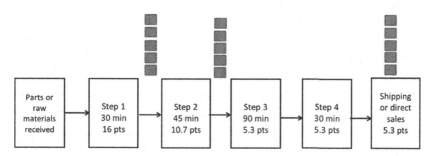

FIGURE 1.11
Maximizing efficiency and its effect on WIP.

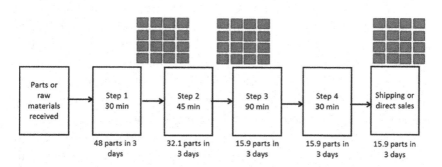

FIGURE 1.12
Process WIP after three eight-hour days.

should be running at the same speed as the constraint (i.e. 1 part every 90 minutes)?" "In order to increase the output rate of this process, Step 3's processing time must be reduced because it is the system constraint. What happens if we focus our improvement efforts on Step 3 only?" The Operations Manager spoke up and said, "By focusing our improvement efforts on Step 3 only, we get an immediate increase in the throughput of this process." The CEO smiled and said, "This is the essence of the Theory of Constraints ... it provides the necessary focus for improvement efforts. So now let's move on to a comparison of Cost Accounting and Throughput Accounting."

COST ACCOUNTING VERSUS THROUGHPUT ACCOUNTING

The CEO first explained the basics of Throughput Accounting (TA) by stating that in TA, Throughput (T) was equal to Revenue (R) minus Totally Variable Costs (TVC) and that Net Profit was equal to Throughput minus Operating Expense, or T – OE. Finally, he explained that Return on Investment (ROI) was equal to NP/Inventory (I). With this brief training behind them, he then challenged his staff to tell him what they needed to have in place to satisfy this profitability goal both today and tomorrow. That is, what must be in place to maximize net profit now and in the future?

After much discussion, his staff offered three Critical Success Factors which the CEO inserted beneath the Goal in the Goal Tree (Figure 1.13). After learning the basics of TOC's concept of the constraint and basic TA, his staff knew that because they needed to increase Net Profit (T – OE), then maximizing throughput had to be one of the CSFs. They also concluded that in order to maximize net profit, minimizing OE had to be another CSF. And finally, because ROI was equal to Net Profit divided by their Investment (i.e. NP = T ÷ I), they needed to include minimum investment as one of the CSFs. The CEO felt very good about the progress they had made with their first Goal Tree, but it was time for lunch, so they decided to break and come back later to complete the Goal Tree.

When his staff returned from lunch, they reviewed what the CEO had presented on TA, just so it was fresh in their minds as they began again to review and construct their Goal Tree.

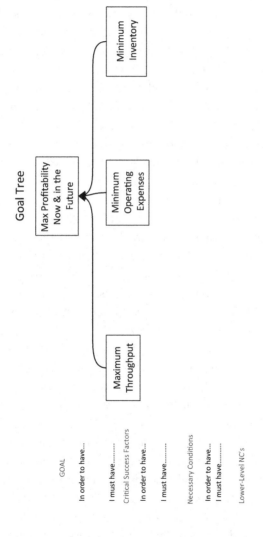

FIGURE 1.13
Goal Tree with three CSFs.

The CEO stated, "So, in order to maximize profitability now and in the future, we must have maximum Throughput, minimum Operating Expense and minimum Investment which is mostly inventory." "Are there any others?" he asked. His staff looked at each other and agreed that these are the three main CSFs. The CEO knew that what was needed next were the corresponding NCs so he started with Maximum Throughput. "In order to have maximum Throughput, what do we need?" His CFO put his hand up and said, "We need to maximize our revenue stream." Everyone agreed, but the Junior Accountant immediately raised her hand and said, "That's only half of it!" The CEO and CFO looked at her and said, "Tell us more." She explained, "Well you explained that Throughput was revenue minus Totally Variable Costs, so minimal Totally Variable Costs has to be a Necessary Condition too." The CEO smiled and said, "So, let me read what we have so far." "In order to have maximum Throughput, we must have maximum Revenue and minimal TVCs" and everyone agreed.

The CEO continued, "In order to maximize Revenue, what must we do?" The Operations Manager said, "We must have satisfied customers," and before he could say another word, the Marketing Director added, "We must also have sufficient market demand." The CEO smiled, scanned the room for acceptance again and added these two NCs to the Goal Tree. The CEO thought to himself, I am so happy that I chose to use the Goal Tree rather than the full Thinking Process analysis.

The CEO then said, "Let's stay with the satisfied customer's NC … in order to have satisfied customers, we must have what?" The Quality Director raised his hand and said, "We must have the highest quality product." The Logistics Manager added, "We must also have high on-time delivery rates." And before the CEO could add them to the tree, the Customer Service Manager added, "We must also have a high level of customer service." The CEO smiled again and said, "Slow down so I don't miss any of these everyone." Everyone laughed. The CEO looked at the lower-level NCs for satisfied customers and asked if they needed anything else. Everyone agreed that if they had the highest quality product with high on-time delivery rates and a high level of customer service, then the customers should be highly satisfied.

The CEO decided to continue on beneath the CSF for Maximum Throughput and asked, "So what do we need to supplement or support sufficient market demand?" The CFO said, "We need a competitive price point and by the way, I think that would also help satisfy our customers." The CEO added both NCs and connected both of them to the upper-level NC of sufficient market demand. The CEO stepped back and admired the work they had done so far, but before he could say anything, the Sales Manager said, "If we're going to have sufficient market demand, don't you think we also need effective sales and marketing?" Again, everyone nodded their heads in agreement, so the CEO added that NC as well.

Before the CEO could say anything more, the Junior Accountant raised her hand and added, "I was thinking that three of the ways we could have effective sales and marketing would be related to the three lower-level NC's assigned to satisfied customers. I mean, can we do that in a Goal Tree?" The CFO was the first person to speak and he added, "I think that's a fantastic idea!" The CEO thanked her and added the connecting arrows. Figure 1.14 is their semi-finished Goal Tree.

The CEO then said, "Great job so far, but what's a good way for us to minimize TVC?" Without hesitation, the Quality Manager said, "That's easy, we need to minimize our scrap and rework." The Quality Manager then said, "I think that would also be an NC for one of our other CSFs, minimum operating expense." Everyone agreed, so the CEO added

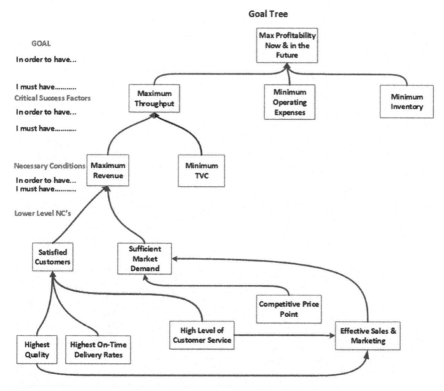

FIGURE 1.14
Semi-finished Goal Tree.

both the NC and the second connecting arrow. Once again, the Junior Accountant raised her hand and added, "I think that we should add another NC to the CSF, minimum operating expense and that we should say something like optimum manpower levels and maybe also minimized overtime." The CEO smiled and added both of the NCs to the tree.

"So, what about our CSF, Minimum Investment?" asked the CEO. The Plant Manager raised his hand and said, "How about minimized WIP and Finished Goods inventory?" The CEO looked for objections, but when nobody objected, he added it to the tree. He then asked, "What about an NC underneath that one?" The Plant Manager looked at him and said, "We need to synchronize our production around the constraint and demand." "What do you mean?" asked the CEO. "I mean we need to stop producing parts on speculation and start building based on actual orders. I've been reading about TOC's version of scheduling, referred to as Drum-Buffer-Rope, and I think we need to move in that direction," he added. And with that, the CEO added his comments to the now completed Goal Tree/IO Map (Figure 1.15).

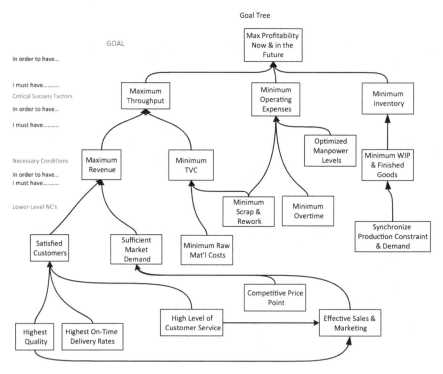

FIGURE 1.15
Completed Goal Tree.

When he was finished adding the new items to the Goal Tree, he turned to the group and began clapping his hands in appreciation for their effort. He explained, "I've been doing this for quite some time now, but I have never seen a group come together more than you have today." He added, "I was a bit apprehensive when we began today that maybe some of you would push back and not contribute, but I was totally wrong." The CFO raised his hand and said, "For me, I have never seen this tool before, but going forward I will be using it a lot. In fact, I was thinking that this tool can be used to develop individual department improvement plans." "Tell us more," said the CEO. "Well, if an NC, for example, applies mostly to a specific group like Production or Sales & Marketing, then that could be seen as the Goal for that group. I'm very happy to have been here today to complete this exercise," said the CFO. Everyone else agreed with him. The CEO then said, "Ladies and gentlemen, this exercise is not over yet." "What else is there to do?" came a question from the CFO. "We'll get back together tomorrow morning and I'll explain the next steps," he explained.

USING THE GOAL TREE AS AN ASSESSMENT TOOL

Bright and early the next morning, the executive team began filing into their conference room, full of anticipation on just what they would do with their completed Goal Tree. The CEO hadn't given them any instructions on how to prepare for the day's work, so they were all eager to have the events of the day unfold. When everyone was seated, the CEO welcomed them and offered his congratulations again on the great job they had done the day before. "Good morning everyone," he said as everyone responded with a "good morning" back to him. As he scanned the room, he noticed that there was one person missing, the Junior Accountant. When he asked the CFO where she was, he explained that she was working on the monthly report and wouldn't be joining them today. The CEO looked the CFO square in his eyes and told him that nothing was more important than what they were going to do today. "Go get her!" he stated emphatically. The CFO left and returned minutes later with the Junior Accountant and the CEO welcomed her. He then said, "We created this as a complete team and we're going to finish it as a complete team."

The CEO explained, "When the Goal Tree was originally created by Bill Dettmer, it was to be used as a precursor to the creation of a Current Reality Tree (CRT) [2]. That is, he used it as the first logic tree in TOC's Thinking Processes to help create the CRT." He continued, "And although I fully support this approach, I have found a way to use it to accelerate the development of an improvement plan." The CEO passed out copies of the completed Goal Tree and began.

"I want everyone to study our logic tree, focusing on the lower level NCs first," he explained. "As we look at these NCs, I want everyone to think about how we are doing with each of these," he continued. "By that I mean, is what we said needed to satisfy a CSF or upper-level NC, in place and functioning as it should be. We're going to use a color-code scheme to actually evaluate where we stand on each one," he said. "If you believe that what we have in place is good and that it doesn't need to be improved, I want you to color it green. Likewise, if we have something in place, but it needs to be improved, color it yellow. And finally, if each NC is either not in place or is not 'working' in its current configuration, color it red," he explained. "Does everyone understand?" he asked, and everyone nodded in agreement. "It's important that we do this honestly, so be truthful or this exercise will all be for not."

The CFO raised his hand and asked, "How will we use our color-coded tree?" "Good question," said the CEO. Once we have reviewed our Goal, CSFs, and NCs, we will start with the red entities first and develop plans to turn them into either yellows or greens. Likewise, we'll then look at the yellows and develop plans to turn them into green ones," he explained. As he was explaining his method, the CEO could see heads nodding in the affirmative meaning that everyone understood his instructions. With that, the CEO passed out green, yellow, and red pencils. "I want everyone to do this individually first and then we'll discuss each one openly until we arrive at a consensus," he explained. "While you're considering the state of each entity, I also want everyone to also think about a way we can measure the status of many of these in the future," he said. "I'll be back in a couple of hours, so please feel free to discuss your color selections as a group," he added. With the instructions complete, the team began reviewing their Goal Tree and applying the appropriate colors to each entity.

Right on schedule, the CEO returned and asked how the session was coming. The Plant Manager spoke first, "I was amazed at how much disagreement we had initially, but after we discussed each item, we eventually came to an agreement on how we believe we're doing." The CFO jumped into the conversation and added, "I was amazed at how we came together as a team just by creating our Goal Tree." "I have to admit that when you told me to go get our Junior Accountant, I was a bit taken back. But at the end of the day, she was a very important addition to this team," he added. And with that, the Junior Accountant was somewhat embarrassed but thanked the CFO for recognizing her contribution to the effort.

"So, where is it?" asked the CEO. "Where is your finished product … your Goal Tree?" The CFO went to the flip chart and there it was. The CEO then asked, "Did you also discuss what kind of metrics we might use to measure how we're doing?" "Yes, we did," said the CFO. "And?" the CEO asked. "We need to do more work on that," he answered. "So, what's next?" asked the CFO. After studying the finished product, the CEO thanked everyone for their effort and then said, "Let's take a break and come back later and I'll explain how we can use this tree to develop our final improvement plan," said the CEO.

The team reassembled later that day to discuss their next steps. Everyone seemed enthusiastic about what they would be doing going forward. When everyone was seated, the CEO turned to the group and asked, "So how does everyone feel about this process so far?" The Plant Manager was the first to respond, "I can't speak for anyone else, but the development of the Goal Tree was a real eye-opener for me. I never imagined that we could have analyzed our organization so thoroughly in such a short amount of time. I mean think about it, when you add up the total amount of time we've spent so far, it's not even been a full day's work!" As he spoke, everyone was nodding their heads in agreement.

The CFO was next to speak and said, "I can absolutely see the benefit from using this tool and one of the things that impressed me the most is that everyone contributed. But what really captivated me is that for the first time since I started working here, we actually are looking at the system rather than isolated parts of it. One of the things that I will take away from this is that the total sum of the localized improvements does not necessarily result in an improvement to the system. The Goal Tree forces us to look at and analyze all of the components of our organization as one entity." Figure 1.16 is their Goal Tree after completing their assessment on how each entity was functioning.

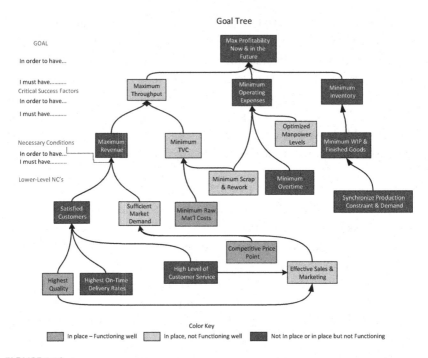

FIGURE 1.16
Goal Tree after assessment.

"OK, let's get started," said the CEO. "Today we're going to plan on how to turn our problem areas, those we defined in red, into, hopefully, strengths," he said. "Does anyone have any ideas on how we can turn our bottom three reds into either yellows or greens?" "In other words what can we do that might positively impact delivery rates, customer service and synchronize production to the constraint and demand?" he asked.

The Plant Manager was the first to speak and said, "If we can come up with a way to schedule our production based upon the needs of the constraint, it seems to me that we could really have a positive result for on-time delivery rates and at the same time it would reduce our WIP and Finished Goods (FG) levels?" he said more in the form of a question. The CFO then said, "Since you mentioned Drum-Buffer-Rope (DBR) yesterday, I've been reading more about it and it seems that this scheduling method is supposed to do exactly what you just described," he said directly to the Plant Manager.

The CEO responded by saying, "He's right, DBR limits the rate of new product starts because nothing enters the process until something exits the constraint." "So, let's look at what happens to the reds and yellows if we were to implement DBR," he added and pointed at the Goal Tree up on the screen. "The way I see it is, if we implement DBR, we will minimize WIP. If we minimize WIP, we automatically minimize FGs which minimizes our investment dollars which positively impacts our profitability," he explained enthusiastically. "We should also see our on-time delivery rates jump up, which should result in much higher levels of customer satisfaction," he added. "This should also allow us to be more competitive in our pricing and stimulate more demand and with our ability to increase throughput, we will positively impact profitability," he explained. The Junior Accountant then said, "Last night I read more about the Theory of Constraints, and it seems to me that one thing we could do is stop tracking efficiency in our non-constraints, and if we do that, we should also reduce our WIP."

The Quality Director spoke up and said, "I'm thinking that if we effectively slowdown in our non-constraints, we should see our scrap and rework levels improve significantly because our operators will have more time to make their products. And I also believe that we should implement TLS." "What is TLS?" asked the CFO. "It's an improvement method which combines the Theory of Constraints, Lean, and Six Sigma," the Quality Director explained. "This improvement will reduce our scrap and rework levels and in conjunction with DBR will reduce both our operating expenses and TVC. The combination of these improvements will both contribute to our profitability," he added.

"One other thing is that we should see our overtime levels drop which will also improve profitability," said the CFO. "I am just amazed that by making these three basic changes, we could see a dramatic financial improvement," he added.

The stage was set for major financial gains by first developing their cause-and-effect relationships and by looking at their organization as a system rather than making improvements to parts of it and that's an important message for everyone to glean from all of this. Not all improvement efforts will happen rapidly like it did in this case study, but it is possible to make rapid and significant improvements to your organization by looking at it from a holistic point of view. The fact is, isolated and localized improvements will not typically result in improvement to the system. So, let's get back to our case study where the subject of performance metrics is explained. The team continued working on their Goal Tree until it was complete (Figure 1.17).

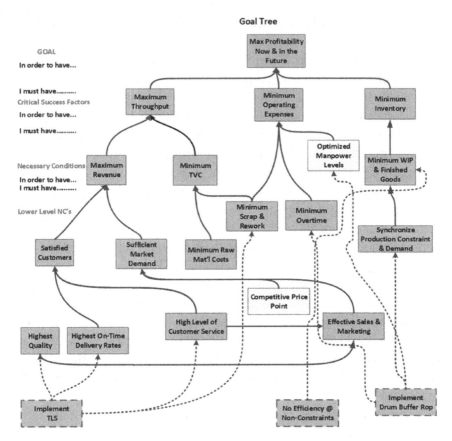

FIGURE 1.17

Goal Tree after implementing improvement ideas.

PERFORMANCE METRICS

The CEO began to explain, "Before we develop our performance metrics, let's first discuss the purposes of an organization's performance metrics. In general, we need some type of feedback mechanism that tells us how we're doing, a way to be able to know that the direction we're traveling is on course in the event that we need to make any midcourse corrections. These performance metrics should be system related in that they tell us how the system is performing rather than how individual processes are functioning. Remember, our focus is on system performance and not individual performance. So, think about what our performance metrics should be? But before we answer that question, let's talk about their purpose."

The CEO continued, "Performance measures are intended to serve at least six important functions or roles," as he wrote them on the flip chart:

1. First, and foremost, the measures should stimulate the right behaviors.
2. The performance measures should reinforce and support the overall goals and objectives of the company.
3. The measures should be able to assess, evaluate, and provide feedback as to the status of the people, departments, products, and the total company.
4. The performance measure must be translatable to everyone within the organization. That is, each operator, manager, engineer, etc. must understand how their actions impact the metric. Performance metrics are intended to inform everyone, not just the managers!
5. The performance metrics chosen should also lend themselves to trend and statistical analysis and, as such, they shouldn't be "yes or no" in terms of compliance.
6. The metric should also be challenging, but at the same time be attainable. There should be a stretch involved. If it's too easy to reach the target, then you probably won't gain nearly as much in the way of profitability. If it's too difficult, then people will be frustrated and disenchanted.

The CEO continued, "So with these functions in mind, let's now look at how we can use our Goal Tree to create our series of performance metrics. If we use the Goal Tree as our guide, we should start with our goal, Maximize Profitability Now and in the Future, and create our first tracking metric," he explained. "Earlier in our discussion, I introduced you to Throughput Accounting, which defined Net Profit as Throughput minus Operating Expense or $NP = T - OE$. The metric of choice for this Goal Tree, then, should be NP which we insert into our 'goal box.' In addition, I prefer to give most of the metrics a target to shoot for. With this metric, I believe that our Net Profit should be greater than twenty-five percent ($NP > 25\%$)," he stated. The CEO continued, "We must then look at each CSF and NC and select appropriate performance metrics and targets for as many as might be appropriate. Keep in mind that not every box will have a defined metric, but let's get as many as we can," he explained. The CEO then told the executive team that he wanted them to work on the rest of the metrics as a team and that he would return later.

Because the operational status of companies varies from company to company, there is no standard set of metrics and targets to recommend, but for the company in this case study, the team stayed focused and was able to identify appropriate metrics and targets. They started with the Goal, then worked through the CSFs and then onto the NCs. Let's get back to the case study and see what they were able to do.

The CFO was the first to speak and said, "It's clear to me that having performance metrics for the three CSFs is imperative since they are the three components of profitability." The team decided to first determine which entities could actually have metrics tied to them. After they had determined all of the metrics, they would then develop targets for each specific performance metric. Figure 1.18 is the Goal Tree with appropriate metrics defined by this executive team.

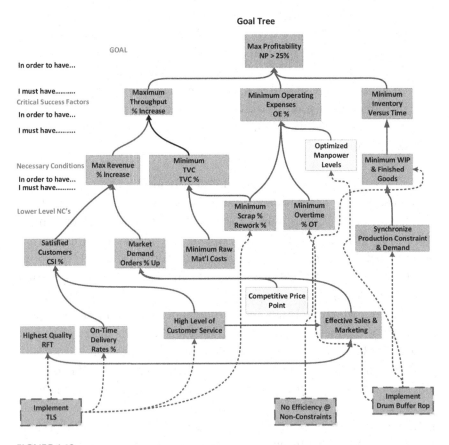

FIGURE 1.18
Goal Tree with performance metrics.

All of the team members contributed to this effort and were all amazed at the finished product they had developed. As they were admiring their Goal Tree with the performance metrics they intended to track, the CEO entered the room. He studied the completed Goal Tree and then moved to the front of the room. He thanked everyone for their effort and told them that they could return to their offices. The CFO stood and said, "With all due respect sir, we haven't finished yet." "We have identified the key metrics we want to track, but we must now develop our targets for each metric." The CEO just smiled and told them he would be back later to see their finished product.

The CFO stood, faced the group and asked, "Where do you think we should start? I mean should we start at the top with the Goal or should we start at the bottom and work our way up?" The Junior Accountant raised her hand and said, "I think we should start at the lower levels and work our way to the top." "Why do you feel that way?" asked the CFO. "If we follow the direction of the arrows and set and reach our target, then the level directly above will be the net result of our efforts," she replied. "Could you give us an example?" asked the CFO. "OK, for example, if we set our target for Highest Quality, Right the First Time (RFT) at greater than 99 percent and we achieve it, plus our on-time delivery rate to 99 percent and we achieve that, then we have a great chance of having our Customer Satisfaction Index (CSI) be greater than 99 percent. So, it's kind of like sufficiency-type logic using if-then statements," she explained.

The Quality Director then spoke up and said, "I can see your point, but I can also make the argument based on necessity-based logic." "By that I mean, we could start with the Goal and give it a target of 25 percent. So, with necessity-based logic, we could say that in order to have a profitability of 25 percent, we must have a Throughput improvement of at least 20 percent, while holding our operating expenses to less than 10 percent and holding our on-hand inventory to less than one day." The CFO re-entered the conversation and said, "I see both points of view, but I must tell you I like following the direction of the arrows on our Goal Tree. I say this because when we implement Drum-Buffer-Rope and TLS we drive improvement upward and our metrics respond to what we're doing."

The Junior Accountant then said, "I don't think it matters which direction we go because, at the end of the day, the metrics will tell us how we're doing." Everyone nodded their heads in agreement and they got busy setting their targets for each defined performance metric. When they finished, they recorded them in a PowerPoint slide for presentation to the CEO.

A short while later, the CEO returned to the conference room to find the completed Goal Tree with metrics and targets posted on the screen at the front of the conference room. He studied it, turned to the group and asked someone to explain it to him. The CFO turned to the Junior Accountant and said, "I think since you contributed most to our success that you should be the one to do that." The Junior Accountant just smiled and said she would be happy to and did so with confidence, agility, and a seemingly true understanding of this new tool (Figure 1.19). She finished her presentation by telling the executive team that this tool will serve her well in her new position as CFO with her new company.

The Goal Tree is an amazingly simple tool to not only learn, but in my experience, it's a tool that most people feel comfortable with using. As you

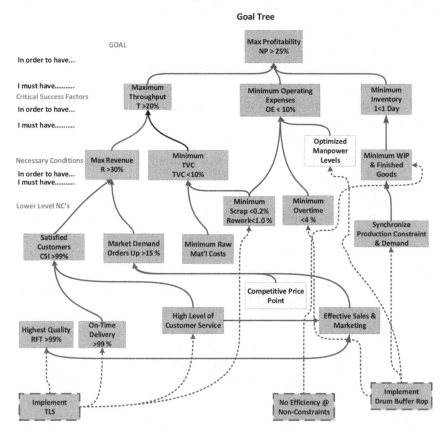

FIGURE 1.19
With metrics and targets.

learned, in a very short amount of time, this team not only learned how to create their Goal Tree, they were able to use it to develop their strategic and tactical improvement plan. I am forever grateful to Bill Dettmer for providing us with this amazing tool, and I encourage everyone to read Bill's book, *The Logical Thinking Process: A Systems Approach to Complex Problem Solving* [2]. Now let's look at an overview of the other Logical Thinking Process tools. For a detailed description of these LTP tools, once again I recommend Dettmer's book.

OVERVIEW OF TOC's LTP TOOLS

One of the important learnings from the Theory of Constraints is the concept of entities referred to as Undesirable Effects, otherwise known as UDEs. In order to understand what UDEs are, we must first understand that they must be considered in the context of an organization's goals, necessary conditions, and performance metrics. For example, suppose the organization's goal is to make money now, and in the future, and its necessary conditions are things like keeping its employees happy and secure, keeping customer satisfaction high, achieving superior quality and on-time delivery, and so on. Further suppose that the organization measures its performance with metrics like on-time delivery, some kind of productivity measurement, the cost to produce products, a customer satisfaction index, and quality through parts per million (ppm) defective. Any organizational effect that moves the organization away from its stated goal, or violates one of the necessary conditions, or drives a performance metric in a negative direction with respect to its target, is considered undesirable. So, think for a minute about what UDEs might exist in your company.

The tool Goldratt developed to expose system type problems, or policy constraints, is referred to as the Current Reality Tree (CRT). The CRT is used to discover organizational problems, or UDEs, and then works in reverse to identify at least one root cause that will usually lead us to most of the UDEs. Dettmer defines a root cause as, "the lowest cause in a chain of cause-and-effect at which we have some capability to cause the break" [2]. His point being that the cause-and-effect chain could continue on indefinitely, but unless the cause lies within the span of control of the organization, it will not be solved. I happen to believe Dettmer's definition of a root cause is the finest characterization I have ever observed. Dettmer further explains that two characteristics apply to root causes:

1. It's the lowest point at which human intervention can change or break the cause.
2. It's within our capability to unilaterally control, or to influence, changes to the cause.

The CRT begins by identifying UDEs or negative symptoms that exist within an organization that let us know that a core problem exists. Core problems are unique in that if the root cause or causes can be found, they can usually be traced to an exceptionally large percentage of the undesirable effects. Actually, Dettmer suggests that this percentage could be as high as 70 percent and maybe even higher. Dettmer refers to a CRT as a "snapshot of reality as it exists at a particular moment in time." Dettmer further explains, "As with a photograph, it's not really reality itself, just a picture of reality, and, like a photo, it encloses only what we choose to aim at through the camera's viewfinder."

By aiming our "logical camera" at the undesirable effects and their root causes, we are essentially eliminating all of the details that don't relate to them. In other words, the CRT helps us focus in on and pinpoint core problems. There are several different versions of the CRT available in the literature on the subject, but they all provide the same end product, at least one actionable core problem. The bottom line is that Current Reality Trees tell us what to change that will have the greatest positive impact on our system.

The next tool in TOC's arsenal of Logical Thinking Process tools is referred to as the Evaporating Cloud (EC), also known as a conflict resolution diagram (CRD). The EC is used primarily to resolve hidden conflicts that have a tendency to perpetuate chronic problems. The EC is based upon the idea that core problems exist because of some disagreement (i.e. conflict) which prevents resolution of a problem. Another use of the EC is that it can be a creative engine for generating new ideas to solve nagging problems with breakthrough solutions. It helps us answer the question of what to change.

Next in the LTP tool kit is the Future Reality Tree (FRT) which serves two primary purposes. First, it permits us to verify that some kind of action we'd like to take will produce the desired result of our action. Second, it helps us identify unforeseen consequences that could occur as a result of our action. These two purposes provide us with two distinct benefits. First, it allows us to, in effect, test our potential solution before we actually implement it. The other benefit is that it helps us look into the future so as to avoid making the situation worse. The FRT helps us answer the question of what to change to by changing UDEs into Desirable Effects (DE).

Once we are confident in our proposed course of action, we now turn our attention to the next tool, the Prerequisite Tree (PRT). The PRT helps us develop the sequence of actions we need to take in order to implement our solution. In addition, the PRT helps us identify any unforeseen obstacles we may run into as we implement our solution and suggests ways to overcome them. The PRT begins to answer the question of how to change.

The final tool in the Logical Thinking Process tool kit is the Transition Tree (TT). The intended purpose of the Transition Tree is to provide a detailed step-by-step process used to implement our intended improvement plan. In addition, the TT provides the rationale behind each step. Dettmer likens it to a detailed road map used to achieve our objective. The Transition Tree provides the second part of how to make the change [2].

Before leaving our discussion on the Logical Thinking Process tools, we need to also discuss the "logical glue" that aims to hold the LTP tools together. This logical glue is known as the Categories of Legitimate Reservation (CLR) which are basically eight rules or tests of your logic that oversee both the construction and review of each of these logic trees. As Dettmer explains, "To be logically sound, a tree must be able to pass the first seven of these tests" [2]. These eight tests are as follows:

1. *Clarity*: Be certain that the individual words used are understood, that there is comprehension of the idea, and that there is a clear connection between the cause and the effect.
2. *Entity Existence*: When constructing the graphic blocks (entities) we must be certain that the text is a complete grammatical sentence that we have not created a compound sentence, and the idea contained in the sentence is valid.
3. *Causality Existence*: Cause-and-effect relationships must be direct and unavoidable.
4. *Cause Insufficiency*: Be certain that you have identified and included all major contributing causes.
5. *Additional Cause*: Each time you observe or imagine an effect, you must consider all possible independent causes.
6. *Cause-Effect Reversal*: Don't mistake an effect for a cause.

7. *Predicted Effect Existence*: Most of the time, causes have multiple effects, so make certain all effects are considered.
8. *Tautology*: Don't take the effect as unequivocal proof alone that the cause exists without considering other alternatives.

So, to summarize our discussion on the Logical Thinking Process tools, Dettmer explains that they are intended to answer four basic questions [2]:

1. What is the desired standard?
2. What to change?
3. What to change to?
4. How to cause the change?

Figure 1.20, taken from Dettmer's book, summarizes which tool to use to answer these four basic questions [2].

CASE STUDY ON HOW TO CONSTRUCT AND USE THE CURRENT REALITY TREE

The example I will present in this section is a company that was having a problem generating enough throughput (i.e. capacity constraint). They had plenty of orders to fill but were unable to produce enough parts to satisfy their market demand. It is clear to me that many of the problems organizations encounter on a daily basis are really interconnected, systems-related problems. It is further clear that by focusing on these core problems, organizations can essentially kill multiple birds with a few stones!

State of Change	Applicable Logic Tree
What's the desired standard?	Intermediate Objectives Map
What to change?	Current Reality Tree
What to change to?	Evaporating Cloud, Future Reality Tree
How to cause the change?	Prerequisite Tree, Transition Tree

FIGURE 1.20
State of change versus logic tree.

CONSTRUCTING A CURRENT REALITY TREE

I said earlier that it was not my intention to present an in-depth discussion of the Logical Thinking Tools, but one of the tools I will discuss is CRT. To demonstrate this tool, I will present a simple case study example that I developed following the recommended steps for creating a CRT according to Dettmer [2]. The company involved here produces flexible tanks used to hold and transport volatile organic liquids. This company had serious problems generating enough throughput to satisfy the volume and delivery requirements of their customers. By creating and using a CRT, this company was able to pinpoint specific system problems that were constraining their throughput and then take actions to alleviate the problem. The following are the steps used to create this CRT as developed by Dettmer [2].

1. Define the system boundaries, goals, necessary conditions, and performance measures. Because we are talking about a system, it is important that we avoid sub-optimization. That is, we must always avoid trying to optimize individual processes and assume that if we do so we will have optimized the system. This assumption or belief that the sum of individual process step optimizations will result in optimization of the total system, is completely invalid.

   All organizations exist for some purpose or goal which is simply the end toward which effort is being directed. Usually, this goal is to make money now and in the future. The necessary conditions, on the other hand, are vital success factors that must be satisfied as we achieve our goal. The performance measurements are simply those organizational metrics that tell us how the organization is performing as it pursues its goal. The following are the actual boundaries, goals, necessary conditions, and performance measures from our case study:

   a. Boundary: Manufacturing and Assembly Area
   b. Goal: Make money now and in the future
   c. Necessary conditions:
      i. Minimize customer returns and complaints
      ii. Achieve at least 95 percent on-time delivery to all customers
      iii. Provide a safe, comfortable, and secure work environment for all employees

     iv. Meet budget Profit & Loss expectations for the board of directors

     v. Performance measures:

- On-time delivery
- Rework hours per tank
- Sales $s per labor hour
- Accident rate
- Workstation efficiency
- Throughput/revenue operating expense

2. State the System Problem: In order to develop a meaningful problem statement, we should always formulate it as a "why?" question. Whatever the biggest issue that you don't like about your system's performance, simply state it as a why question.

   a. Problem statement: Why is our throughput/revenue so low?

3. Create a Causes, Negatives, and Whys Table (CNW Table): This is done by first creating three columns and then listing in the Negatives column (center column), the things you don't like about the way your system is currently performing, which includes all of the things that make your job more difficult to perform. My advice to you is, don't try to solve world hunger. List no more than five to eight Negatives, otherwise the CRT will become unmanageable.

    Table 1.1 is from our case study and as you can see, there are eight entries listed as "Negatives" in the center column. It is important to remember that each of the negatives should be considered in the context of our problem statement, which was, "Why is our throughput/revenue so low?"

    Next, sequentially number all of the negatives and then explain why you believe the negative is considered a negative. This is done so by asking the question, "Why is this negative a bad thing for our goal, necessary conditions or performance measurements?" Although Dettmer suggests that if you have multiple whys, then you should add a lowercase letter to the appropriate number, I have always added a lowercase letter to the number even if I had only one why, like the example in Table 1.2. I find that it helps me distinguish the negatives, whys, and causes as we construct the CRT.

    Once the why column of the table has been completed, move to the "Cause" column and, for each negative, ask the following question,

TABLE 1.1

CNW Table with Negatives Listed

Causes (What Is Causing This Negative?)	Negatives (What I Don't like about the Current Situation)	Why Is This Negative Bad for Our Goal, Necessary Condition, or Measurement?
	1. Absenteeism is high and unstable. 2. Processes are not stable and predictable. 3. Operators don't/won't follow specifications. 4. Product build cycle times are excessively long. 5. Equipment breaks down frequently. 6. Incoming materials are frequently nonconforming. 7. QA inspections are inconsistent between inspectors. 8. Problems are never really solved.	

TABLE 1.2

CNW Table with Negatives and Whys Listed

Causes (What Is Causing This Negative?)	Negatives (What I Don't like about the Current Situation)	Why Is This Negative Bad for Our Goal, Necessary Condition or Measurement?
	1. Absenteeism is high and unstable. 2. Processes are not stable and predictable. 3. Operators don't/won't follow specifications. 4. Product build cycle times are excessively long. 5. Equipment breaks down frequently. 6. Incoming materials are frequently nonconforming. 7. QA inspections are inconsistent between inspectors. 8. Problems are never really solved.	1a. P&A is forced to overstaff operations which drives up operating expenses due to excessive overtime. 2a. Wet cement and grout drive cycle times higher. 3a. Excessive rework causes higher operating expense. 4a. Throughput rates are too low causing late P&A deliveries to customers. 5a. Cycle times are extended causing late deliveries to P&A customers. 6a. Product cycle times are extended causing late deliveries to customers. 7a. Excess repairs drive up operating expenses and delay shipments. 8a. Repetitive defects occur which result in excessive repair time which drives up OE.

"What is causing this negative?" or "Why does this negative exist?" It's important to remember that there could very well be more than one cause responsible for creating this negative and if there are, make sure you list them. Table 1.3 includes the Negatives, Whys, and Causes. For each Cause, place an upper-case letter beside the appropriate number, again, to distinguish between negatives, causes, and whys. When this table is complete, you are now ready to construct your current reality tree. All of the Causes, Negatives, and Whys will serve as your initial building blocks for your CRT.

TABLE 1.3

Completed CNW Table

Causes (What Is Causing This Negative?)	Negatives (What I Don't like about the Current Situation)	Why Is This Negative Bad for Our Goal, Necessary Condition or Measurement?
A1. Attendance policy is not enforced by HR and/or operations.	1. Absenteeism is high and unstable.	1a. P&A is forced to overstaff operations which drives up operating expenses due to excessive overtime.
A2. Effective process control system does not exist.	2. Processes are not stable and predictable.	2a. Wet cement and grout drive cycle times higher.
A3. Specifications are vague, not current, and difficult to understand	3. Operators don't/won't follow specifications.	3a. Excessive rework causes higher operating expense.
A4. Material dry/cure times are excessively long.	4. Product build cycle times are excessively long.	4a. Throughput rates are too low causing Late P & A deliveries to customers.
A5. Preventive maintenance on key equipment is inconsistent or ineffective.	5. Equipment breaks down frequently.	5a. Cycle times are extended causing late deliveries to P&A customers.
A6. Suppliers are not always held accountable to produce in-spec material.	6. Incoming materials are frequently nonconforming.	6a. Product cycle times are extended causing late deliveries to customers.
A7. Clear and concise acceptance standards do not exist.	7. QA inspections are inconsistent between inspectors.	7a. Excess repairs drive up operating expenses and delay shipments.
A8. Most problem-solving efforts focused on treating the symptoms instead of the root cause(s).	8. Problems are never really solved.	8a. Repetitive defects occur which result in excessive repair time which drives up OE.

4. Convert all Negatives, Whys, and Causes to CRT Entities (Graphic Blocks): Using the alphanumeric entries from Table 1.3, word your Negatives, Whys, and Causes in such a way that they will fit neatly inside the graphic blocks or boxes. The information inside the block should be complete statements and should leave no ambiguity as to its meaning. Figure 1.21 is an example of what your graphic blocks should resemble. Note that the information is a complete statement, and its content leaves no doubt about what is negative.

5. Identify and Designate the Undesirable Effects: After you have converted all of the Negatives, Whys, and Causes into graphic blocks, it's time to determine which of the negatives and whys are UDEs. UDEs are those whys and negatives that are negative in relation to the organization's goal or necessary conditions or the key measures of progress toward achievement of the goal. Normally, all of the whys will be considered UDEs and probably some of the negatives will as well. In some cases, even some of the root causes could be considered UDEs. The key point to remember is whether or not the contents of the graphic block would be considered negative at face value or detrimental to the achievement of the system's goal. If they are, then designate them as a UDE. Once they are designated as a UDE, assuming you are using a drawing software (e.g., Visio), mark the UDE in some fashion so as to make it visual. In my example, I have changed the wall thickness of the graphic block to designate which of them are UDEs.

6. Group the Graphic Blocks into Clusters: To quote Dettmer, "From this point on, building the CRT is going to be very much like assembling a jigsaw puzzle with the graphic blocks being the puzzle pieces." Grouping is done by aligning the Whys (now a UDE) at the top of the page, appropriate Cause directly beneath the corresponding Negative, as shown in Figure 1.22.

   Table 1.3 permits us to group together related graphic blocks. Actually, constructing the CRT is very similar to constructing an affinity diagram for those of you familiar with this tool.

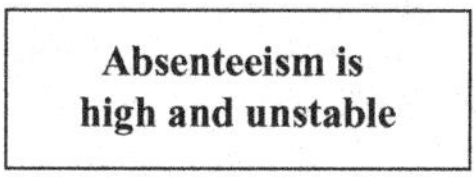

> **Absenteeism is high and unstable**

FIGURE 1.21
Graphic block example.

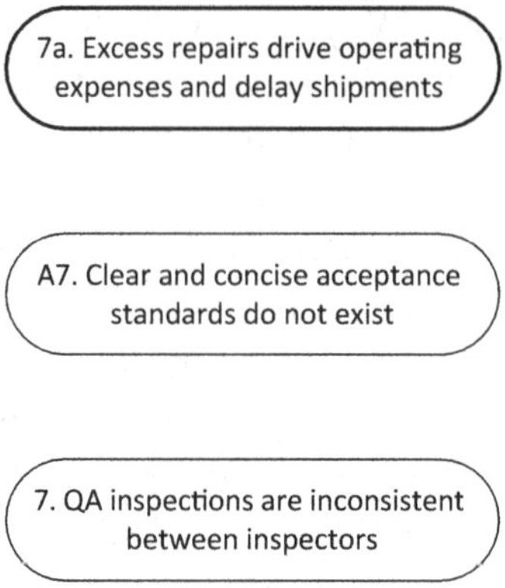

7a. Excess repairs drive operating expenses and delay shipments
A7. Clear and concise acceptance standards do not exist
7. QA inspections are inconsistent between inspectors

FIGURE 1.22
Graphic blocks in clusters.

7. Connect the Causes, Negatives, and Undesirable Effects: Using dotted or dashed lines, connect the negatives individually to each of the UDEs and then connect the causes to the negatives as demonstrated in Figure 1.23.

   Figure 1.24 contains all of the connected clusters (i.e. a cluster is defined as the connected UDEs, Negatives, and Causes) from our example. Note that the UDEs are designated by thicker walls on the graphic blocks.
8. Group Related Clusters Together: In this step, we need to search for clusters that appear to be related in some way and then place them in close proximity to each other. From our example, we see that UDE

7a. Excess repairs drive operating expenses and delay shipments
A7. Clear and concise acceptance standards do not exist
7. QA inspections are inconsistent between inspectors

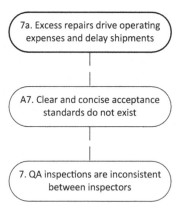

FIGURE 1.23
Causes, negatives, and UDEs.

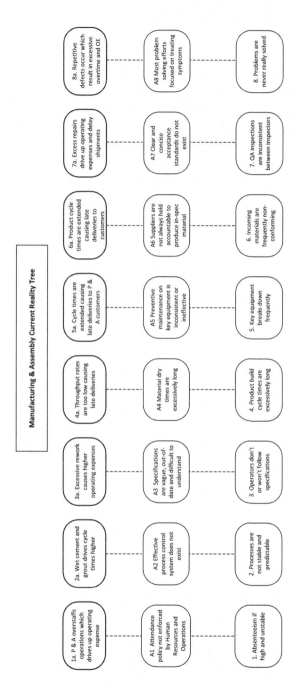

FIGURE 1.24
Connected clusters.

7a states that "excess repairs drive up operating expenses and delay shipments." That is closely related to UDE 8a, "Repetitive defects occur which result in excessive overtime and OE." We then look for connection points between the two clusters. In this particular example, the connection point appears to be at the UDE level so we place a dotted line to connect the two clusters at the connection point as shown in Figure 1.25.

In a similar fashion, we search for other related clusters and connection points and then connect them. This activity is not as simple as it may sound simply because much thought must go into how the clusters are related and where the connection point is located. My recommendation is that if you aren't sure, seek out other opinions or do more research. Figure 1.26 displays how the clusters are related from our example. Don't worry about how pretty your grouped cluster arrangement is, just try to connect them in a way that is legitimate and makes sense. It's always a good idea to seek out an objective opinion to make sure what you've constructed makes sense.

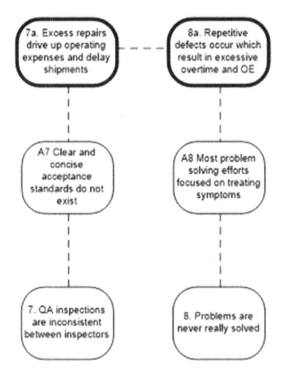

FIGURE 1.25
Connected clusters.

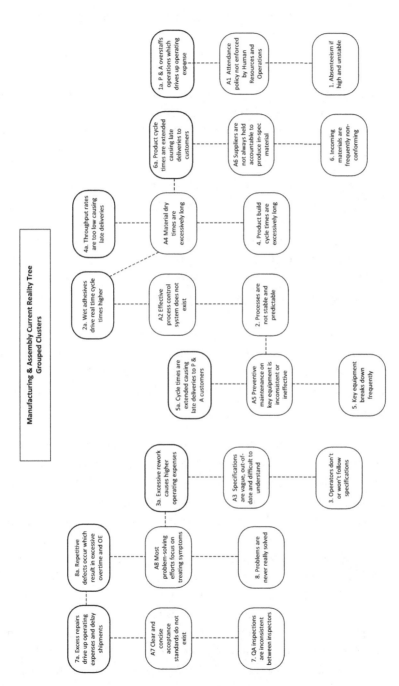

FIGURE 1.26
Three grouped clusters.

As you can see in Figure 1.26, there are three separate grouped clusters. As we continue building our CRT, it is not unusual for the final CRT to show linkages between each cluster as we add additional cause-and-effect relationships. Remember, what you will eventually discover is that only a few core problems will exist and when these few are solved, many of the UDEs will simply go away.

9. Scrutinize and Finalize the Connections: I mentioned earlier that I had no intentions of providing detailed instructions of how to construct current reality trees, so I highly recommend Dettmer's book, *The Logical Thinking Process*, for a detailed description of how to construct CRTs [2]. This is especially true from this step forward as we construct the Current Reality Tree. Dettmer emphasizes the need to use the Categories of Legitimate Reservation (CLR) to solidify the logic of each causal connection. The CLRs help us construct our own logical relationships and they enable us to evaluate the logic of others. That is, the CLRs help us avoid errors in logic as we construct our Current Reality Tree.

The eight categories of legitimate reservation act as the "rules-of-engagement" as we construct our current reality trees, so be certain to use them as you check your logic. Dettmer explains that we must pick a cluster and, beginning with the cause at the bottom, ask ourselves three basic questions.

a. Could this cause by itself create that effect or would it need help from another cause that we haven't yet acknowledged? If there is another contributing cause, place it in a graphic block beside the original cause, add an ellipse, and pass both causes through the ellipse.

b. Is there a step (graphic block) missing between this cause and that effect that would better explain what is happening? If there is, then create a new graphic block and insert it between the cause and the effect and then recheck both connections for cause sufficiency. That is, does it need help from another dependent cause to create the effect or is it a stand-alone, independent cause?

c. Is there another independent cause that could produce the same effect, without any assistance from the one already listed? If there is, then create another graphic block and insert it beside the original cause and connect it to the effect.

d. Look for Additional Causes: As additional causes and connections are determined, add them to the CRT and solidify the logical connection as demonstrated in Figure 1.27. You are able to distinguish the additional causes added as the graphic blocks without numbers or letters assigned to them.

Dettmer recommends the use of ellipses to show cause sufficiency or bow ties to show magnitudinal effects when they're needed. Magnitudinal effects are similar in nature to interactions in designed experiments (DOEs). That is, there may be several independent causes creating an effect, but when more than one is present at the same time, the effect is actually amplified. Once you are satisfied that a connection is logically sound enough to survive the criticism of someone else, make them permanent

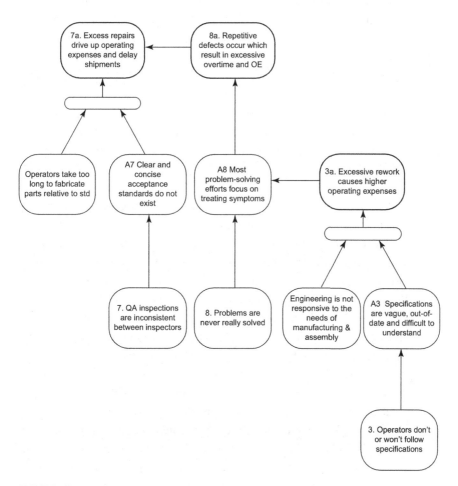

FIGURE 1.27
Current Reality Tree (CRT) with additional causes.

by changing the dotted lines to solid lines. Continue in this manner until all connections are considered to be solid and incontrovertible.

Figure 1.28 is the finalized version of the Current Reality Tree complete with highlighted Undesirable Effects, ellipses, and connecting errors. The clusters in the Current Reality Tree have been tested according to the categories of legitimate reservation so we are now ready for the next step.

a. Redesignate Undesirable Effects: Now that all of the clusters are joined into a tree and new causes have been added, it is now time to review everything you've done, starting with your UDEs. It's entirely possible that some of the UDEs that you considered to be UDEs might not seem undesirable any longer. Or, as you've added new graphic blocks to the tree, there could be new effects that are considered undesirable. Dettmer advises us to ask two basic questions as we're revisiting the CRT.

   i. Are all of my original UDEs bad enough to still be considered undesirable? If they are, don't change their designation. If they aren't, then remove them.

   ii. Have I added any new effects that might now qualify as undesirable effects using the same guidelines that we used to identify the original ones? If there are, then incorporate them into the tree.

b. Look for Negative Reinforcing Loops (NRL): A negative reinforcing loop is a scenario where a negative effect of some cause reinforces the cause. For example, suppose an inspector records a defect, based upon his or her interpretation of an ambiguous acceptance standard, and he or she is praised for doing so. Since the inspector was praised, the expected behavior one might expect to see from this inspector is interpreting other ambiguous acceptance standards so as to find a new defect. It could be that this condition has been acceptable for years, but because of the first event (i.e. finding the first defect) was positively reinforced, the apparent defect might now be looked at differently. Although not common, a good place to look for these are situations are where effects seem to be disproportionately magnified.

c. Identify All Root Causes and a Core Problem(s): In this step, we are interested in identifying the root causes upon which we can take action and, hopefully, identify a single core problem. Remember Dettmer's definition of root causes? A root cause is the lowest cause in a chain of cause-and-effect at which we have some capability to cause the break. This means that it's the lowest point at which human intervention can change or break a cause that is within our capability to control or influence. That is to say, we have no control over things like the weather because it's outside our capability to control or influence it.

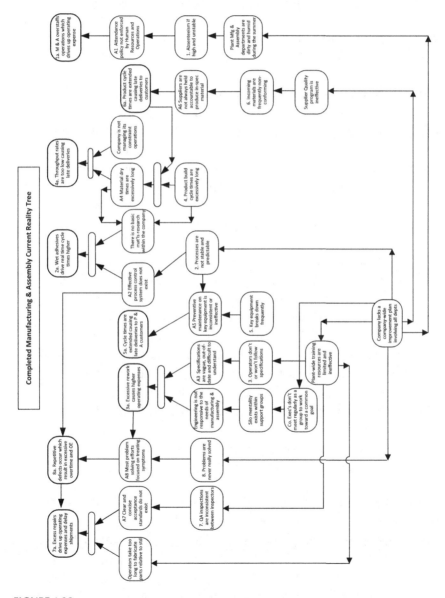

FIGURE 1.28
Completed Current Reality Tree (CRT).

A core problem, on the other hand, is a unique kind of root cause because it can be traced to an extraordinarily large number of undesirable effects (maybe as high as 70 percent). If we are fortunate enough to have located a core problem, just imagine what would happen to our system's problems if we were to resolve it? In one fell swoop, we could eliminate most of our UDEs, so it's important to be methodical in the development of our CRT. But having said this, what if the core problem is beyond our scope of influence or control? If it is, then elevate it! I haven't met many leaders that wouldn't be interested in solving a core problem when the potential results are so enormous!

In our example (see Figure 1.28), there are actually two core problems identified. The company lacks a comprehensive improvement plan that involves most of the other departments in the company and the company's attendance policy isn't followed. If we were to attack these two problems, there is a good chance that most of the UDEs identified could simply go away. The silos could be broken, specifications could be updated and be less vague, excessive rework could be reduced, problems could be solved, attendance could be reduced, and so on.

    d. Trim Non-essential Graphic Blocks: Although I don't believe this step is critical, if you have rendered some branches of your CRT neutral, Dettmer recommends that you, for housekeeping purposes, should eliminate any of these neutral branches.

    e. Choose the Root Cause to Attack: As just discussed, if there is a core problem to solve, then clearly you should attack it. But suppose there isn't one? Which root cause should you assail? Dettmer provides three "rules-of-thumb" to guide us in this selection.

       i. The one with the highest probability of your being able to influence

      ii. The one that accounts for the greatest number of UDEs

     iii. The one that accounts for the most precarious UDE

In my opinion, it is always better to attack the problem that is causing the most serious UDE for several reasons. First, the positive impact on the organization will be felt and realized immediately. Second, by solving this problem, it could serve as a rallying point to achieve future buy-in for this approach to problem identification and resolution. Third, if you have chosen the root cause that has the largest financial impact on the organization, it may very well be used to fund other solutions to other more complex root causes that might require a capital expenditure. Finally, leaders want to see results as quickly as possible.

As I said in our example, there are two key core problems to solve. The first one involves the lack of a comprehensive improvement plan that ties together all of the individual groups working to achieve the goals of the company. The real problem as it related to throughput was the excessively long cure times of the various adhesives used to produce the tanks. The second problem related to the specifications supplied by the engineering group. This problem wasn't so much that the specifications didn't exist but rather a problem associated with updating the specifications to reflect better ways of producing products as these new ways were developed. If this company could solve both the specification clarity and update problem and discover ways to reduce the long cure times, then both should automatically result in significant throughput gains simply because rework and cycle times should be reduced. So, the question becomes one of coming up with simple solutions to these two core problems (Figure 1.29).

RESOLVING CONFLICTS

Now that we have a completed Current Reality Tree, and have identified and selected the root causes and/or core problem to attack, what's next? Just how do we go about attacking a system's problem or a policy constraint? We do so by developing simple breakthrough ideas and solutions. But with every problem, there are conflicts that seem to get in the way of our ideas for problem resolution. There are three primary types of conflict that we must deal with as we work to resolve problems or more specifically, system's problems and policy constraints.

1. The first conflict is one where one force is pulling us to do one thing, but an equal and opposite force pulls in the opposite direction. Dettmer refers to this type of conflict as Opposite Conditions [2].
2. The second type of conflict is one in which we are forced to choose between different alternatives which Dettmer calls, quite appropriately, Different Alternatives.
3. The third type of conflict is what I refer to as The Hidden Agenda conflict. In a hidden agenda conflict, there is generally a personality involved and typically is manifested in a desire or inherent need to hold onto some kind of power.

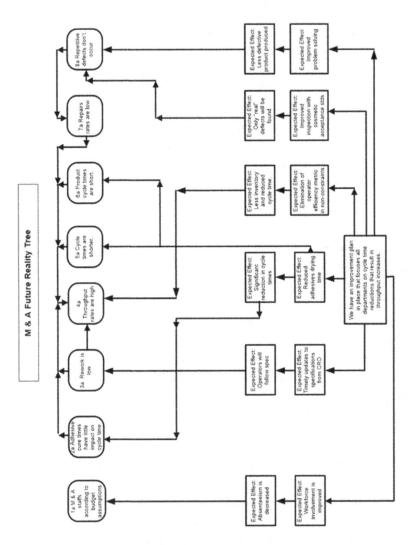

FIGURE 1.29
Completed Future Reality Tree.

In attempting to resolve conflicts, it is important to recognize that there are three types of resolution that can be achieved; win-win; win-lose; or compromise. Of the three possibilities, we should always attempt to achieve a win-win solution, but sometimes it isn't practical. In a win-lose situation, one side typically gets just about everything it wanted, while the other side gets very little. This type of solution serves to create antagonistic or hostile attitudes and your chances of success are diminished because the losing side might attempt to sabotage your solution. Not openly, mind you, but rather covertly or surreptitiously.

In the case of a compromise, generally, the solution ends up being sub-optimized because you are attempting to satisfy most of the requirements of both parties engaged in the conflict. But having said this, a compromise is better than a win-lose or imposed solution, but remember, it generally results in a sub-optimized solution. The solution for a hidden agenda conflict is much like what happens in a win-lose conflict in that someone works against you behind the scenes in hopes of holding on to their apparent power. So how do we resolve these conflicts?

Goldratt developed a tool he refers to as a Conflict Resolution Diagram (CRD) or as we discussed earlier, it is also known as an Evaporating Cloud (EC) [1]. The EC identifies and demonstrates the relationship between the key elements of a conflict and then suggests ways to resolve it. For a detailed description of how to create and use a CRD, read Dettmer's book, *The Logical Thinking Process* [2]. Figure 1.30 is the basic structure of the CRD.

From our CRT, here is an example of one of the conflicts being resolved using the CRD.

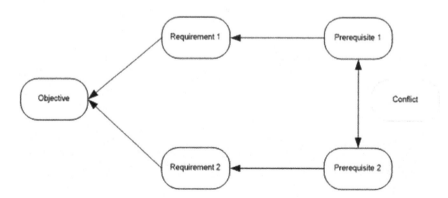

FIGURE 1.30
Basic structure of CRD.

In Figure 1.31, both sides want Minimal Rework. The CRD uses sufficiency-based logic and is read as follows: One side says, "In order to have minimal rework, we must have operators follow shop floor specifications," and "in order to have operators follow shop floor specifications, we must have clear, unambiguous & up-to-date specifications." The other side of the conflict is as follows: "In order to have minimal rework, we must focus resources on new product development," and "in order to focus resources on new product development, we must reduce the time spent writing shop floor specifications." This conflict had to be resolved, and it was by adding additional clerical help.

Now that you have developed a Current Reality Tree and resolved one of the conflicts with a Conflict Resolution Diagram, what now? Obviously, what we would like to have happen is to remove all or many of the undesirable effects and solve core problems. One tool we can use to do this is an FRT. Future Reality Trees are used to map out our future opportunities. We do this by first inserting an idea or injection that we developed to break our current reality problem or core conflict. A Future Reality Tree helps us look into the future, so we see and test the future outcomes of our cause-and-effect analysis before we actually implement any new ideas.

In its simplest form, an FRT could be envisioned as our current reality with all of the undesirable effects changed to desirable effects. By injecting new ideas into the current reality tree, we can see how our idea might change our current reality from the undesirable effects in the present to desirable outcomes in the future. The future reality tree is a tool for gaining

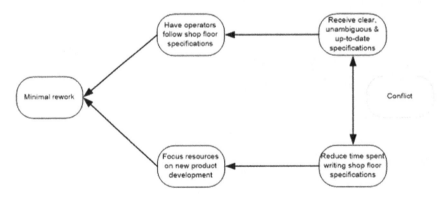

FIGURE 1.31
Identifying the conflict to be resolved.

a "warm and fuzzy" about the solutions we are intending to implement. So how do we construct an FRT? Once again, for details on how to construct and use an FRT, read Dettmer's book, *The Logical Thinking Process* [2]. The FRT from our case study is seen in Figure 1.32.

The FRT allows us the opportunity to test the effectiveness of our actions before we invest time in them, so as to avoid a wasteful use of our limited resources. And for the companies that have limited resources, this is an important benefit. While the CRT answers the question of what to change, the FRT answers the question of what to change to.

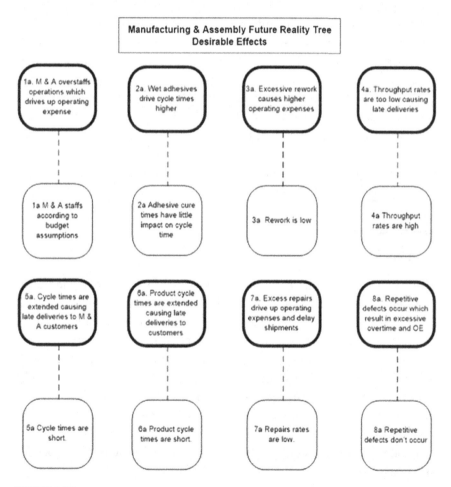

FIGURE 1.32
Future Reality Tree with desirable effects.

PREREQUISITE AND TRANSITION TREES

The final two trees in the Logical Thinking Process tool kit are the Prerequisite Tree (PT) and the Transition Tree (TT). The Prerequisite Tree is, in reality, an implementation planning tool which helps us structure the multifaceted activities associated with the execution of a policy change. The component activities and tasks which happen first and the obstacles that must be overcome are laid-out in the sequence required for execution. What you will see with a finished Prerequisite Tree typically illustrates an inter-reliant network of activities that should be easily translatable into a project activity network. Or to quote Dettmer, "In other words, change implementation can be managed as a formal project, with discrete performance, cost, and schedule parameters" [2].

A Transition Tree works to translate the Prerequisite Tree into a step-by-step guide for completing essential tasks. The Transition Tree can be very useful when the individual tasks must be completed by people who are not accustomed to the steps for doing so. It also helps explain why the individual steps must be accomplished in a specific order.

SUMMARY

LTP is truly a tool kit of unique capability. LTPs are controlled and governed by the Categories of Legitimate Reservation and provide a logical cause-effect-cause picture of your system's current reality, as well as how it might look in the future. The Logical Thinking Process surpasses all other tools in its ability to reveal the complex interconnectedness and interdependencies between both the components of the system, as well as between the system and its environment. As I've indicated numerous times in this chapter, I highly recommend Dettmer's classic book, *The Logical Thinking Process: A Systems Approach to Complex Problem Solving*. No book that I have ever read does a better job of laying out the Logical Thinking Processes.

REFERENCES

1. Eliyahu M. Goldratt and Jeff Cox, *The Goal: A Process of Ongoing Improvement*, North River Press, Great Barrington, MA, 1984.
2. H. William Dettmer, *The Logical Thinking Process: A Systems Approach to Complex Problem Solving*, Quality Press, Milwaukee, WI, 2007.

2

What Is This Thing Called Lean Manufacturing?

In this chapter, we will explore the basic principles, tools, and actions that take place when companies attempt to implement Lean Manufacturing. I will not go into depth when describing those things associated with Lean, but rather take a look at the basics that companies should understand when attempting to implement Lean.

Womack and Jones begin their classic book, *Lean Thinking: Banish Waste and Create Wealth in Your Corporation* with one word, *muda* [1]. They go on to explain that it's the one word of Japanese you really must know:

> In a single word, muda is the Japanese word meaning waste, which is defined by the authors specifically as any human activity which absorbs resources but creates no value. Things like mistakes which require rectification, production of items that no one wants so that inventories and remaindered goods pile up, processing steps which aren't actually needed, movement of employees and transport of goods from one place to another without any purpose, groups of people in downstream activity standing around waiting because an upstream activity has not delivered on time, and goods and services which don't meet the needs of the customer.

Jamie Flinchbaugh and Andy Carlino in their book, *The Hitchhiker's Guide to Lean: Lessons from the Road* have defined waste as, "Anything beyond the absolute minimum amount of materials, manpower, and machinery needed to add value to a product or service" [2]. Both sets of authors have provided a clear definition of waste for readers to ponder.

So, what both sets of authors are defining are those things that negatively impact the ultimate value of products and services, which is ultimately defined by the customer. Value is produced by the producer, but it is clearly defined by the end user.

Lean manufacturing is a whole-systems approach that focuses on identifying and eliminating non-value-added activities within a process. Lean attempts to involve everyone in the organization in the quest to eliminate any and all forms of waste everywhere in the process. Although eliminating waste is a good thing, too many times I have seen this maniacal focus on immediately eliminating waste anywhere and everywhere in the process, creating disorganization problems that can by and large result in chaos. Customers know what they want, when they want it, where they want it, the price they are willing to pay, and the quantities and varieties they want while demanding exceptional quality. The bottom line is, if you don't give customers all of this, then they will simply go elsewhere.

Lean's objectives are to use less human effort, less inventory, less space, and less time to produce high-quality products as efficiently and economically as possible while being highly responsive to customer needs and demands. Lean thinking starts with a conscious effort to define value in very specific terms through constant dialogue with customers. So, just exactly what is value? Surprisingly, value is not always an easy thing to define. Womack and Jones [1] tell us that "part of the reason value is hard to define for most producers is that most producers want to make what they are already making and partly because many customers only know how to ask for some variant of what they are already getting. They simply start in the wrong place and end up at the wrong destination." Womack and Jones further explain that another reason firms find it hard to get value right is "that while value creation often flows through many firms, each one tends to define value in a different way to suit its own needs." The basic definition that I have always used to define value is whatever the customer feels good about paying for. If they are questioning why they should pay for something, then it simply isn't value. Think about it, why should a customer pay for things like excess inventory or a defective product? At the end of the day, value clarifies itself!

Lean Manufacturing has been generally recognized as one of the most effective business-improvement strategies in the world today, but many of the Lean initiatives are either failing or stagnating. Lean's focus is on the complete elimination of waste everywhere within an organization with waste being defined as "any activity (human, equipment, policy, etc.) which absorbs resources but creates no value." When you stop and think about all this could include, the list kind of becomes mind-boggling. Things like mistakes that require repair or modification, production of items that haven't been ordered or that nobody wants, transportation of products within a facility that travel great distances to get from one process step to another, idle time of one process step created by downtime at another or just differences in processing times, defective or scrap materials, and the list could continue through many pages of this book. In some companies, or should I say many companies, listing the actual activities that do create value, or those steps which are said to be value-added, would probably not fill a single page! And if you calculate the ratio of value-added to non-value-added activities in your process, you will be shocked, surprised, and maybe even embarrassed.

Taiichi Ohno, a Toyota executive and intense opponent of waste [3], was really the first to identify and classify seven different categories of waste with corresponding examples as follows:

1. *Overproduction*: Producing items for which there are no orders. That is, making more, earlier, or faster than is required by the next customer. Overproduction generates other wastes like overstaffing, storage, and transportation costs because overproduction always results in excess inventory.

2. *Waiting (time on hand)*: Workers having to stand around waiting for parts from upstream process steps, tools and supplies that they need to process the parts, instructions on how to process the parts, equipment downtime, defective products from the internal and external suppliers, inspections results, and even information. As you will see later on, waiting accounts for the highest amount of non-value-added time in almost all processes.

3. *Unnecessary transport or conveyance*: Having to transport raw material, Work-In-Process (WIP), or finished goods long distances or moving products in and out of storage or between process steps. Unless the product being produced proceeds, uninterrupted, from one step to another and isn't stacked or shelved, then it is considered unnecessary transport or conveyance.

4. *Over-processing or incorrect processing*: Having unnecessary or unneeded steps or extra effort within a process that adds little or no value. This includes things like over-working or over-inspecting a part in an attempt to make it "perfect" when perfection isn't required by the customer.

5. *Excess inventory*: Any part or supply that is in excess of one-piece-flow through the manufacturing process. This includes excess raw material, work-in-process, or finished goods that cause excessive lead times, obsolescence, damaged parts, and transportation and storage costs. In addition, inventory hides problems like defects, machine downtime, flow problems, and so on.

6. *Unnecessary movement*: Any motion of operators, tooling, or equipment that adds no value. This includes things like looking for parts or supplies, stacking and un-stacking of parts, walking to get something, reaching, unnecessary twisting and turning, and so on.

7. *Defects*: Production of products that results in repairs or scraps, replacement production, re-inspection, late deliveries, or that requires extra inspection, sorting, scrapping, downgrading, or replacement.

Although these are the original seven categories of waste, others have added waste of people's creativity as an eighth category which is simply not fully utilizing employees or more explicitly operator's brainpower, creativity, and experience.

From the 10,000-foot view, implementing Lean typically follows the following five steps or principles of Lean:

1. Define value from the end customer's perspective with value being defined by the customer.

2. Identify the value stream which is all of the actions required to bring products from a concept, through detailed design, to an order, to delivery of the products, to the customer. Womack and Jones state that "value stream analysis will almost always show that three types of actions are occurring along the value stream: (1) Many steps will be found to unambiguously create value; (2) Many other steps will be found to create no value, but to be unavoidable with current technologies and production assets; and (3) Many steps will be found to create no value and to be immediately avoidable" [1]. Translated, these three actions are (1) value-added, (2) non-value-added but necessary, and (3) non-value added. For the non-value-added steps, Lean advocates eliminating them immediately, but I don't necessarily agree that immediate elimination is the right approach.

3. Once value has been defined and precisely specified and the value stream analyzed with obvious non-value-added steps removed, make the remaining, value-creating steps flow. In this step, the focus is on

maximizing value by producing only what's needed in the shortest time possible with the fewest resources needed.

4. Pull to customer demand by producing only at the rate of customer orders and no more. In other words, don't overproduce.

5. Pursue perfection by empowering employees with waste elimination tools to create a culture of continuous improvement.

In order to better understand how and why Lean works, it's a good idea to also understand the basic Lean building blocks. These are the basic tools, techniques, and methods that are used during a Lean implementation which include:

1. *5S*: A 5-step procedure aimed at fashioning workplace organization and standardization with each step starting with the letter S. The five Ss originated in Japan and are (with the English translation) Seiri (Sort), Seiton (Set in Motion), Seison (Shine), Seiketsu (Standardize), and Shitsuke (Sustain).

2. *Visual controls*: The assignment of all tools, parts, production procedures, performance metrics, orders, and so on in plain view so that the status of a process step can be understood in fewer than 30 seconds. Typically, one might expect to see things like lights or different colored flags that indicate at a glance the process status.

3. *Standardized work*: A physical description (many times including photos) of exactly how to perform each job according to prescribed methods (developed with operator assistance), with the absolute minimum of waste.

4. *Cellular layout*: The layout of a process (machines, materials, supplies, and people) performing different operations in a tight sequence (a manufacturing cell).

5. *One-piece flow*: The flow of product through a sequence of process steps that passes one piece at a time, with few interruptions, backflows, scrap, rework, or accumulated inventory.

6. *Quality at the source*: Quality is the responsibility of the person producing the product with inspection and process control done at the source by the operator prior to passing the product onto the production step.

7. *Quick changeover*: Being able to change from tooling set or fixtures to another rapidly, on a single machine, to permit the production of multiple products in small batches on the same equipment.

8. *Pull and kanban*: A system of production and delivery instructions sent from downstream operations to upstream operations that is done so only after a signal, usually in the form of a small card.

9. *Total Productive Maintenance* (TPM): A series of maintenance methods that assures process equipment will always be available when needed for as long as it is needed with minimal amounts of downtime.

BASIC LEAN TOOLS

Value Stream Map

It is assumed, by now, that most of you understand the concept of value and what a value stream is, but in case you have missed it along the way or haven't been exposed to it, in simplistic terms, the value stream is simply all those things we do to convert raw materials into a finished product that creates value. Value is simply all of those things that a customer is willing to pay for [4]. Rother and Shook tell us, "Taking a value stream perspective means working on the big picture, not just individual processes, and improving the whole, not just optimizing the parts." I categorically agree with Rother and Shook and further emphasize that improving the whole, not just optimizing the parts is paramount to the success of any for-profit business or organization.

As a tool or technique, the Value Stream Map (VSM) uses a variety of symbols, or a sort of short-hand notation if you will, to depict various elements within the process. For example, a triangle with a capital "I" inside of it represents inventory, with the amount of inventory entered directly beneath the triangle. There are various material flow icons, general icons and information flow icons used to represent all of the specific elements within the process. I highly recommend Rother and Shook's, *Learning to See* for details on the specifics of their methods and styles for producing a VSM and the various icons they use [4]. From my perspective, it's not as important to get the VSM perfect as much as it is to get it functional. Figure 2.1 is an example of a completed value stream map which exhibits information flow, material flow, and lead times.

The actual Value Stream Map can take many different forms, so you shouldn't get hung up on creating the perfect VSM. Just keep your

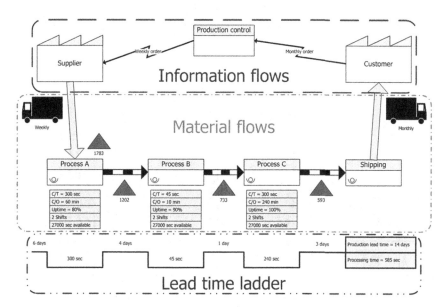

FIGURE 2.1
Example of a value stream map.

objectives in mind and create your own version of this tool to guide you. Figure 2.2, for example, is a sample of a very simple VSM that I created for a company that produces flexible tanks used to hold volatile organic fluids. The typical lead time to build one of these tanks from start to finish is measured in weeks (i.e. 6 to 10 weeks, depending upon the size and complexity of the tank). The process consists of Operations 1 through 6 that are used to manually construct a top and a bottom for each tank in a stationary mold. The top and bottom halves of the tank are then joined in Operation 7 in one of two joining molds. The point is that when you create a VSM, don't be limited and be creative.

Why is Value Stream Mapping such an essential tool? Rother and Shook [4] have answered that question with a list of eight reasons:

1. It helps you visualize more than just the single-process level, i.e. assembly, welding, etc., in production. You can see the flow of the process and the information.
2. Mapping helps you see the sources of waste in your value stream that may not be obvious to you without visualizing it.
3. It provides a common language for talking about manufacturing processes.

VSM Constraint Analysis

Tank Type	Schedule	Oper 10	Oper 9	Oper 8	Mold 1 / Oper 7	Mold 2	Ready Inventory	Oper 6	Oper 5	Oper 4	Oper 3	Oper 2	Oper 1
A	1-Delq 4-March 4-April 2-May 4-June 4-July 4-Aug	1 Tank		4 Tanks	1 Tank	1 Tank	3 Tops 3 Bottoms	3 Tops 3 Bottoms		1 Top 2 Bottoms	2 Tops	2 Bottoms 1 Top	1 Top
B	3-Delq 4-March 6-April 0-May 6-Jun 4-Jul 4-Aug	1 Tank		1 Tank	Empty	1 Tank	2 Bottoms 1 Top	4 Tops	2 Tops	5 Bottoms 1 Top	3 Bottoms 1 Top	1 Bottom	1 Bottom
C	3-Delq 3-March 7-April 4-May 8-June 8-July 8-August			1 Tank	Empty	1 Tank	5 Bottoms 1 Top		1 Top	1 Top	3 Tops	EMPTY	1 Bottom

	Oper 10	Oper 9	Oper 8	Mold 1	Mold 2	Oper 6	Oper 5	Oper 4	Oper 3	Oper 2	Oper 1
Yield	Y=100%	Y=99%	Y=99%	Y=85%	Y=83%	Y=95%	Y=99%	Y=99%	Y=99%	Y=100%	Y=100%
Cycle Time	C/T 2 Days	C/T 1 Day	C/T 2 Days	C/T 6 Days	C/T 8 Days	C/T 3 Days	C/T 1 Days	C/T 1 Day	C/T 2 Days	C/T 2 Days	C/T 1 Day
Lead Time	LT 3 Days	LT 4 Days	LT 3 Days	LT 9 Days	LT 9 Days	LT 34 Days	LT 2 Days	LT 3 Days	LT 2 Days	LT 2 Days	LT 1 Day

✂ = # FULL PERSON ASSIGNED ✂ = 1/2 PERSON ASSIGNED

FIGURE 2.2

Value stream map example.

4. It makes decisions about the flow apparent, so you can discuss them. Otherwise, many details and decisions on your shop floor just happen by default.

5. It ties together lean concepts and techniques, which help you avoid "cherry picking."

6. It forms the basis of an implementation plan. By helping you design how the whole door-to-door flow should operate—a missing piece in so many lean efforts—value stream maps become a blueprint for lean implementation. Imagine trying to build a house without a blueprint!

7. It shows linkage between the information flow and the material flow. No other tool does this.

8. It is much more useful than quantitative tools and layout diagrams that produce a tally of non-value-added steps, lead time, distance traveled, the amount of inventory, and so on. Value stream mapping is a qualitative tool by which you describe in detail how your facility should operate in order to create flow. Numbers are good for creating a sense of urgency or as before/after measures. Value stream mapping is good for describing what you are actually going to do to affect those numbers.

Although I agree with most of these eight reasons listed above, I have added a ninth reason to this list, which, I might add, is actually first on my list and trumps the first eight. The reason I consider most important is to identify the current and next constraint operation! In my opinion, this step is the quintessential starting point in any improvement process for all of the reasons I outlined in Chapter 1.

Another point that I absolutely agree with Rother and Shook on is that value stream mapping is a "pencil and paper tool" that helps you see your way through your own value stream. VSMs are not intended to be pretty or even "artsy," they are meant to be functional. You cannot create a value stream from your office, and you can't do it effectively in a vacuum, because it won't be accurate or even complete. For this reason, please don't create a value stream map by yourself. Instead, other resources like hourly operators, material handlers, and so on should assist you to make sure you've included all facets of the flow of information and product.

The next question to be answered is which products should I map? All of them? Some of them? If you are producing only a single product, then it's a simple selection as to what you should map. But if your company produces multiple products, then it's always best to select a product family to map. My recommendation is that you spend some time practicing VSMs until you have learned to capture everything that you need, but again, it isn't about making your VSM pretty!

So just what should be included in your value stream map? Well, think about what you are trying to accomplish? If your goal is to make money now, and in the future, then one thing you want to be able to identify is the operation that is limiting your throughput. Additionally, you want to be able to identify any opportunities that will reduce both inventory and operating expense. With this in mind, what are the things that are important to answer these three profit essentials? Obviously, inventory stacked up is an excellent indicator of where your constraint operation might be, so inventory must be listed. What about processing and cycle times? Cycle times certainly can have an impact on the rate of generation of throughput, don't they? How about delays, don't they negatively impact throughput? How about equipment downtime? And let's not forget inspection sites as well as defect rates and rework locations. I have created my own list of things that I include in my version of a value stream map that don't necessarily agree with Rother and Shook's version. Just remember what you are attempting to determine. You want to identify the operation that is constraining your throughput and all of the other opportunities that could be used to reduce inventory and operating expense. My list of entries that you might use (note: I don't use all of these all of the time) and a brief explanation of each is as follows for each process step:

1. Identification of the product or product family being studied.
2. Identification of each individual process step listed by the name of the function (e.g., assembly, drilling, etc.).
3. Step-by-step value-added time, wait times, processing times, cycle times and lead times.
   a. *Value-Added-Time*: The average total time taken to transform the product into value (note: this does not include wait times).
   b. *Wait Time*: The average time that a part waits within a process step before being able to move to the next process step. This might include any drying or curing times, waiting for an inspection to occur, etc.
   c. *Processing Time*: The average length of time it takes for a single part to be completed by a single-process step which should equal a plus b.

     d. *Cycle Time*: The average length of time it takes from release of raw materials into the process to completion of finished goods ready to ship.

     e. *Lead Time*: The average total elapsed time from receipt of the order from the customer to the receipt of the order by the customer.

4. Inventory Levels: The number of individual pieces or parts waiting to be processed in each step of the process.
5. Capacity: The average number of pieces or parts that a process step is able to produce in a given unit of time.
6. Actual Demonstrated Capacity: The average total pieces or parts produced/unit of time minus total average scrapped during the same time. This can be any unit of time depending upon the overall speed of the process.
7. Percent Repaired: The average number repaired compared with the average total produced for any unit of time.
8. Customer demand or order rate.
9. Actual rate to be produced compared with order rate (i.e. takt time).
10. Average defect rates and the actual defects based upon inspection data for a given period of time (Pareto chart).
11. Inspection points and average inspection time required.
12. The average downtime rates and a description of actual downtime based upon maintenance history (Pareto chart).
13. The number and location of operators (i.e. how many and where they are).
14. The average travel time and distance traversed per any unit of time (use a Spaghetti diagram).
15. The average percent Order On-Time Completion.

As you can see, I have included items that should help us first, answer where the constraint operation is, and then, where and how we might be able to improve the throughput, operating expense and inventory within the constraint. Remember, unless you improve the throughput of the constraint operation, you will not be improving the overall system!

One final point, that I'm sure will draw criticism, are the boundaries I establish when preparing VSMs. Since I am looking for ways to increase throughput within the factory, I don't always include suppliers. The obvious exception to this is if I know that a particular supplier is the constraint. That is, if I am frequently waiting for raw materials to begin production, or the quality of the incoming raw materials is poor, and I am confident that this supplier is constraining my throughput, then it's easy to determine my focus. Typically, I am concerned with what goes on inside the walls of the facility that limits throughput. It doesn't mean that I ignore suppliers, it only means that most of the time the problems I see with limited throughput and less than optimal margins are related to internal issues, not external ones.

Although I support Shook and Rother's approach to VSM [4], I also believe that it can be overwhelming to companies that are just starting their improvement initiative. The long-term goal of an organization should be to eliminate waste and reduce variation, but don't get beleaguered at the outset. Keep it simple in the beginning.

IMPLEMENT 5S WORKPLACE ORGANIZATION

One of the keys to reducing waste in your process is to organize it; 5S is a tool specifically designed to help establish effective organization of tools, equipment, and so on, so that time isn't wasted looking for things needed to produce product and that wasted motion is reduced. The term 5S is a reference to a list of five Japanese words which start with the letter "S." Those five Japanese words plus their translation and meaning are as follows:

1. Seiri—Separating—Refers to the practice of going through all of the tools, equipment, supplies, materials, etc., and then assigning each one to a specific location close to the point-of-use.
2. Seiton—Sorting—Refers to the practice of arranging the tools, equipment, materials, etc., according to an order that promotes workflow through unnecessary movement or motion.
3. Seiso—Shining—Refers to the practice of keeping the workplace neat and clean on a daily basis.
4. Seiketsu—Standardize—Refers to operating in a consistent and standardized way so that everyone understands what their responsibilities are.
5. Shitsuke—Sustain—Refers to maintaining the standards completed in the previous four Ss and to not permit any backsliding.

Davis has developed his own version of 5S which he refers to as his 6Cs [5]. Davis believes that "there is an important step not included in 5S." Table 2.1 contains Davis' 6Cs with each step labeled in the order in which they are performed. Davis also tells us, "whereas 5S tends to be used as a group of things to do, with no special order as to which is prescribed first, second or third other than what might be assumed, the steps and levels noted are an extremely important factor in applying the 6C's [sic]." Davis explains that "unlike 5S, the scoring approach is absolutely critical for determining the effectiveness of each of the of 6C's [sic] steps [...] For any plant or operation that has not gone through the process of putting true workplace organization (WPO) in place, the initial 6C score will always be zero." Davis says this because he believes that workplace organization is truly the foundation for continuously improving an operation and that it is a step-by-step effort, rather than a one-time event. In other words, you don't start Level II (Confine) until you have completed Level I (Clear). I absolutely agree with Davis in that I have seen many 5S initiatives fall short of achieving workplace organization simply because the effort was seen as a one-time event and clearly it isn't. For a detailed description of Davis' 6C approach to workplace organization, I recommend that you read his book.

Davis [5] further explains why he is so adamant that workplace organization being the foundation for continuous improvement for five reasons:

1. Without WPO, you can exert wasted efforts in dealing with things that are not absolutely needed, thus expending time and energy that could be applied elsewhere.
2. Until an area is rid of things not absolutely required, it is impossible to see the real workplace.
3. Time wasted trying to find things on the shop floor distracts from productivity.
4. A tidy and orderly work area provides the appearance of efficiency which can have a positive influence on the perception of the organization by customers who visit the plant and on the attitude of employees.
5. Applying WPO in an area of the factory where it has not existed before provides a stark contrast to the way things are run in the rest of the factory, thus visualizing the level of change underway.

TABLE 2.1

Davis's 6Cs

Step	Activity	Level
Step one	Clear	Level I
Step two	Confine	Level II
Step three	Control	Level III
Step four	Clean	Level IV
Step five	Communicate	Level V
Step six	Continue	Level VI

Whether you are applying 5S or 6C you will be doing so in the constraint operation and you will see improvements in both constraint efficiency and throughput just by organizing your workplace.

IMPLEMENT VISUAL CONTROLS

Earlier, I discussed 5S and workplace organization and closely related to these two activities is the concept of visual controls. A visual control is any communication method or device that is used to tell us at a glance how work should be done and what its status is. In everyday life, a common example of a visual control is a traffic light. We know intuitively that green means it is safe to proceed, yellow means that we can continue with caution, and red means it is not safe to proceed. Effective visual controls help employees see immediately things like the status of work-in-process, the location and quantity of different items, and what the standard procedure for performing a job is. The primary reason for using visual controls is to define the desired state (i.e. the standard) and then to quickly recognize any deviation from that standard.

One common example of a visual control in manufacturing are andon lights that are used to visualize the status of work-in-process. Like traffic lights, andon lights typically utilize the color green to indicate no problems, yellow to indicate potential problems, and red to indicate a serious problem that is preventing the operation from producing product. Andon lights permit the easy identification of the status of an operation even from an area not close to the operation. The flag system I discussed in a previous section is basically a manual version of the andon light concept.

Other common examples of visual controls are the use of shadow boards to show the location of each tool required in a particular operation, having clearly visible indicators of minimum and maximum levels for inventory, process control boards with well-designed performance charts and graphs located within a work cell, kanban cards or bins to control the flow of materials in a pull system, and even outlines on the floor to designate where items should be placed.

Toyota uses visual control so that no problems are hidden. Even in a world that is dominated by electronic data, if you walk into a Toyota facility you will see things like paper kanban cards circulating through the factory, paper flip charts being used for ad hoc problem-solving, and manual paper charts and graphs that are updated manually by the operators in the work cell. Toyota believes that people are visual creatures that need to be able to look at their work, their parts, and their product flow, just to make sure they are performing to Toyota's standards. The key to creating effective visual controls is to use your imagination and consider the visual needs of the people that will be using them.

DESIGN AND IMPLEMENT WORK CELLS

We're all familiar with the positive effects of implementing Cellular Manufacturing (CM) in our workplaces such as the improved flow through the process, overall cycle time reduction, throughput gains as well as other benefits. But there is one other positive effect that can result from implementing Cellular Manufacturing that isn't discussed much. This potential positive impact is what Cellular Manufacturing can do to reduce variation.

In many companies that I have visited over the years, it is not uncommon for products to travel great distances from machine to machine because of the equipment layout scheme. In one particular company located in France that produced pinions for things like turn-signal levers, the distance traveled was actually measured in miles! And this did not include the distance traveled to send parts outside the company for heat treatment! Why so much travel distance?

The distance problem was manifested in the individual pieces of equipment used to produce the pinions (i.e. all of the turning, drilling, hobbing, grinding, reaming, washing, and crack-detection machines) being set up as functional islands located throughout three different factories! (Functional islands are like machines that are used for the same function that are all placed in close proximity to each other in the same area of the plant.) Because of the location of the equipment, it was not uncommon for the parts to travel back and forth between the factories as they made their way through the process sequence. This company also produced their parts in relatively large batches and didn't transfer the parts to the next operation until the containers used to transport them were full. Because of the location of the equipment, it was not uncommon for the parts to travel back and forth between the factories as they made their way through the process sequence.

The deleterious effects of this protracted distance traveled, and large batch sizes, were prolonged cycle times that were proportional to both the distance traveled and the size of the transfer batch. These long-drawn-out distances and inflated times translated directly into routine delays throughout the process, with the ultimate consequence being late deliveries and missed shipment to customers. To make matters worse, when quality problems were eventually detected, it was not uncommon for very large numbers of defective pinions to be found requiring massive sorting, re-inspection of parts, and a large number of repairs and scrapped parts. This was due in large part to a phenomenon referred to as "paths of variation."

When multiple machines performing the same function are used to produce identical products, there are potentially multiple paths that parts can take from beginning to end as the parts progress through the entire process. There are, therefore, potential multiple paths of variation. These multiple paths of variation can significantly increase the overall variability of the process.

Even with focused reductions in variation, real improvement might not be achieved because of the number of paths of variation that exist within a process. Paths of variation, in this context, are simply the number of potential opportunities for variation to occur within a process because of potential multiple machines processing the parts. And the paths of variation of a process are increased by the number of individual process steps and/or the complexity of the steps (i.e. number of sub-processes within a process).

The answer to reducing the effects of paths of variation should lie in the process and product design stage of manufacturing processes. That is, processes should/must be designed with reduced complexity and products should/must be designed that are more robust. The payback for reducing the number of paths of variation is an overall reduction in the amount of process variation and ultimately more consistent and robust products. Let's look at a real case study.

Many years ago, I had the opportunity to consult for a French pinion manufacturer located in southern France. (Fortunately for me, years before this, I had worked for Michelin Tire and had spent a year in France, so the language barrier did not exist which proved to be very helpful.) For those of you who are not familiar with pinions (i.e. pignons in French), a pinion is a round gear used in several applications: usually the smaller gear in a gear drive train. Figure 2.3 is a drawing of what a pinion might look like, and as you might suspect, pinions require a complicated process to fabricate.

When our team arrived at this company, based on our initial observations, it was very clear that this plant was being run according to a mass production mindset. I say this because there were many very large containers of various-sized pinions stacked everywhere.

The actual process for making one particular size and shape pinion was a series of integrated steps from beginning to end as depicted in Figure 2.4. The company received metal blanks from an outside supplier which were fabricated in the general shape of the final product. The blanks were then passed through a series of turning, drilling, hobbing, etc. process steps to finally achieve the finished product (Figure 2.3).

The process for this particular pinion was highly automated with two basic process paths, one on each side of this piece of equipment. There

FIGURE 2.3
Example of a pinion.

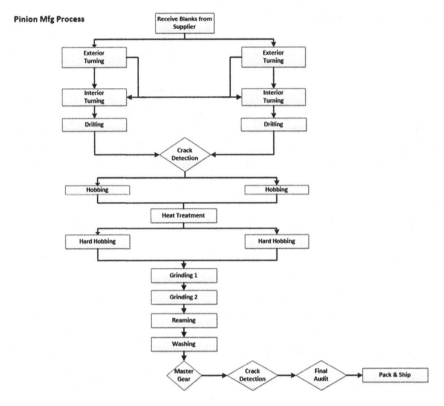

FIGURE 2.4
Pinion manufacturing process.

was an automated gating operation that directed each pinion to the next available process step as it traversed the entire process which consisted of 14 steps. It was not unusual for a pinion to start its path on one side of the machine, move to the other side and then move back again which meant that the pinion being produced was free to move from side to side in random fashion. Because of this configuration, the number of possible combinations of individual process steps, or paths of variation, used to make these pinions was very high. Figure 2.4 is the layout of this manufacturing process.

The process for this particular pinion was automated with two basic process paths, one on each side of this piece of equipment. There was an automated gating operation that directed each pinion to the next available process step as it traversed the entire process which consisted of 14 steps. As I said earlier, it was not unusual for a pinion to start its path on one side of the machine, move to the other side and back again which meant that the pinion being produced was free to move from side to side in random fashion. Because of this configuration, the number of possible combinations of machines used to make the pinion, or paths of variation, was very high. Let's take a look now at the number of paths of variation that existed on this machine as seen in Figure 2.5.

The first step in the process for making this style pinion was an exterior turning operation with two exterior turning machines available to perform

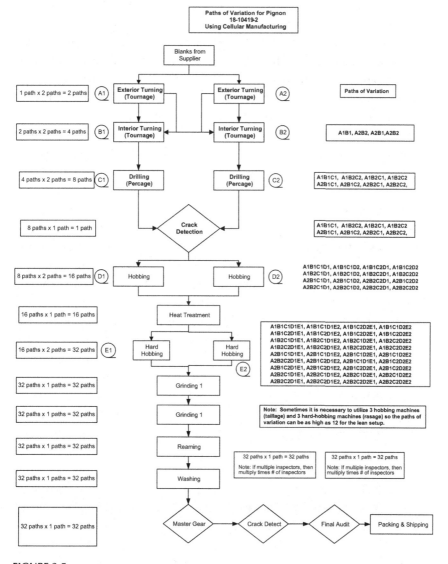

FIGURE 2.5
Current state pinion manufacturing process.

this function (labeled A1 on one side of the machine and A2 on the other side of the machine as shown in Figure 2.5). The purpose of this first step, like the others to follow, was to shave metal from the blank to ultimately achieve its final shape and critical dimensions.

The next step in the process is referred to as interior turning and, again, there are two interior turning machines labeled B1 and B2, one on each side. In the third step, there were two possible choices for drilling, C1 and C2. After the pinion was automatically inspected for cracks (with one, common automated gage), it then progressed to one of two hobbing machines, D1 and D2. The parts were then collected in storage bins and sent as large batches to an outside vendor for heat treatment. Upon return from heat treatment, the pinions then proceeded to hard hobbing, E1 and E2, and then on through the remainder of the process as indicated in Figure 2.5. Hobbing is a machining process used for gear cutting, cutting splines, and cutting sprockets on a hobbing machine, which is a special type of milling machine. The teeth or splines are progressively cut into the workpiece by a series of cuts made by a cutting tool called a hob. Compared with other gear forming processes, it is relatively inexpensive but still quite accurate, thus it is used for a broad range of products.

The boxes to the right in Figure 2.5 represent the possible paths that the pinion could take as it makes its way through the process. For example, for the first two process steps, there are four possible paths, A1B1, A1B2, A2B1, and A2B2. The parts then move to the third step, drilling where you now see there are eight possible paths of variation which are listed on the right side of Figure 2.5.

As you can see, as the part continues on, the possible paths continue until all 32 potential paths are seen. Do you think that the pinions produced through these multiple paths will be the same dimensions or will you have multiple distributions? Here are two important questions for you to consider:

- Do you think that the pinions produced through these multiple paths will be the same dimensions or will you have multiple distributions?
- What if we were able to reduce the number of paths of variation from 32 down to 2? Do you believe the overall variation would be less and how many distributions would you have now? Or another way of saying it, do you believe the part-to-part consistency would be greater?

In Figure 2.6, I have created what I refer to a "virtual cell," meaning that we limited the paths of travel that an individual pinion can take by removing the possibility for a part to traverse back and forth from side to side of this machine configuration. In simple terms, the part either went down side 1 or side 2 rather than allowing the gating operation to select the path. In Figure 2.6, you can see that pinions passing through exterior

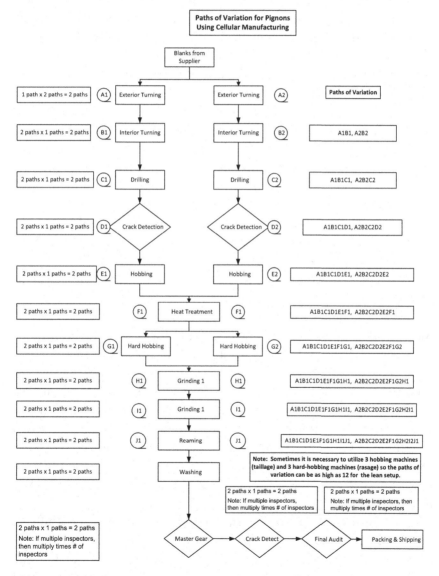

FIGURE 2.6
Modified pinion manufacturing process.

turning machine A1 are only permitted to proceed to internal turning machine B1. Those that pass through internal turning machine A2 are only permitted to proceed to turning machine B2. In doing so, the number of paths of variation for the first two process steps was reduced from four to two. Continuing, the parts that were turned on A1 and B1 can only pass through drilling machine C1, crack detection D1, and hobbing machine E1 while those produced on A2 and B2 can only be processed on drilling machine C2, drilling machine D2, and hobbing machine E2. To this point, the total paths of variation remain at 2 instead of the original number of paths of 16.

The part continues to hard hobbing where there are, once again, two machines available. The parts produced on A1B1C1D1E1 can only proceed to the G1 hard-hobbing machine while those produced on A2B2C2D2E2 can only be processed on hard-hobbing machine G2. We also instructed the heat-treater to maintain batch integrity and not mix the batches. So, at this point, because we specified and limited the pinion paths, the total paths of variation decreased from 32 to only 2! So, what do you think happened to variation when we created our virtual cell?

The key response variables for this process were five individual diameters, measured along the surface of the pinion. As a result of limiting the number of potential paths of variation, the standard deviation for the various diameters was reduced by approximately 50 percent on each of the diameters!

But even though we were very successful in reducing variation, there was a problem associated with making this change, sort of an unintended consequence, if you will. Remember in the original configuration, pinions could move to the next available machine (i.e. either side) as they proceeded along the flow of the process. With the new configuration, they could no longer do this. Prior to this change, when there was downtime on one side of the machine, the automation and/or operator simply diverted the pinion to the same machine on the other side so as to keep the parts moving. With the new configuration, when a machine in the cell went down unexpectedly, the parts now had to wait until the machine was repaired.

The immediate short-term result of this change was a significant reduction in throughput of pinions because of unplanned downtime. However, in the longer term, it forced the company to develop and implement a preventive maintenance system which eventually reduced the unplanned downtime to nearly zero. When this happened, the new throughput surpassed the original throughput and the variation was reduced by 50 percent! In addition, the scrap levels for this process were reduced by 40–50 percent! And the great part was, not a single dollar—or should I say Euro—was spent in doing this, yet the payback was huge. So, as you are studying your process for variation reduction, keep the concept of paths of variation foremost in your mind, because it can make a huge difference in some circumstances.

Cellular manufacturing and work cells lie at the heart of Lean Manufacturing with the general benefits being things like simplified flow, cycle time reductions, improved quality, improved intra-process communication, and so on. In cellular manufacturing, equipment and workstations are arranged in close proximity to each other in the normal process sequence. Once processing begins, products move directly from workstation to workstation with the result typically being significant improvements in overall cycle times and vastly improved teamwork and quality. This arrangement of workstations supports a smooth flow of products and components through the process with minimal transport and delays. In addition, arranging the equipment into manufacturing cells makes it much easier to reduce the transfer batch size.

A manufacturing cell is comprised of the people, equipment, and workstations, arranged in the logical sequence required to produce the end product. The positive effects of cellular manufacturing, if done correctly, include smaller batch sizes, one-piece flow, flexible production, reduced travel time for parts, less equivalent manpower, improved quality, less damaged product, less required space, less obsolescence, immediate identification of problems, reduced walking time, and less lead time, all of which can translate to decreased cycle time, increased throughput, and reduced inventory and operating expense.

I mentioned that one-piece flow is one of the positive benefits of cellular manufacturing. In a one-piece flow production environment, parts are moved immediately to the next operation for processing making it arguably the most efficient way to process material through a factory. When done in conjunction with the establishment of work cells, one-piece flow works very well. Imagine what happens to the lead time of products being produced in work cells with one-piece flow, providing we have calculated the correct critical WIP.

I recognize that some equipment is simply too large and bulky to be moved into and included in a cell, but even with this scenario, there is a solution. If the equipment is too large and difficult to move, then build the work cell around this limiting piece of equipment. Large screw machines or stamping presses, for example, might not be possible to move, but don't let that stop you. Either arrange the equipment around these machines or arrange the equipment that can be moved into a cellular arrangement.

In the French company I discussed earlier, we faced this situation just described. We simply left the large screw machines where they were and arranged the remainder of the equipment (i.e. drilling, hobbing, grinding, reaming, washing, and crack-detection machines) into functional cells and the result was significantly reduced space, less cycle time, dramatic reductions in distance traveled, increased throughput, improved quality, reduced inventory, and much-improved on-time delivery. As a matter of fact, the on-time delivery improved from approximately 70 percent to over 90 percent while PPM's decreased from over 20,000 to around 200 in a little over 3 months.

So where was the system constraint in this case study? In this case, we weren't dealing with a physical constraint in this manufacturing system. In actuality, we were dealing with a *policy constraint.* Remember how I explained that the process for this particular pinion was highly automated with two basic process paths, one on each side of this piece of equipment? I explained that there was an automated gating operation that directed each pinion to the *next available process step,* as it traversed the entire process which consisted of 14 steps. And when one step went down, the operator could move the part to the other side of the machine. By removing this decision portion of the procedure, we could effectively streamline this process and throughput could jettison upward, along with this company's profitability. In other words, we identified and exploited this policy constraint. So now the question becomes, where did the constraint become next?

As I explained, in the original configuration, pinions could move to the next available machine (i.e. either side) as they proceeded along the flow of the process. With the new configuration, they could no longer do this. I also explained that prior to this change, when there was downtime on one side of the machine, the automation and/or operator simply diverted the pinion to the same machine on the other side, so as to keep the parts moving. With the new configuration, when a machine in the cell went down unexpectedly, the parts now had to wait until the machine was repaired. I also explained that the immediate short-term result of this change was a significant reduction in throughput of pinions because of unplanned downtime and the parts now had to wait until the machine was repaired. This lack of preventive maintenance now became the new system constraint! The exploitation of the new constraint was the implementation of a comprehensive preventive maintenance plan and when this was implemented, throughput and profitability jettisoned upward as predicted.

Once we determined the new system constraint, we then applied the tools and techniques of both Lean and Six Sigma to optimize this process. The important point to remember here is that not all constraints are physical in nature, so it's important to thoroughly review the process or system being improved to determine what type of constraint you are dealing with and react accordingly.

REFERENCES

1. James P. Womack and Daniel T. Jones, *Lean Thinking: Banish Waste and Create Wealth in Your Corporation*. Free Press, New York, NY, 1996.
2. Jamie Flinchbaugh and Andy Carlino, *The Hitchhiker's Guide to Lean: Lessons from the Road*. Society of Manufacturing Engineers, Dearborn, MI, 2006.
3. Taiichi Ohno, *Toyota Production System, Beyond Large-Scale Production*. CRC Press, Taylor and Francis Group, Boca Raton, FL, 2012.
4. Mike Rother and John Shook, *Learning to See: Value Stream Mapping to Create Value and Eliminate Muda*. Lean Enterprise Institute, Boston, MA, 1999.
5. Charles Standard and Dale Davis, *Running Today's Factory: A Proven Strategy for Lean Manufacturing*. Hanser Gardner Publications, Cincinnati, OH, 1999.

3

What Is This Thing Called Six Sigma?

SIX SIGMA PRINCIPLES, TOOLS, AND METHODS

When I read one of my first books on Six Sigma, there was one quote that drove home what Six Sigma is all about, at least for me. Mikel Harry told us something about the power of measurements with the following [1]:

> To know the truth is to know all of the facts.
> To know the facts requires investigation.
> Investigation is driven by questions.
> A question (Q) always precedes an answer (A), thus $A = f(Q)$.
> Questions lead, and answers follow.
> Without the question, an answer is merely information, not an answer.
> The same question invariably leads to the same answer.
> To change the answer is to change the question.
> We won't change the question without reason to do so.
> We can only reason from what we know.
> What we know is based on facts.
> Every fact is an answer to some question.
> Facts are discovered, not created.

These words, although elegant and simple, deliver a very compelling message to all of us about first questioning, then searching for answers, and then measuring to find the answers. The fact is, if we don't measure, we simply will not improve. This is the powerful and dynamic message of Six Sigma. Wheeler and Chambers explain, "You can make calculated guesses and assumptions based on experience, but without hard data, conclusions are based on insufficient evidence" [2]. Or maybe a simpler message is, "Without data you're just another person with an opinion."

The first step in the Six Sigma roadmap is the identification of core or primary processes and key customers. As a rule of thumb, most companies have four to eight really high-level, essential core processes that represent the backbone of how the company functions. These typically include things like customer acquisition, order administration, order fulfillment, customer service and support, new product/service development, and invoicing and collections. If you consider each of these in the context of the goal of the company, to make money now and in the future, and although they all contribute, each could also be a system constraint. If you were, for example, producing product and shipping it according to order rates, but you were not receiving the revenue in a timely manner, then invoicing and collections could be the operation that is constraining or restricting your organization's revenue stream. Or maybe your order fulfillment process is preventing you from moving closer to your goal.

Six Sigma uses "projects" to make improvements and these projects can be located in any of the core processes, or support processes, or even external to the company. Pande, Newman, and Cavanaugh list three criteria for understanding what will qualify as a "Six Sigma" project as follows [3]:

1. There is a gap between current and needed/desired performance.
2. The cause of the problem isn't clearly understood.
3. The solution isn't predetermined, nor is the optimal solution apparent.

These three criteria seem logical, but only if they are applied to performance issues or problems within the operation that is constraining your organization. At the risk of sounding redundant, any action taken in operations outside the constraint operation, or that process step that is limiting throughput, is in my opinion, a somewhat wasted use of valuable resources. And although you might move closer to your goal, your rate of movement will be much slower than it could or should be.

One of the key teachings of Six Sigma is the concept of sigma levels which, in a nutshell, refer to the quality level of the product produced, or service delivered. Quality is measured and tracked as defects per million opportunities (DPMO). In Table 3.1, Harry and Schroeder estimated the cost of quality as a percent of sales for each level of sigma [1]. Harry and Schroeder believe that a typical corporation operates at a three to four sigma level with DPMO levels ranging from 66,807 down to 6,210. They also believe companies that operate below three sigma usually don't

TABLE 3.1

The Cost of Quality

The Cost of Quality		
Sigma Level	Defects Per Million Opportunities (DPMO)	Cost of Quality
2	308,537 (Non-competitive companies)	Not applicable
3	66,807	25–40% of sales
4	6,210 (Industry average)	15–25% of sales
5	233	5–15% of sales
6	3.4 (World class)	<1% of sales

survive, clearly because their cost of quality prevents them from being competitive.

The concept of measuring processes on the basis of defective product (or service) is an important one because even a shift from 4 sigma to 4.5 sigma represents a big improvement to the bottom line. Harry and Schroeder further explain that "[t]he improved quality that results will translate not only into cost reductions but into increased sales and quantum leaps in profitability."

Although I agree, in spirit, with the comment regarding increased sales and "quantum leaps in profitability," I would add that Harry and Schroeder's comment is only this impactful if the improvement efforts are focused in the constraint operation. However, if your operation already has excess capacity, then clearly an improvement in your product's quality level could be leveraged to improve your ability to land new orders and therefore new revenue.

When Harry and Schroeder introduced their Six Sigma methodology, there were eight steps in their process as follows [1]:

1. (R) Recognize functional problems that link to operational issues.
2. (D) Define the processes that contribute to the functional problems.
3. (M) Measure the capability of each process that offers operational leverage.
4. (A) Analyze the data to assess prevalent patterns and trends.
5. (I) Improve the key product/service characteristics created by the key processes.
6. (C) Control the process variables that exert undue influence.
7. (S) Standardize the methods and processes that produce best-in-class performance.
8. (I) Integrate standard methods and processes into the design cycle.

Somewhere along the way, these eight steps have been distilled into the familiar DMAIC methodology that we now see in most texts. In so doing, I believe many companies are missing a golden opportunity to get the most of their efforts. For example, suppose that there is a problem with the billing process that delays incoming revenue. All the improvement in the world in other areas will not increase the rate of revenue generation if the billing process is flawed. Some will contend that by making this statement, I am backing away from my belief that we should be focusing on the constraint operation when in reality all I am saying is that the billing process could be the constraint operation. Remember, the constraint operation is the one that is preventing us from moving closer to our goal of making more money now and in the future. The billing process, in this example, would provide the operational leverage to the rest of the process. As we present the individual steps in the Ultimate Improvement Cycle [4], we will be able to see the relevance of this point.

The real power of Six Sigma lies in its disciplined structure and use of statistical tools, techniques, and methods. In 1925, H. G. Wells wrote, "Statistical thinking will one day be as necessary for efficient citizenship as the ability to read and write." Wells was clearly a visionary and what separates Six Sigma from other improvement methodologies is the use of statistical analysis tools and techniques to translate operational data into usable decision-making information. I agree with Wells and believe that the training provided by many of the Six Sigma Black Belt certifications is now a business imperative.

But while the use of statistical tools and techniques is vital, they can be "over-used" to the detriment of many improvement initiatives. In fact, many companies have experienced information overload and analysis paralysis, whereby there is a failure to launch into solutions. That is, companies sometimes spend so much time analyzing data that their improvement initiative never seems to get off the ground, or if it is launched, there are too many equally rated problems and participants end up drowning in a sea of data. Companies must always guard against trying to collect and analyze more data and information than they need to in order to make improvements to their process. For this reason, I believe that there are six simple tools and one a bit more complicated that are critical to master, but more importantly critical to use. These six simple tools are:

1. Run Charts
2. Pareto Charts

3. Cause-and-Effect Diagram
4. Causal Chains
5. Control Charts
6. Check Sheets

The more complicated tool is Design of Experiments (DOEs) which really isn't difficult, but it is perceived to be. Since many people believe DOEs are too advanced for them because of the use of statistics, they tend to shy away from using it. The reality is that with the statistical software that exists today (e.g., Minitab), DOEs are relatively straightforward to design, run, and analyze. Minitab even has a feature that explains in very simple terms, the purpose of each step of the DOE process and how to interpret the results of the study. If this sounds to you like an endorsement for Minitab, then you're absolutely right. As I write today, I can state that of all the statistically based software on the market today that I have used, Minitab is clearly the most user-friendly one available, and I highly recommend it.

Each of the six simple tools plays a valuable role in the improvement process and, as such, each has a distinct purpose. The run chart serves several important purposes. First, it provides a history of where the process or product variable has been, where it is operating right now, and where it could likely be in the future. When changes are made to the process, the run chart lets us know the impact of changes and from a problem-solving perspective, being able to relate changes to shifts in the response variables we are attempting to improve is invaluable. By recording the changes that you are making, or have made, directly onto the run chart, you get a visual presentation of the impact of the change.

Pareto charts serve a much different purpose than run charts in that they help us identify, focus on, and prioritize the defects, problems, and so on that offer the greatest opportunity for improvement. By seeing things in priority order, we have less of a tendency to squander our resources.

Cause-and-Effect Diagrams help us organize potential causes of defects, problems, and so on, while Causal Chains facilitate the logical dissection of problems by continuing to ask why until we arrive at potential root causes of the problem we are attempting to solve.

Control Charts provide us with the opportunity to identify sources and types of process variation, help us reduce process variation, let us know whether or not our processes are in a state of statistical control, and then allow us to predict what future results might be.

Check sheets help us pinpoint where on the object the problem or defect is occurring. DOEs are an important part of our improvement initiative and will help us identify which factors and interactions are most responsible for creating defects and excessive variation. DOEs also facilitate the optimization of our process and corresponding response variables. Every successful improvement tool kit must contain DOEs.

TYPES OF VARIATION

In a manufacturing environment, there are two completely different categories of variability that have profoundly different impacts on a manufacturing process. The first one, processing time variability (PTV), is primarily concerned with the speed that parts progress through an individual process step, or the time required to actually process materials to produce the products (or deliver services) or components. The second category is process and product variability (PPV) which involves the variation associated with the physical process used to produce the product and variability of the actual product produced. By process, in this context, I am referring to the physical process parameters or machine settings used to produce the product. By product, I am referring to the physical characteristics or critical to quality characteristics that we measure on the product being produced.

Because each category of variability presents completely different challenges for a company, I have elected to treat each one separately in our discussion of variability. However, as will become apparent, PPV has a profound influence on PTV. Let's look at product and process variation first.

MEASURING VARIATION

In order to reduce variation, you must be able to accurately and precisely measure it. This means that you must have a measurement system that is capable of measuring your products and processes both accurately and precisely. I am assuming that the reader understands basic measures of variation like Range (R), Standard Deviation (σ), and Variance ($\sigma2$), and basic measures of central tendency like population mean (μ) and sample mean ($\bar{x}$), but in the event that you don't, here are some basic definitions for each measure.

- Range is the highest value minus the lowest value
- Variance is a measure of absolute variability
- Standard deviation is the square root of the variance and is a measure of relative variability
- μ is the average of the population

$\bar{x}$ is the average of a sample from the population

Process and product variation consist of the actual variation of the product's physical characteristics or process parameters plus the variation of the measurement system plus any other error not accounted for. Mathematically this concept looks as follows:

$$\sigma^2 \text{ Total} = \sigma^2 \text{ Process} + \sigma^2 \text{ Measurement System} + \varepsilon^2$$

Solving for σ:

$$\sigma = \sqrt{\sigma^2 \text{ Process} + \sigma^2 \text{ Measurement System} + \varepsilon^2}$$

Measurement system errors can be classified into two distinctly different categories: *accuracy* and *precision*:

1. *Accuracy (or Bias)*: A measure of the difference between the average value of the measurements on the parts studied and the "True Value" or "Master Value" of the parts. Having an acceptable accuracy guarantees that the measurements on parts are close to what their true value is. Clearly, we want our measurement device to be as accurate as possible.
2. *Precision*: Precision is the variation you see when you measure the same part repeatedly with the same measurement device. Obviously, we want precision to be very low compared with part variation so that we can detect differences between parts.

With any measurement system, you want measurements to be both accurate and precise, but that doesn't always happen. For example, you may have a measurement device that measures parts precisely, but not accurately. Or, you may have a device that is accurate, but not precise (i.e. measurements have a large amount of variation). You can also have a device that is neither accurate nor precise. Precision is further broken down into two components:

a. *Repeatability* assesses whether the same tester can measure the same part multiple times with the same measurement device and get the same value. Repeatability is the variability associated with the measurement device.

b. *Reproducibility* assesses whether different testers can measure the same part/sample with the same measurement device and get the same value. Reproducibility is the variability associated with the operator of the measuring device.

Mathematically speaking, the formula for these two components of precision is as follows:

$$\sigma^2 \text{ Measurement System} = \sigma^2 \text{ Gage} + \sigma^2 \text{ Operator}$$

Solving for σ:

$$\sigma = \sqrt{\sigma^2 \text{ Gage} + \sigma^2 \text{ Operator}}$$

Visually, accuracy, and precision are demonstrated in Figure 3.1.

The accuracy of a measurement system can be further reduced into two additional components:

1. *Stability*: The capacity of a measurement system to produce the same values over time when measuring the same sample or part. Stability means that no special cause variation is present in the measurement process and that only common cause variation is present.

2. *Linearity*: A measure of the consistency of accuracy (bias) over the expected range of the measurement device. For example, if a bathroom scale is under by 2 pounds when measuring a 150-pound person but is off by 10 pounds when measuring a 200-pound person, the measurement device (or system) is not linear over the expected range of use.

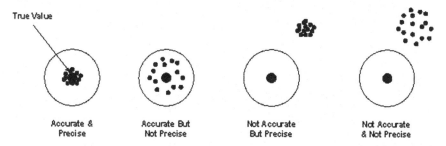

FIGURE 3.1
Graphic of accuracy and precision.

There are two additional properties that must be considered in order to have an acceptable measurement system as follows:

3. *Resolution*: The ability of a measurement device to discriminate between parts. As a rule of thumb, the measurement system should have a resolution of at least 1/10th the smaller of either the specification tolerance or the process spread. If the resolution is not fine enough, process variability will not be recognized by the measurement system.
4. *Number of Distinct Categories*: Ratio of the standard deviation of the parts to standard deviation of the measurement system. The number of distinct categories estimates how many separate groups of parts or samples the measurement system is able to distinguish.

   Number of Distinct Categories = σ parts/σ measurement system

Needless to say, PPV originates from many different sources within the process and includes things like lot-to-lot differences of raw material, differences in operator technique, differences in machines, temperature changes, and so on. Figure 3.2 is a graphical presentation focused primarily at variation associated with the measurement system. Keep in mind that the various sources of variation associated with part-to-part variation are not included here. Is it no wonder why measurement system problems exist?

A measurement system analysis, or Gage Repeatability and Reproducibility (GR&R) study, assesses the properties of a measurement system to ensure its adequacy for a given application. The details of how to perform a measurement system evaluation are beyond the scope of this book, but there are many excellent sources available for the reader.

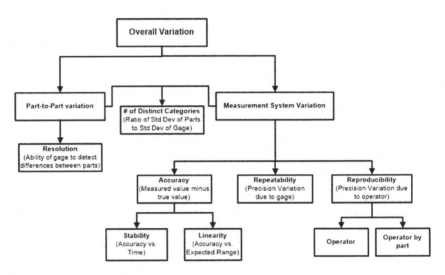

FIGURE 3.2
Graphical presentation of overall variation.

Back in their day, variation was declared "Public Enemy Number 1" by both Goldratt and Deming. But just exactly what is variation? Although you may not be able to define variation, you most certainly experience its effects every day in your life. Variation interferes with and hinders our ability to plan things. We might have planned to go to a baseball game only to have it canceled by rain or inclement weather. Sure, we checked the weather forecast ahead of time, but we all know how inaccurate the weather forecasts can be. Or maybe we wanted to renew our passport, but because of new laws regarding travel outside the United States, the time required to complete the process is highly variable and, therefore, unpredictable. I'm sure that you have and will continue to experience the negative effects of variation every day in your personal life.

From a throughput perspective, variability of processing time hinders our ability to meet production requirements that translates directly into delivery performance. This form of variability comes from both internal and external sources such as equipment downtime (planned and unplanned), inconsistent or non-standardized work methods, absenteeism, long equipment set-up times, late deliveries from suppliers, and a host of other sources.

Standard and Davis explain that there are three ways to handle variability: eliminate it, reduce it, or adapt to it [5]. Since it is impossible to eliminate variability, whenever and wherever possible, we must reduce variability as much as possible and then adapt to the remaining variation. Reducing overall process cycle time variability and lead time is, in some respects, the single most important manufacturing strategy of all simply because reducing it typically leads to improvements in throughput, revenue, delivery performance, factory congestion, inventory levels, production costs, and repeat orders. While cycle time variability is important, variation within processes creates all sorts of problems, especially when it's located in the constraint operation. And as I mentioned earlier, PPV has a profound impact on PTV.

From a process perspective, we might have planned to produce and ship "x" number of widgets today, but our equipment unexpectedly went down, or maybe a quality problem sprang to life and forced us to miss our delivery date to a customer. Variation has been defined as an unwanted condition and is the difference between where you are (current state) and where you'd like to be (desired end-state). My definition is much simpler in that variation is defined by one word, inconsistency. If variation exists, then consistency does not! How much variation that exists determines how consistent (or inconsistent) your processes will be.

How serious are the effects of variation? Variation creates all sorts of problems for us both on and off the job. Variation is serious enough for W. Edwards Deming to have said, "If I had to reduce my message to management to just a few words, I'd say it all has to do with reducing variation" [6]. These words from Dr. Deming are so profound and insightful, but he had more to say on the subject. "The central problem in management, leadership and production, as my friend Lloyd S. Nelson put it, is failure to understand the nature and interpretation of variation." If you assume that the specifications your products are being judged against are functional and were correctly established, then up or down deviations from the target value will always result in changes to your product's performance, for better or worse. How much worse is dependent upon how far your process deviates from its target. In effect, you will be creating defective product resulting in either rework or scrap, both of which negatively impact lead time, inventory, operating expense, throughput, capacity, and so on. In either case, when the throughput of the constraint operation is infected with the variation virus, the system throughput and profitability suffer.

Variation has existed since the early days of the industrial revolution and there are plenty of reasons why. The fact is, no two things are ever exactly alike and even if they were, we probably couldn't confirm it with measurements because no two measurement devices, measuring the same thing, will ever provide the same results. The fact that differences do exist compels us to develop a strategy on how to deal with variation effectively. Shewhart, for example, suggested that in order to master variation, we should "minimize variation so that it will be so insignificant that it does not, in any way, affect the performance of our product" [7].

On the other hand, Taguchi suggests that we should, "Construct (design) the product in such a way that it will be robust to any type of variation" [8]. Shewhart's approach is to focus on variation during the production phase while Taguchi's approach focuses on the design phase [7]. So who's right? Actually, they both are. In order to maximize your variation reduction efforts, both methods work to reduce process variation. Taguchi offers a way to create a more robust process that will mitigate noise effects, while Shewart teaches us how to systematically reduce all forms of variation present in our process. Let's now turn our attention to the other form of variability impacting throughput, PTV.

CYCLE TIME AND PROCESSING VARIABILITY

Now that we have a better understanding of PPV, what about PTV? Hopp and Spearman, in their breakthrough book, *Factory Physics*, provide valuable insights into variability by providing us with seven fundamental points to remember [9]. If you don't have a copy of this book, I suggest you purchase one. These seven points are as follows:

1. Variability is a fact of life. From a management perspective, it is clear that the ability to recognize and deal effectively with variability is perhaps the most critical skill to develop for all managers and engineers. Without this skill, your decisions will be full of uncertainty and might even be wrong most of the time.
2. There are many sources of variability in manufacturing systems. Process variability comes at us in many different forms. It can be as simple as work method variations or as complex machine setups and changeovers, planned and unplanned downtime, or scrap and rework. Flow variability is created by the way we release work into the system or how it moves between stations. The result of variability present in a system can be catastrophic if its underlying causes aren't identified and controlled.

3. The coefficient of variation is a key measure of item variability. The coefficient of variation, given by the formula, $CV = \sigma/\mu$, is a reasonable way to compare the variability of different elements of a production system. Because it is a unitless ratio, we can make rational comparisons of the level of variability in both process times and flows. In workstations, the CV of effective process time is inflated by equipment downtime and setups, rework and scrap, and a host of other factors. Interruptions that cause long, but infrequent periods of downtime will increase CV more than ones that cause short, frequent periods of downtime as long as the variability remains somewhat constant.

4. Variability propagates. If the output of a workstation is highly variable, then downstream workstations receiving products will also be highly variable.

5. Waiting time is frequently the largest component of cycle time. Two factors contribute to long waiting times: high utilization levels and high levels of variability. It follows then that increasing the effective capacity and decreasing variability will reduce cycle times.

6. Limiting buffers reduces cycle time at the cost of decreasing throughput. Because limiting inventory between workstation is the equivalent of implementing a pull system, it is the primary key reason why reducing variability reduction is so critical in Just In Time (JIT) systems.

7. Variability pooling reduces the effects of variability. Pooling variability will dampen the effects of variability because it is less likely that a single occurrence will dominate performance.

The inevitable conclusion is that variability degrades the performance of a manufacturing organization. Once again, I encourage the reader to seek out a copy of Hopp and Spearman's book for detailed explanations and proofs of these manufacturing fundamentals as they apply to variability [9].

Where does this variability come from? Before we attempt to identify and locate sources of variation, it is important to first understand the causes of variability. It is equally important to be able to quantify it and we can do this by using standard measures from statistics to define variability classes. Hopp and Spearman report that there are three classes of processing time variability as seen in Table 3.2 [9].

When we think about processing times, we have a tendency to consider only the actual time that the machine or operator spends on the job

TABLE 3.2

Three Classes of Processing Time Variability

Variability Class	Coefficient of Variation	Typical Situation
Low (LV)	$CV_t < 0.75$	Process times without outages (e.g., downtime)
Moderate (MV)	$0.75 \leq CV_t < 1.33$	Process times with short adjustments (e.g., setups)
High (HV)	$CV_t \geq 1.33$	Process times with long outages (e.g., failures)

actually working (i.e. not including failures or setups) and these times tend to be normally distributed. If, for example, the average process time was 20 minutes and the standard deviation was 6.3 minutes, then $CV_t = 6.3/20 = 0.315$ and would be considered a low variation (LV) process. Most LV processes follow a normal probability distribution. Suppose the mean processing time was 20 minutes, but the standard deviation was 30 minutes. The value for $CV_t = 30/20 = 1.5$. This process would be considered highly variable.

You may be wondering why we care whether a process is LV, MV, or HV? Suppose, for example, that you have identified a constraint that is classed as a LV process with an average process time of 30 minutes and a standard deviation of 10 minutes. The calculated value of the coefficient of variation, $CV_t = 10/30 = 0.33$. Suppose that the non-constraint operation feeding the constraint has an average processing time of one-half that of the constraint, 15, but its standard deviation was 30 minutes. The calculated value for $CV_t = 30/15 = 2.0$ and is considered a HV process. A value of 2.0 from Table 3.2 suggests that this process probably has long failure outages which could starve the constraint! When developing your plan of attack for reducing variation, using the coefficient of variation suggests that you include non-constraint processes that feed the constraint operation if they are classified as HV.

Hopp and Spearman present five of the most prevalent sources of variation in manufacturing environments as they apply to processing times [9]:

1. *Natural variability*: Includes minor fluctuations in process time due to differences in operators, machines, and material and, in a sense, is a catch-all category, since it accounts for variability from sources that have not been explicitly called out (e.g., a piece of dust in the operator's eye). Because many of these unidentified sources of variability are operator-related, there is typically more natural

variability in a manual process than in an automated one. Even in a fully automated machining operation, the composition of the material might differ, causing processing speed to vary slightly. In most systems, natural processing times are low variability, so CV_t is less than 0.75.

2. *Random outages*: Unscheduled downtime can greatly inflate both the mean and the coefficient of variation of process times. In fact, in many systems, this represents the single largest cause of variability. Hopp and Spearman refer to breakdowns as preemptive outages because they occur whether we want them to or not (e.g., they can occur right in the middle of a job). Power outages, operators being called away on emergencies, and running out of consumables are other possible sources of preemptive outages.

Hopp and Spearman refer to non-preemptive outages as stoppages that occur between, rather than during jobs and represent downtime that occurs, but for which we have some control as to when [9]. For example, when a tool begins to wear and needs to be replaced, we can wait until the current job is finished before we stop production. Other common examples of non-preemptive outages include changeovers, preventive maintenance, breaks, meetings, and shift changes. So how can we use this?

Suppose we are considering a decision of whether to replace a relatively fast machine requiring periodic setups with a slower, flexible machine that does not require setups. Suppose the fast machine can produce an average of one part per hour but requires a two-hour setup every four parts on average. The more flexible machine takes 1.5 hours to produce a part but, requires no setup. The effective capacity (EC) of the fast machine is:

$$EC = 4 \text{ parts/6 hours} = 2/3 \text{ parts/hour}$$

The effective process time is simply the reciprocal of the effective capacity, or 1.5 hours. Thus, both machines have an effective capacity of 1.5 hours. Traditional capacity analysis would consider only mean capacity and might conclude that both machines are equivalent. Traditional capacity analysis would not recommend one over the other, but if we consider the impact on variability, then the flexible machine, requiring no setup, would be my choice (and that of Hopp and Spearman [9]). Replacing the faster machine with the more flexible machine would serve to reduce the process time CV and therefore make the line more efficient. This, of course, assumes that both machines have equivalent natural variability.

3. *Setups*: The amount of time a job spends waiting for the station to be set up for production. Setups are like changeovers in that they contain internal and external activities. Internal activities are those that must be done while the equipment is shut down while external activities can be completed while the equipment is still running. The key to reducing setup time is to turn as many internal activities into external activities, thus reducing waiting time.

4. *Operator availability*: The amount of time a job spends waiting for an operator to be available to occupy the workstation and begin to produce product. The best way to reduce this type of time delay is to create a flexible workforce. Having to wait for a specialist operator is no longer acceptable. Companies today must cross-train operators so that if one is called away or is absent, another can step in and perform his or her tasks. This is especially critical in the constraint operation.

5. *Recycle*: Just like breakdowns and setups, rework is a major source of variability in manufacturing processes. If we think of the additional processing time spent "getting the job right" as an outage, it's easy to see that rework is completely analogous to setups because both rob the process of capacity and contribute greatly to the variability associated with processing times. Rework implies variability which in turn causes more congestion, Work-In-Process (WIP), and cycle time.

One of the keys to understanding the impact of variability is that variability at one station can affect the behavior of other stations in the process by means of another type of variability referred to as flow variability. Hopp and Spearman [9] explain that flow refers to the transfer of jobs or parts from one station to another and if an upstream workstation has highly variable process times, the flow it feeds to downstream workstations will also be highly variable. In other words, variability propagates!

The concepts of processing time variability and flow variability are important considerations as we attempt to characterize the effects of variability in production lines, but it's important to understand that the actual processing time (including setups, downtime, etc.) typically accounts for only about 5 to 10 percent of the total cycle time in a manufacturing plant [9]. The vast majority of the extra time is spent waiting for various resources (e.g., workstations, transporting, storage, operators, incoming parts, materials and supplies, etc.). Hopp and Spearman refer to the science of waiting as queuing theory, or the theory of waiting in lines [9]. Since jobs effectively "stand in lines" waiting to be processed, moved, and so on, it is important to understand and analyze why queuing exists in your process. Doesn't it make sense that if waiting accounts for the vast majority of time a product spends in the system, then one of the keys to throughput improvement is to identify and understand why waiting exists in your process?

A queuing system combines the impact of the arrival of parts from other processes and received parts from outside suppliers, the production of the parts, and the inventory or queue waiting to be processed. Hopp and Spearman go into depth on this subject [9], and I suggest you read their work, but the important thing to remember is the following. Since limiting interstation buffers is logically equivalent to installing a kanban, this property is a key reason that variability reduction (via production smoothing, improved layout and flow control, total preventive maintenance, and enhanced quality assurance) is critical to reducing variability.

In this section, we have identified and discussed a number of causes of variability and how they might cause congestion in a manufacturing system. We said that one way to reduce this congestion is to reduce variability by addressing its causes. Hopp and Spearman [9] point out that:

> another, and more subtle way to deal with congestion effects is by combining multiple sources of variability known as variability pooling. An everyday example of this concept is in financial planning. Virtually all financial advisers recommend investing in a diversified portfolio of financial instruments. The reason, of course, is to hedge against risk. It is highly unlikely that a wide spectrum of investments will perform extremely poorly at the same time. At the same time, it is unlikely that they will perform extremely well at the same time. Hence, we expect less variable returns from a diversified portfolio than from a single asset.

Hopp and Spearman [9] go on to discuss how variability pooling affects batch processing, safety stock aggregation, and queue sharing, but the important point to take away is this: pooling variability tends to reduce the overall variability, just like a diversified portfolio reduces the risk of up and down swings in your earnings. The implications are that safety stocks can be reduced (less holding costs) or that cycle times at multiple-machine process centers can be reduced by sharing a single queue.

There are two basic but fundamental laws of factory physics relevant to variability provided to us by Hopp and Spearman [9].

1. *Variability Law*: Increasing variability always degrades the performance of a production system. This is an extremely powerful concept since it implies that variability in any form will harm some measure of performance. Consequently, variability reduction is central to improving performance.
2. *Variability Buffering Law*: Variability in a production system will be buffered by some combination of:
   a. Inventory
   b. Capacity
   c. Time

This law is an important extension of the variability law because it specifies the three ways in which variability impacts a manufacturing process and the choices we have in terms of buffering for it.

The primary focus of this section was the effect of PTV on the performance of production lines. The primary points, conclusions, or principles are provided, once again, by Hopp and Spearman [9]:

1. *Variability always degrades performance.* As variability of any kind is increased, either inventory will increase, or lead times will increase, or throughput will decrease or a combination of the three. Because of the influence of variability, all improvement initiatives must include variability reduction.
2. *Variability buffering is a fact of manufacturing life.* If you can't reduce variability, then you must buffer it or you will experience protracted cycle times, increased levels of inventory, wasted capacity, diminished throughput, and longer lead times, all of which will result in declining revenues and customer service.
3. *Flexible buffers are more effective than fixed buffers.* By having capacity, inventory, or time available as buffering devices permits the flexible combination of the three to reduce the total amount of buffering needed in a given system. Examples of each type of buffer are included in Table 3.3.
4. *Material is conserved.* Whatever flows into a workstation must flow out as either acceptable product, rework, or scrap.

TABLE 3.3

Three Classes of Flexible Buffer Types

Flexible Buffer Type	Buffer Example
Flexible Capacity	Cross-trained workforce—by moving flexible workers to operations that need the capacity, flexible workers can cover the same workload with less total capacity than would be required if workers were fixed to specific tasks.
Flexible Inventory	Generic WIP held in a system with late product customization. That is, having a product platform that results in potentially different end products.
Flexible Time	The practice of quoting variable lead times to customers depending upon the current backlog of work (i.e. the larger the backlog, the longer the quote). A given level of customer service can be achieved with shorter average lead time if variable lead times are quoted individually to customers instead of uniform fixed lead time quoted in advance. This is possible if you significantly reduce your cycle time to the point that the competition can't match it.

5. *Releases are always less than capacity in the long run.* Although the intent may be to run a process at 100 percent of capacity, when true capacity, including overtime, outsourcing, etc., is considered, this really will never occur. It is always better to plan to reduce release rates before the system "blows up," simply because they will have to be reduced as a result of the system "blowing up" anyway.

6. *Variability early in a line is more disruptive than variability late in a line.* Higher front end process variability of a line using a push system will propagate downstream and cause queuing later on in the process. By contrast, stations with high process variability toward the end of the process will affect only those stations.

7. *Cycle time increase non-linearity in utilization.* As utilization approaches 100 percent, long-term WIP and cycle time will approach infinity.

8. *Process batch sizes affect capacity.* Increasing batch sizes increases capacity and thereby reduces queuing, while increasing batch size also increases wait-to-batch and wait-in-batch times. Because of this, the first focus in serial batching situations should be on setup time reduction, enabling the use of small, efficient batch sizes. If setup times cannot be reduced, cycle time may well be minimized at a batch size greater than one. In addition, the most efficient batch size in a parallel process may be between one and the maximum number that will fit into the process.

9. *Cycle times increase proportionally with transfer batch size.* Because waiting to batch and un-batch is typically one of the largest sources of cycle time length, reducing transfer batch sizes is one of the simplest and easiest ways to reduce cycle times.

10. *Matching can be an important source of delay in assembly systems.* Lack of synchronization caused by variability, poor scheduling, or poor shop floor control will always cause significant build-up of WIP, resulting in component assembly delays.

DEFECT IDENTIFICATION

Thus far in this chapter, we have discussed how to identify and locate variation, primarily in our constraint process. Let's now turn our attention to the subject of identifying defects within our process. If you talk to an expert on Six Sigma, they will probably mention terms like defects per opportunity (DPO), defects per million opportunities (DPMO), or sigma measure. One of the features that Six Sigma brings to the improvement table is how to determine defect opportunities. In *The Six Sigma Way*, Pande, Newman, and Cavanaugh present a three-step procedure for defining the number of opportunities [3]:

1. Develop a preliminary list of defect types.
2. Determine which are the actual, customer critical, specific defects.
3. Check the proposed number of opportunities against other standards.

In the same book, Pande, Newman, and Cavanaugh summarize guidelines for figuring opportunities for your products or services as follows [3]:

1. Focus on "standard" problem areas.
2. Group closely related defects into one opportunity.
3. Make sure the defect is important to the customer.
4. Be consistent.
5. Change only when needed.

Although I support these guidelines, remember right now we are only interested in correcting problems that limit throughput in the constraint operation. My advice to you is to simply analyze the defect data, develop a Pareto chart of the defects, prioritizing them based upon which is having the most detrimental effect on the output rate of the constraint operation (or downstream operations) and decide how you are going to attack them. Once you've resolved the highest priority defect, move to the next one and so forth. You cannot simultaneously attack all defects and you cannot afford to have your available resources working on problems that aren't going to give you pay back in the constraint operation. If you want to start a fire with a magnifying glass, you have to be able to focus the rays of the sun in one location. So too with improving the output of the constraint operation. It's really all about being able to focus.

So, now that we have discussed the three major components of what I refer to as the Ultimate Improvement Cycle, in the next chapter we will now turn our attention to how best to combine these three methodologies into a very powerful improvement method.

REFERENCES

1. Mikel Harry and Richard Schroeder, *Six Sigma: The Breakthrough Management Strategy Revolutionizing the World's Top Corporations*, Doubleday, New York, 2000.
2. Donald J. Wheeler and David S. Chambers, *Understanding Statistical Process Control*, SPC Press, Knoxville, TN, 1986.
3. Peter S. Pande, Robert P. Newman, and Roland R. Cavanaugh, *The Six Sigma Way: How GE, Motorola, and Other Top Companies Are Honing Their Performance*, McGraw-Hill, New York, 2000.
4. Bob Sproull, *The Ultimate Improvement Cycle*, CRC Press, Taylor & Francis Group, Boca Raton, FL, 2009.
5. Charles Standard and Dale Davis, *Running Today's Factory: A Proven Strategy for Lean Manufacturing*, Hanser Gardner Publications, Cincinnati, OH, 1999.
6. W. Edwards Deming, *Out of the Crisis*, Massachusetts Institute of Technology, Center for Advanced Engineering Study, Cambridge, MA, 1982, 1986.
7. Walter A. Shewhart, *Economic Control of Quality of Manufactured Product*, D. Van Nostrand Company, Inc., Princeton, NJ, 1931.
8. Genichi Taguchi, Elsayed A. Elsayed, and Thomas Hsiang, *Quality Engineering in Production Systems*, McGraw-Hill Publishing Company, New York, 1989.
9. Wallace J. Hopp and Mark L. Spearman, *Factory Physics: Foundations of Manufacturing Management*, second edition, McGraw-Hill, New York, 2001.

4

How to Integrate Lean, Six Sigma, and the Theory of Constraints

IMPROVEMENT INITIATIVES TODAY

The Lean Enterprise Institute has conducted annual surveys about how well Lean implementations are going, and based on the results of these surveys, the results seem to say that things aren't going too well [1]. The fact is, one of the most recent surveys has indicated that about 48 percent of companies attempting to implement a full-scale Lean initiative were actually backsliding to their old ways of working. With nearly 50 percent of companies reporting backsliding, this is not at a very healthy trend, especially when we consider the amount of money invested in many of the Lean initiatives.

According to industry experts, poor project selection has been one of the key areas where many businesses still continue to struggle. Industry experience suggests that about 60 percent of businesses are currently not identifying key projects that would do the most to benefit their business. Add to that, many Lean consultants attempt to "Lean out" every process across the entire enterprise which ends up resulting in a multitude of incomplete projects or projects that simply don't generate much interest from senior leadership. There is no doubt that process layouts become better with manufacturing cells in place, and usually, there's much less waiting, but the financial results typically don't seem to materialize, or at least not enough to satisfy leadership within many companies. Add to that, even after much hard work, not only are positive bottom line results not happening, but orders are still arriving late to intended customers.

In the case of Six Sigma initiatives, the results have been somewhat more impressive, but not as inspiring as they could be. In a Six Sigma survey, carried out by Celerant Consulting [2], generating responses from managers across all business sectors, the results were generally more positive than negative, but there were several problems that surfaced. The survey suggested that businesses which are new to Six Sigma find that running effective projects has been a significant challenge on many occasions. It's not unusual for projects to take up to six months or sometimes even longer to complete and, like Lean implementations, the training costs aren't providing an adequate return on investment.

So, what happens when Lean and Six Sigma are combined? One would think that the best of both initiatives would generate much better results. According to Mohit Sharma from iSixSigma, in his June 16, 2015, paper entitled, *Has the Era of Lean Six Sigma Gone?* [3],

> Now in 2014 we are at the brink of another paradigm shift as organizations are little restless with LSS methodology as well. This methodology is not a differentiator for companies anymore. Practitioners are saying that organizations using Lean Six Sigma are destined to wrestle for nickels. In today's dynamic business environment, organizations now need disruptive thinking and innovative problem-solving techniques. New Methodology of innovation with a revised nomenclature would possibly use decent portions of LSS methodology and a few selected new tools. This would be a perfect analogy to the popular adage – "old wine in a new bottle."

I happen to agree with Mohit Sharma in that combining Lean and Six Sigma will not deliver the kind of results that leadership is expecting, or at least hoping for. In my way of thinking, both Lean and Six Sigma, although both quite effective when used correctly, are missing the one ingredient needed to deliver that kind of results that would justify spending the needed capital to implement either one individually or in combination. This missing link is the focal point for all improvement initiatives that provides the needed leverage to maximize profitability for companies. So, what's the answer?

THE ULTIMATE IMPROVEMENT CYCLE

Based upon what I've written so far, it would appear that I haven't painted a very glowing picture of either of these two improvement initiatives. One might conclude from my remarks up to now that I am advocating abandonment of both of these initiatives. The fact of the matter is, that while I am a huge supporter of both Lean and Six Sigma, as I said earlier, both of these initiatives are lacking the focus and leverage required to deliver improvements that result in profit maximization. So, if not Lean and Six Sigma, what do I recommend? Enter the Theory of Constraints (TOC). TOC became famous in the mid-1980s through Eli Goldratt and Jeff Cox's book *The Goal* (1986) [4].

TOC teaches us that within any process or system, there is a factor that we must identify and exploit if we are to maximize system throughput and its corresponding profitability. As I explained in Chapter 1, the Theory of Constraints is characterized by its five focusing steps:

1. Identify the system constraint
2. Decide how to exploit the system constraint
3. Subordinate everything else to the constraint
4. If necessary, elevate the constraint
5. Return to Step 1, but don't let inertia create a new constraint

These five steps form a different type of Process of On-Going Improvement (POOGI) that provides the focus and leverage missing from both Lean and Six Sigma initiatives. What would happen if we were to combine Lean and Six Sigma with the Theory of Constraints and form a new style POOGI? In what I call the Ultimate Improvement Cycle (UIC) [5], I have done just that. By focusing the Lean and Six Sigma principles, tools, and techniques on the operation that is limiting throughput, your profits will grow at an unprecedented rate and on-time deliveries will skyrocket. In fact, one double-blind study of 21 electronics plants has confirmed that an integrated TOC-Lean-Six Sigma methodology improved profits roughly 22 times that of Lean and 13 times more than Six Sigma compared with both if these were singular initiatives [6]. The fact is, the profits realized from these two initiatives or even the hybrid Lean-Sigma, pale in comparison with what can happen when TOC, Lean, and Six Sigma are combined. So, how does this integrated methodology work?

Figure 4.1 graphically represents what I have christened the Ultimate Improvement Cycle [5]. What you see are three concentric circles representing three different cycles of improvement. The inner or core cycle represents the TOC process of on-going improvement from Goldratt and Cox. TOC provides the essential focus that is missing from Lean and Six Sigma improvement initiatives. Based on my experience and results, the key to successful improvement initiatives is focusing your

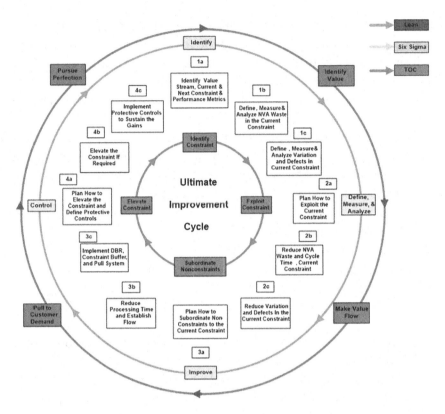

FIGURE 4.1
The ultimate improvement cycle.

improvement efforts on the right area, the system constraint. Remember, the constraint dictates your throughput rate which ties directly to bottom-line improvement.

The second circle represents the Six Sigma roadmap popularized by the authors of two books (Pande, Neuman, and Cavanaugh and Harry and Schroeder [7,8]). Here you will recognize the now famous D-M-A-I-C roadmap associated with Six Sigma. The outer circle depicts the Lean improvement cycle popularized by Womack and Jones (2003) [9]. The fact of the matter is both Six Sigma and Lean are absolutely necessary for my methodology to work, the only difference being where and when to apply them.

Figure 4.2 summarizes the tools and actions needed to effectuate the improvement in the constraint and a general idea of when to use them. Keep in mind that all processes are not the same, so the type of tool or action required and the order of use will probably be different. This is clearly situation-dependent. Figures 4.1 and 4.2 should be self-explanatory,

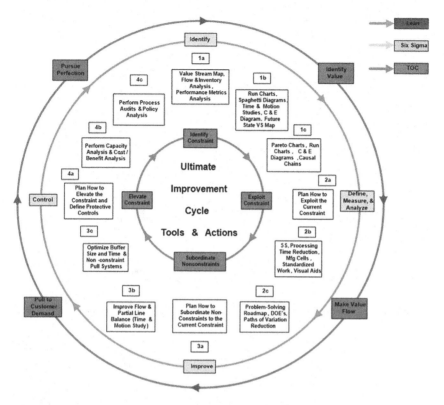

FIGURE 4.2
The tools and actions of the ultimate improvement cycle.

so let's move on to Figure 4.3, the UIC Deliverables. When this section is complete, we'll look at a brief case study to see just how the UIC works.

Figure 4.3 is a graphical summary of what I refer to as the UIC Deliverables or what I believe you should end up with when the Ultimate Improvement Cycle is implemented correctly. As Box 1a clearly states, you should have a complete picture of the system you are trying to improve in terms of flow, the predicted behaviors that you should see from the people working within the system, and efficiency (or utilization) only being measured in the designated constraint.

Moving along, you should have a profound knowledge of the location and type of waste, variation, inventory, and information of the defects occurring within the system, as well as the identified core problems within the system. Using all of this information, you should also have a coherent action plan on how you will go about improving the capacity and throughput of the system. This action plan, when executed, should

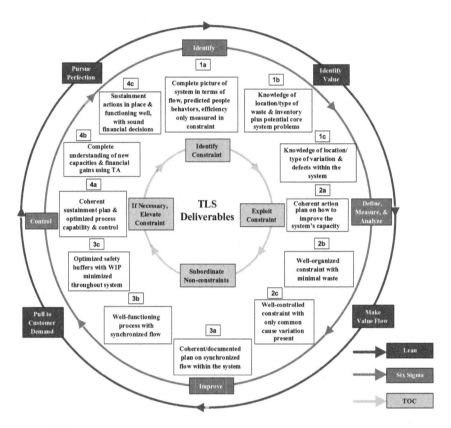

FIGURE 4.3
The UIC deliverables.

result in a well-organized constraint with minimal waste as well as a well-controlled constraint with only common cause variation present.

Another important deliverable will be a coherent, documented plan on how you will synchronize flow within your system. And once executed, you should not only see a process with synchronized flow but with minimal WIP throughput the system. This plan you will have developed will set the stage for a maximum return on your investment.

The final deliverable is a coherent sustainment plan with guaranteed optimal process capability and total control of your process. And when this plan is implemented, you will have a complete understanding of your new capacity which will have resulted in significant financial gains using Throughput Accounting to drive your profitability. The final piece of the UIC pie is the sustainment actions in place and the functioning based upon sound financial decisions. So, with this explanation of the UIC, let's look at a case study where I used this methodology.

A CASE STUDY

This case study involves a company that had been manufacturing truck bodies for the transportation industry since 1958 and was one of the recognized industry leaders. The company had a staff of 17 full-time engineers, with engineering performance measured by the number of hours of backlog waiting to pass through engineering (it seems odd to me that a negative performance metric was being used). A new VP of Quality and Continuous Improvement (Me) had been hired because the company was losing market share as well as experiencing significantly high missed delivery dates. In addition, morale within engineering was apparently at an all-time low. Upon arriving at this company, I was informed that, in addition to being responsible for all Continuous Improvement activities, I would also have responsibility for the engineering group. The company had apparently fired their former VP of Engineering because the backlog of quotes for potential orders had risen from their normal 300 hours to roughly 1400 hours just in the previous two months.

In keeping with the instructions for the UIC, my first step was to create a Lean-based, high-level Process Map (P-Map) and a Value Stream Map (VSM) to better understand what was happening. It was immediately clear to me that the constraint was the order entry system. It seems that the process of receiving a request for a quote and delivering it back to the customer was consuming an alarming 40 days! Since it only took two weeks to produce and mount the truck body, it was clear to me why market share was declining at such an alarming rate. I then created a lower-level Process Map of the quoting process to better understand exactly what was consuming so much time.

My next step was to develop a run chart to get some history of the quoting process. Figure 4.4 shows historical backlog hours for the previous year-and-a-half. When I first looked at the data, I was very confused. Confused because I first observed a steady and rapid decline in backlog hours beginning in May of the previous year through October, and then an equally rapid increase through the current year. Further investigation revealed that the decline in backlog was associated with mandatory engineering overtime, and the ascent occurred when the overtime had been canceled. The previous engineering VP hadn't solved the problem; he had just treated the symptoms with mandatory overtime.

The next step for me was to create another run chart going back further in time. I reasoned that if I was going to solve this problem, I needed to

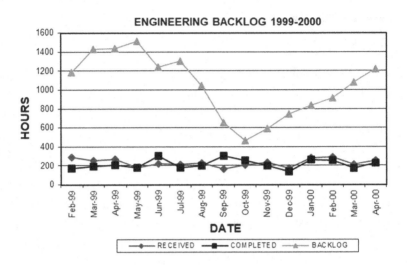

FIGURE 4.4
The engineering backlog 1999–2000.

understand when this volatility actually began. Figure 4.5 is the second run chart I created, and it became clear that the backlog problem was relatively recent, so the key to solving this dilemma was to determine what had changed to cause the deterioration of this performance metric.

It turned out that somewhere around the beginning of the previous year, the incumbent VP of Engineering had decided to move on to another position outside the company. The first new VP apparently didn't like the way the engineering group was arranged, so he changed the structure.

The company produced three basic types of truck bodies and historically had three different groups of engineers to support each type. These groups were staffed based upon the output ratio of each type of truck body. For the previous four years, the company had maintained a very stable level of backlog hours. But when the new VP of Engineering consolidated the three groups into a single unit, the backlog began to grow exponentially. Several months later, the company fired him and hired yet another new VP. This second new VP had used mandatory overtime to bring the backlog hours down, which meant that the root cause of the increase was still present. A significant part of the problem was the performance metric that was in place, which caused abnormal and unacceptable behaviors.

The fix was clear for me and so was the constraint. What we were looking at was a policy constraint, so if I wanted to correct this problem,

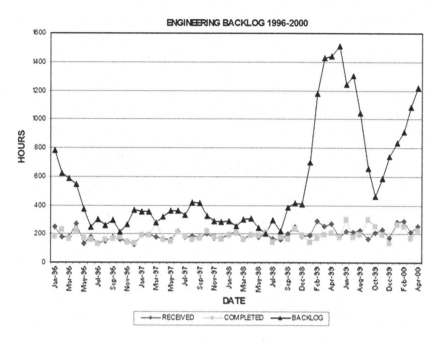

FIGURE 4.5
The engineering backlog 1996–2000.

I had to change the policy. In other words, I had to return to the previous engineering configuration and drive down the backlog hours by removing waste and reducing and controlling the variability. The results were swift and amazing—the backlog decreased from 1200 hours to 131 hours in approximately five weeks and remained within an acceptable maintenance level after that. In fact, because of Lean, much of the waste was eliminated within the engineering process, and as a result, the time required to process orders through engineering decreased from 40 days to an astounding 48 hours! Much of this waste was in the form of waiting, waiting for an available engineer. Figure 4.6 shows the final results of this team effort. Not only had the number of backlog hours decreased to levels never seen before, the number of quotes completed shown here were at all-time highs for this company.

The key to success in this case was first to identify the operation that was constraining throughput; second, to decide how to exploit the constraint by applying various Lean and Six Sigma tools to the constraint; third, to subordinate everything else to the constraint and then if need be, break the constraint by spending money. Thanks to Lean and Six Sigma, there was no need for additional expenses. And the best news is both market

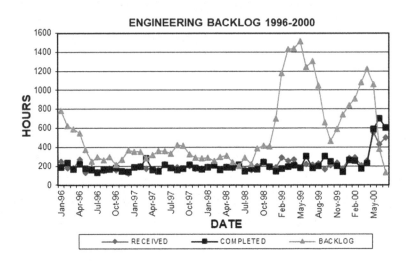

FIGURE 4.6

The engineering backlog 1996–June 2000.

share and profitability increased dramatically by simply integrating Lean and Six Sigma with the Theory of Constraints. This company learned the hard way about the importance of focus and leverage.

The conclusion one should draw here is that if these three improvement initiatives are to work, they need to be done in concert with each other—a symbiosis or interdependence if you will. The Theory of Constraints provides the needed focal point for improvement while Lean and Six Sigma provide the necessary tools for improvement of the process and system. In isolation, these initiatives only provide part of what is needed, but in their integrated state, they represent the most powerful improvement methodology available today.

REFERENCES

1. Lean Enterprise Institute, *Surveys on Lean Manufacturing*, 2004, 2005.
2. Celerant Consulting Survey, 2004.
3. Mohit Sharma, iSixSigma, in his June 16, 2015 paper entitled, *Has the Era of Lean Six Sigma Gone?*
4. Eliyahu M. Goldratt, *The Goal*. North River Press, Great Barrington, MA, 1986.
5. Bob Sproull, Reprinted with permission from *The Ultimate Improvement Cycle: Maximizing Profits through the Integration of Lean, Six Sigma, and the Theory of Constraints*. CRC Press, Taylor & Francis Group, Boca Raton, FL, 2009.
6. Reza M. Pirasteh and Kimberly S. Farah, The top elements of TOC, Lean, and Six Sigma (TLS) make beautiful music together. *APICS Magazine*, May 2006.

7. Peter S. Pande, Robert P. Newman, and Roland R. Cavanaugh, *The Six Sigma Way: How GE, Motorola, and Other Top Companies are Honing Their Performance.* McGraw-Hill, New York, 2000.
8. Mikel Harry and Richard Schroeder, *Six Sigma: The Breakthrough Management Strategy Revolutionizing the World's Top Corporations.* Doubleday, New York, 2000.
9. James P. Womack and Daniel T. Jones, *Lean Thinking: Banish Waste and Create Wealth in Your Corporation.* Free Press, New York, 2003.

5

A Better Way to Measure a System's Success

A system's constraint was defined by Goldratt and Cox as anything that limits the system from achieving higher performance versus its goal [1]. So how should we measure and judge our performance? Since the most common goal of organizations is to make money now, and in the future, doesn't it make perfect sense that at least some of the performance measurements we choose should be monetary metrics? For example, two metrics that we could use are Net Profit (NP) and Return on Investment (ROI). Goldratt explained that in order to judge whether an organization is moving toward its goal, three questions must be answered.

1. "How much money is generated by our organization?"
2. "How much money is invested by our company?"
3. "How much money do we have to spend to operate it?"

In any improvement initiative, the person responsible for the financial well-being of your business should play a crucial role in assuring that the initiative stays focused on the primary goal of most companies—to make money now and in the future. Within the confines of our improvement methodology known as the Theory of Constraints (TOC), in this chapter I will present the details of an alternate form of accounting, known as Throughput Accounting (TA). Throughput Accounting is intended to be used for real-time financial decisions rather than basing decisions on what happened in the past like traditional Cost Accounting (CA) does. Many businesses will emphatically state that the primary goal of their business is to make money and yet they spend the largest portion of their time trying to save money.

The key to profitability is by identifying and focusing on that part of the system that controls and drives revenue higher and higher, rather than through cost-cutting efforts. It matters not if you are a service provider, a small business owner, a distributor, or a manufacturer. What you need is a way to sell more product which increases revenue and, ultimately, profitability. In this chapter, I will systematically compare two accounting methods and demonstrate the superiority of Throughput Accounting in terms of profitability improvement.

Because traditional Cost Accounting is so complicated, in this discussion, I won't go into great detail, but I will cover the highlights of it so that a comparison to TA can be made. Figure 5.1 below illustrates selected elements of CA which is taken from a wonderful book by John Ricketts entitled, *Reaching the Goal* [2], as is much of what is to follow in this chapter.

In his book, *Reaching the Goal*, John Ricketts explains that when Cost Accounting began being used in the early 1900s, labor costs were clearly dominated the scene in manufacturing and workers were typically paid by the piece [2]. That is, they were paid based upon how much they produced. Back then, it made perfect sense to allocate overhead expenses to products on the basis of direct labor costs when preparing financial statements. But since then, automation now dominates manufacturing, and workers are normally paid by the hour, allocation of large overhead expenses, on the basis of small labor costs, has created some very distinct distortions in accounting.

When observed at the enterprise level, product cost distortions do not affect financial statements much at all. Yet if prices are computed as product cost plus standard gross margin, the predominant method in Cost Accounting is that product cost distortions will carry into product pricing. The resulting effect is that it is possible that some products will

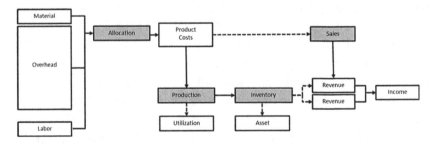

FIGURE 5.1
Selected elements of Cost Accounting.

appear to be profitable when they are not, and conversely, some products that appear to not be profitable, really are.

A second problem with Cost Accounting is that factories are encouraged to produce excess inventory. Why is this? Producing excess inventory usually happens because of Cost Accounting's impulse for higher levels of manpower efficiency and equipment utilization in non-constraints. It is because of this that inventory accumulation can be driven by the counterintuitive effect it has on earnings. So, what does this mean? What happens as a result of this inventory accumulation is that rather than being expensed on the income statement in the accounting period they were incurred, the cost of inventory gets recorded on the balance sheet as an *asset*. The resulting effect is that an inventory profit may be reported, and businesses can use this to enhance their reported earnings. The problem is that it has absolutely nothing to do with real income and profitability. If inventory can't be sold, guess what happens. If it isn't sold, then it becomes a depreciation expense on the income statement and an inventory loss will be the end result.

Ricketts explains that a third problem with Cost Accounting is concerned with management priorities [2]. This means that operating expense will be managed closely because it is well-known and under direct control. Unlike operating expense, revenue is seen as less controllable because of the perception that it is dependent upon the markets and customers. Inventory is a distant third in management priorities because, as just stated, reducing it will have an adverse effect on a company's reported income.

Even though most businesses practice it, the key to profitability is not through how much money a company can save, but rather through how much money a company can make! And believe me, these two concepts are drastically different. Let's now look at a different accounting method referred to as Throughput Accounting, once again by looking at John Ricketts' book, *Reaching the Goal* [2].

Throughput Accounting addresses all of the problems just discussed with Cost Accounting by not using product costs, but rather by eliminating incentives for excess inventory and reversing typical management priorities. It's very important to understand that TA is not a substitute for conventional financial reporting simply because publicly traded companies are required by law to comply with Generally Accepted Accounting Principles (GAAP) requirements. But having said this, TA does provide a way to make "real time" financial decisions. Throughput Accounting will reveal which are the most profitable mix of products, and I promise you will be different than what traditional CA would give you.

Throughput Accounting uses three basic financial measures, namely Throughput (T), Inventory or Investment (I), and Operating Expense (OE). So, let's look at each of these measures in more detail.

- *Throughput* (T): The rate at which the system generates money through sales of products or services or interest generated. If you produce something but don't sell it, it's not throughput, it's just inventory. Throughput is obtained after subtracting the totally variable costs (i.e. cost of raw materials, or those things that vary with the sale of a single unit of product or service) from revenue.
- *Inventory or Investment* (I): All the money that the business has invested in things it intends to sell. Inventory (I) primarily includes the dollars (or whatever currency you use) tied up in Work-In-Process (WIP) and Finished Product Inventory.
- *Operating Expense* (OE): All the money the system spends in order to turn inventory into Throughput including all labor costs. It also includes rent, plus selling and general and administrative (SG&A) costs. Including all labor costs is a huge departure from traditional Cost Accounting.

Throughput is maximized by selling goods or services with the largest difference between revenue and totally variable cost and by minimizing time between spending money to produce and receive money from sales. It's important to understand that TA does not use labor costs to allocate OE. Direct labor is not treated as a variable cost simply because businesses do not typically adjust their workforce every time demand for their product or service changes. It's also important to remember that Throughput is determined by both speed and magnitude.

From the three basic elements of Throughput Accounting, namely T, I, and OE, we can calculate several other important metrics as follows:

- Net Profit = Throughput – Operating Expense or NP = T – OE
- Return on Investment = Net Profit ÷ Inventory or ROI = NP/I
- Productivity = Throughput ÷ Operating Expense or P = T/OE
- Inventory Turns = Throughput ÷ Inventory or i = T/I

An ideal decision using TA would be one that increases T while decreasing or maintaining both I and OE. A good decision increases NP, ROI, P, or i [2]. It's important to remember that NP is net operating profit before interest and taxes. Under TA there are no product costs, but instead, there are constraint measures that should be tracked as follows:

- Throughput per Constraint Unit: T/CU = (revenue – totally variable cost)/units
- Constraint Utilization: U = time spent producing/time available to produce

The best way to maximize T is to maximize these constraint measures. Constraint utilization is important because every hour lost on the constraint is an hour lost for the entire business that can never be recovered. On the other hand, utilization of non-constraints is not tracked because it encourages excess inventory.

Typical decisions based on the metric, T/CU include things like prioritizing use of the constraint (e.g., choosing the best product mix); deciding whether to increase the constraint's capacity through investment; selecting products to introduce or discontinue; and pricing products based on the opportunity cost of using the constraint.

Ricketts eloquently explains that for normal product decisions, T/CU is used to determine the mix that best maximizes T [2]. If producing less of one product in order to produce more of another product would increase T, for example, then that is a good decision. But for major decisions that might shift the constraint or forfeit some Throughput on current products, then TA uses the following decision-support measure:

- Change in Net Profit: $\Delta NP = \Delta T - \Delta OE$ (Note: The Δ symbol stands for difference or change in a comparison between alternatives). Likewise, to show the impact of these investment decisions, the metric Payback: $PB = \Delta NP/\Delta I$ should be used.
- To minimize unfavorable deviations from plans, TA advocates these control measures that should be minimized:
  - Throughput Dollar Days: TDD = Selling price of late order × days late
  - Inventory Dollar Days: IDD = Selling price of excess inventory × days unsold

TDD measures something that should have been done but was not (e.g., ship orders on time) while IDD measures something that should not have been done but was (e.g., create unnecessary inventory).

TA is used to identify constraints, monitor performance, control production, and determine the impact of decisions. Table 5.1 is a manufacturing situation consisting of just three parts with each part requiring the same three steps. Each product requires a different number of minutes per step, but the total time required for each part is the same. Labor costs per minute are the same across all steps.

Part A has the highest price and the lowest raw material cost per part while part C has the lowest price and highest raw material cost per part. Because the same workers will be used to produce any product mix, the best mix would seem to be to produce as much of part A as demanded, then B, then C. Following this priority, the factory will produce 100 units of A, 75 of B, and none of C. Note that Step 2 limits enterprise production regardless of whether it's actually recognized as the constraint. Operating expense includes rent, energy, and labor. Let's look at an example comparing CA with TA's product mix decision as laid out in Table 5.2.

When CA allocates operating expense to products based on their raw material costs, the resulting product costs confirm the expected priority: Product A has a lower product cost than Product B. Unfortunately, with this product mix, this business generates a net loss of $250. Because Part A appears to be profitable while Part B generates a loss, it's tempting to conclude that producing none of B would stop the loss. However, the Operating Expense covered by Product B would then have to be covered entirely by Product A, which would yield an even larger loss. If additional work was started, in an effort to keep the workers at Steps 1 and 3 fully utilized (i.e. to maximize efficiency), work-in-process inventory would grow. The inevitable conclusion, using Cost Accounting, is that this business is not profitable!

TABLE 5.1

Manufacturing System

	Products			Have	Need
	A	B	C		
Demand	100	100	100		
Price	$105	$100	$95		
Raw Material	$45	$50	$55		
Step 1 Time	3	6	9	2,400	1,800 Minutes
Step 2 Time	15	12	9	2,400	3,600 Minutes
Step 3 Time	2	2	2	800	600 Minutes
Total Time	20	20	20		

TABLE 5.2

Cost Accounting Comparison

	Products			Have	Need
	A	B	C		
Demand	100	100	100		
Price	$105	$100	$100		
Raw Material	$45	$50	$55		
Step 1 Time	3	6	9	2,400	1,800 Minutes
Step 2 Time	15	12	9	2,400	3,600 Minutes
Step 3 Time	2	2	2	800	600 Minutes
Total Time	20	20	20		

Cost Accounting	Products			Total
	A	B	C	
Product Cost	$100	$111	0	
Mix	100	75	0	
Step 2 Used	1,500	900	0	2,400
Revenue	$10,500	$7,500	0	$18,000
Raw Material	$4,500	$3,750	0	$8,250
Gross Margin	$6,000	$3,750	0	$9,750
Operating Expense	$5,455	$4,545	0	$10,000
Net Profit	$545	($795)	0	($250)

Let's now look at this same company using TA and see if the results tell us the same things or not as described in Table 5.3. TA provides an entirely different perspective when looking at this business and its potential product mix.

TA ranks product profitability according to Throughput on the constraint per minute (T/CU/t). In addition, it does not allocate OE to products. So, based upon this, Product A yields $4 per minute on the constraint, Product B yields $4.17, and Product C yields $4.44. TA says the priority should be to produce as much of Product C as capacity will allow, then Product B, then Product A (the exact opposite priority of CA). Because Step 2 is the system constraint, producing 100 units of Product C, 100 of Product B, and 20 of Product A is all that can be done. With this product mix from Throughput Accounting, instead of a $250 loss when using Cost Accounting, this business generates a net profit of $200. The only difference being the product mix!

Effective use of Throughput Accounting requires different information than from Cost Accounting, so new report formats must be implemented [2]. For example, a Throughput Accounting earnings statement shows T, I, and OE relative to the constraint, while conventional Cost Accounting reports are oblivious to the constraint. Just as CA and TA rank product profitability differently, they may also rank customer profitability quite differently. Several Throughput Accounting outcomes are noteworthy:

- Financial measures reverse management priorities from OE, T, and I (for Cost Accounting) to T, I, and OE (for Throughput Accounting).
- Performance measures for Throughput Accounting are not distorted by cost allocations for Cost Accounting.
- Constraint measures eliminate conflict between local measures (machine utilization or operator efficiency) and global measures (performance of the business).
- Control measures remove the incentive to build excess inventory and replace it with the incentive to deliver products on time.

Let's now review the primary components of Throughput Accounting, starting with Throughput.

Throughput at your Company is achieved by processing parts, selling or delivering them to customers, and *receiving payment* for all goods you sold. Again, inventory is not throughput!

TABLE 5.3

Throughput Accounting Comparison

	Products			Have	Need
	A	B	C		
Demand	100	100	100		
Price	$105	$100	$100		
Raw Material	$45	$50	$55		
Step 1 Time	3	6	9	2,400	1,800 Minutes
Step 2 Time	15	12	9	2,400	3,600 Minutes
Step 3 Time	2	2	2	800	600 Minutes
Total Time	20	20	20		

Throughput Account	Products			Total
	A	B	C	
T/CU	$60	$50	$40	
T/CU/t	$4.00	$4.17	$4.44	
Mix	20	100	100	
Step 2 Used	300	1,200	900	2,400
Revenue	$2,100	$10,000	$9,500	$21,600
Raw Material (TVC)	$900	$5,000	$5,500	$11,400
Throughput (T)	$1,200	$5,000	$4,000	$10,200
Operating Expense (OE)				$10,000
Net Profit (NP)				$200

Inventory or Investment (I) is primarily the amount of WIP and Finished Goods inventory, but it also includes all purchased parts for sales or the equipment, buildings, and other assets required to produce parts, if you're a manufacturer. The real key to reducing "I" is to stop the practice of pushing orders through your processes and replace it with pulling orders through your processes. Use the concept of nothing comes into your process until something exits the constraint (synchronizing flow). Too much WIP at one time leads to extending the productive cycle time of every part, causing late deliveries of parts and unhappy customers.

Operating Expense is all the money the system spends in order to turn inventory into throughput *including all labor costs*. The key for your Company to reduce labor costs is by improving Throughput at a much faster rate by removing waste and variation within the constraint. In doing so, this will reduce the dependence on overtime to play catch-up and reduce overall dollars spent on overtime. It will also improve the morale of the workforce because you have eliminated the fear of layoffs. Think about it, if you can generate additional Throughput with the same OE, you will return much more to your company's bottom line.

So, there's your comparison of these two distinctly different accounting methods. It should be clear to you that if you continue using traditional Cost Accounting to make your key decisions, like product mix, your company could be missing an opportunity to make more money. And since the goal of most companies is to make money now and in the future, doesn't it make sense to use Throughput Accounting to make your real-time financial decisions?

REFERENCES

1. Eliyahu M. Goldratt and Jeff Cox, *The Goal: A Process of Ongoing Improvement*, North River Press, Great Barrington, MA, 1984.
2. John Arthur Ricketts, *Reaching the Goal: How Managers Improve a Services Business Using Goldratt's Theory of Constraints*, IBM Press, Boston, 2008.

6

TOC's Distribution and Replenish Model

THE SUPPLY CHAIN

One way or another most, if not all, businesses are somehow linked to some kind of supply chain. They need parts or raw materials from somebody else in order to do whatever it is they do and pass it on to the next process step or next manufacturing unit until it finally arrives to the consumer. Depending on what you make and how fast you make it, the supply chain can be your best friend or your worst enemy. If it works well, it's your best friend. If it doesn't work well, it's your worst enemy.

The fundamental problem with most supply chain systems today is that through time they have remained stagnant in their management concepts and thinking, while the reality of business has flexed in a cycle of constant change; sometimes changing at an exponential rate. There are many new supply chain software applications, each proposing that it will solve the problem(s) associated with supply chain management.

These new software applications have come about mostly because of advances in computer technology, but few if any, have solved the real issues of supply chain management. It is true that these systems can provide an enormous amount of data and information very fast, but sometimes the speed at which the information is supplied is less important than having access to the correct information. What difference does it make how fast you get the information if it's the wrong information? The new realities for business have caused a needed change for supply chain systems, but most supply chain systems have not changed to keep pace with business changes. Businesses now are required to build products cheaper, have higher quality, and deliver those products at a faster pace and higher level of on-time delivery. These are the new rules of competition and being able to play in the game requires that your business must learn how to do this. You either play by the rules or you get out of the way. The rules in business have changed and yet many businesses insist on doing business the same "old" way. So, why is this?

When reviewing the reason why businesses still trend to the same old way, the most common answer given is: "Because that's the way we've always done it." The old system and the old rules may have worked for some period of time in the past, but times are changing, and the old rules and old methods no longer apply. If the supply chain system has not changed to align with the new rules, then the chasm between supply chain output and system needs will grow even larger. If the supply chain system is not changed to meet future needs, then there is very little hope of getting different results.

Most supply chain systems were originally designed to solve a problem and the problem they were focused on was the needed availability of parts or raw materials. That is, the right part/material, in the right location, at the right time. A primary function of these supply systems, as designed, was to hold the inventory in check. That is, don't buy too much, but also don't allow stock-out situations to occur. Managing the supply chain, then and now, is a tough job. Within even a small supply chain there can be many variables that require constant attention. You don't want to run out of parts, and yet you still do. You don't want excess inventory, and yet you still have it. These constant negative inventory cycles of sometimes too much and sometimes too little have persisted through time, even with the new supply system technology advancements. The supply problems being encountered years ago are still the same supply problems being encountered today.

THE MINIMUM/MAXIMUM SUPPLY CHAIN

For many companies, the supply chain/inventory system of choice is one often referred to as the Minimum/Maximum system. Parts or raw materials are evaluated based on need and usage to delineate the maximum and minimum levels for each item of inventory. The traditional rules for the minimum/maximum inventory system are usually quite simple:

Rule 1: Determine the maximum and minimum levels for each item.
Rule 2: Don't exceed the maximum level.
Rule 3: Don't reorder until you reach or go below the minimum level.

The original assumptions behind these rules are primarily based in Cost Accounting and cost world thinking. The overriding focus of these rules is to save money and minimize the expenditures for parts/inventory, or at least hold in reasonable check the amount of money you spend on these items. In order to reduce the amount of money you spend on these items, you must never buy more than the maximum amount. Also, in order to reduce the money spent on these items, you must not spend money until absolutely necessary, and order parts only when they reach the minimum level.

These assumptions seem valid as inventory goals and, if implemented correctly and monitored, should provide a satisfactory supply system that controls the inventory dollars spent while maintaining the necessary inventory within the minimum and maximum limits. However, most systems utilizing these rules, even in the perfect world, don't seem to generate the desired or needed results. For a variety of reasons, in most supply chain systems, there always seems to be situations of excess inventory for some items and of stock-out situations for other items. There seem to be the constant gyrations (variation) between too much inventory and too little inventory, especially for some specific items. The entire operational concept behind the supply chain minimum/maximum system was supposed to prevent these kinds of occurrences from happening, and yet they still do. Let's look at why it happens.

CONSEQUENCES OF COST ACCOUNTING METRICS

Perhaps the best way to make this point is with a couple of examples. The first example deals with a company who measured and rewarded their procurement staff based on the amount of money they could save with procurement purchases. For the procurement staff, their primary arrangement to accomplish this objective was to buy in bulk. For the most part, this task was usually quite easy to accomplish. Their suppliers were willing and sometimes demanded that their customers buy in bulk to receive the maximum benefit of "quantity discounts." The more you bought, the less it cost per unit. The assumption being that the purchase price per unit could be driven to the lowest possible level by buying in bulk and that they would save the maximum amount of money on their purchase. It seemed like a great idea and certainly argued as a great way to achieve the lowest cost per unit measure, therefore meeting the objective of saving money.

Sometimes these supply items were procured in amounts well in excess of the maximum quantities allowed, but they got them at a great cost-per-unit price. By employing this "cost-saving" strategy, and rewarding the procurement staff for doing so, this company had a warehouse full of low-cost inventory that equaled a little over $7 million. The problem was that they didn't have enough of the right mix of inventory to build even a single product. They had too many of some items (even though they were all purchased at the lowest price) and not enough of the other items needed for production. The bigger problem was they were out of money to purchase any more parts because of all the money they had saved buying inventory they didn't need. Now they couldn't purchase the parts they desperately needed in order to complete production. Do you suppose they wished they had at least some of the perceived cost savings back, so they could buy the right parts, in the right quantity, at the right time so they could produce products?

Another cost-saving example is the tale of a company that was a contractor to the United States government. In their contract, the government had offered a very lucrative contract clause. This clause, of course, was focused on saving money. During the yearly budgeting process, this company was given a strict budgeted amount to buy parts every year. Based on this budgeted amount, the government had offered to split 50–50 any amount they could underrun their parts budget. Because of this contract incentive, the company decided to take the total budgeted dollar amount and divide it by 12 to establish a monthly parts budget. They also held back an additional 10 percent of the monthly budget so they could claim cost savings and split the savings with the government. Any parts purchase that would have exceeded the targeted monthly budget was postponed until the next month, even if it was urgently needed. The ability of this company to complete their work was severely hampered and their ability to make money slowed dramatically. The bottom line was that they couldn't get the work out on time. There were many jobs waiting for parts that couldn't be finished until the needed parts arrived and the wait times for parts were measured in days or weeks. Their on-time delivery suffered dramatically. This company was literally jumping over dollars to pick up pennies and all because they wanted to save a few dollars on inventory in the hope of making some additional money.

In both of these examples, it's an issue of bad Cost Accounting metrics driving the bad behavior. In both of these cases, cost saving was the primary strategy and each one suffered the consequences. In the first example, the company ultimately went bankrupt and went out of business because they couldn't pay back the loans on the monies they had borrowed to buy raw material for all of the low-cost parts. In the second example, the company avoided bankruptcy because they provided a needed service for the government and were ultimately spared from going out of business by eventually seeing the error of their ways (both contractor and government) and decided instead to spend the allocated budgeted dollars to buy the needed parts.

THE SYSTEM ANALYSIS

If the system as a whole isn't producing the desired results, then what segment of the system needs to be changed to produce the desired results? Perhaps the minimum/maximum levels are the wrong rules to engage and saving money is the wrong financial measure to consider. In order to solve today's problems, we must think at an order of magnitude higher than we were thinking when we developed yesterday's solutions. In other words, any goodness from yesterday's solutions is causing most of today's problems.

One of the most important aspects of any manufacturing, production, or service supply chain system is to have and maintain the ability to supply raw materials or parts at a very predictable level. If the parts availability drops to zero, then production will stop for some period of time and sales activities will require that any orders received are immediately put on back order. The accurate and constant availability of parts implies a supply chain system that contains all of the necessary and robust features to support the customer demand requirements.

THE MOST COMMON SUPPLY CHAIN SYSTEM

The Minimum/Maximum (Min/Max) supply chain system was developed years ago, and at the time had some favorable improvements that it brought forward from previous methods. Then, and now, the functional philosophy behind the supply chain minimum/maximum system is that supplies and materials are distributed and stored at the lowest possible level of the user's chain. In essence, this is a push system that pushes parts through the system to the lowest possible level. It seems to make good sense to do this because parts must be available at the lowest level in order to be used. With this system, the parts are consumed until the minimum quantity is reached or exceeded and then an order is placed for more parts. The part's order goes up the chain from the point-of-use (POU) back to some kind of central supply center, or orders are placed directly back to the vendor/supplier depending on the supply system being used. When the orders are received at the central supply center, they are pushed back down the chain to the lowest POU locations.

Figure 6.1 defines a simplified version of this parts-flow activity. This flow might not be applicable to all situations, but to most, it will make sense. Some companies and smaller businesses will have fewer steps, in that they order directly from a vendor and receive parts back into their business without the need for large, more complex, distribution systems. However, the thinking behind the minimum/maximum system will still

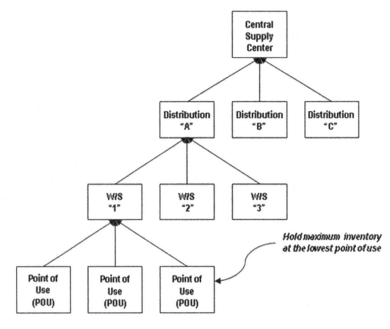

FIGURE 6.1
Parts and inventory flow from central distribution location to POU locations.

apply, even to those smaller businesses. Larger companies, or those with numerous geographical locations, will most likely have developed some type of a central supply and/or distribution locations that feed the next level of the supply distribution system—that is, regional warehouse versus local distribution points. The distribution points in turn feed the companies or business segments that use the raw material and parts at the final POU to build products. Some distribution systems may even be more complex than what is displayed here. But even with increased complexity, the results they are trying to achieve remain the same, which is to get the parts to where they need to be when they need to be there.

The model of a central supply system versus a decentralized system has volleyed back and forth for many years. Some say the supply system should be centralized at the user location to make supply activities easier and more responsive. Others argue that the supply activities should be decentralized to save money and reduce operating expense. Even with these continuing arguments, it seems that the current vogue is for the decentralized model of supply systems.

For all of its intent to save money and reduce operating expenses, the decentralized system can and does cause enormous hardships on the very systems it is designed to support. With all of the intended good this type of system is supposed to provide, there are some top-level rules that drive the system into chaos. Let's look at some of these rules and understand the negative aspects that derive from them. Table 6.1 provides a summary listing of the top-level rules for the maximum/minimum supply system.

Even though the Min/Max system appears to control the supply needs and cover the inventory demands, there are some significant negatives effects caused by using this system. First and foremost, there is the problem of being reactive to an inventory or parts situation, rather than proactive. When minimum stock levels are used as the trigger to reorder parts,

TABLE 6.1

Top-Level Rules for the Minimum/Maximum Supply System

1. The system reorder amount is the maximum amount no matter how many parts are currently in the bin box.
2. Most supply systems only allow for one order at a time to be present.
3. Orders for parts are triggered *only* after the minimum amount has been exceeded.
4. Total part inventory is held at the lowest possible level of the distribution chain—the point-of-use (POU) location.
5. Parts are inventoried once or twice a month and orders placed as required.

some supply chain systems, as they are currently organized and used, will have a difficult time keeping up with the demands being placed upon them. And there is an increased probability that stock-outs will occur, maybe for long periods of time.

Stock-outs occur most often when the lead time to replenish the part exceeds the minimum stock available. In other words, availability of the part between the minimum amount and zero is totally depleted before the part can be replenished from the vendor. Figure 6.2 displays a graphical representation of this stock-out effect. The curved line shows the item usage through time and the possibility of a stock-out situation.

Variation also exists with this scenario and stock-outs can either happen in a shorter or longer time frame, depending on the actual part usage. These stock-out situations are a recurring problem in systems that use minimum stock levels as the trigger to reorder parts.

Of course, when parts are reordered, they are ordered at a level equal to the maximum amount, and the problem appears to quickly correct itself. However, there can be a significantly large segment of time between stock-out and correction, and if the part is urgently needed, its non-availability can cause havoc in the assembly sequence.

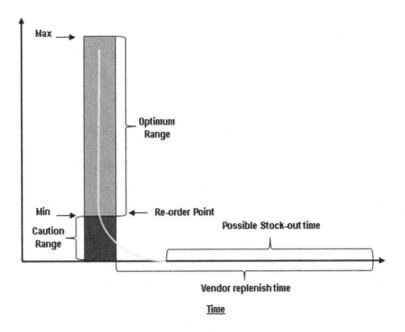

FIGURE 6.2
Minimum/Maximum parts model.

Some might argue that the solution to the problem is to simply increase the minimum amount to trigger a reorder sooner in the process and avoid the stock-out situation. It is possible this solution could provide some short-term relief, but in the long run, it causes inventory levels to go up and stay up. It is also possible that if you raise the minimum level, then the maximum level must also be raised. Many companies use a ratio variable to calculate the spread between minimum and maximum. If that's the case, then total inventory levels will go up, which costs more money to maintain. This is totally counter to the Cost Accounting rules.

The Min/Max supply chain is based totally on being in a reactive mode, waiting for the part to reach minimum stock level before a reorder request is activated. In many companies, the most used parts are managed using the minimum/maximum concepts and can frequently be out of stock. This Min/Max supply system also creates the disadvantage of potentially having several thousand dollars or hundreds of thousands of dollars tied up in inventory that may or may not get used before it becomes obsolete, modified, or dated because of expiration. If additional money is spent buying parts that might not be needed, at least in the quantity defined by the maximum limit, then you have effectively diverted money that could have been used to buy needed parts.

As an example, for purposes of discussion, suppose we pick a random part with a minimum/maximum level already established, and we track this part for a 26-week period using the current system rules and follow the flow and cyclical events that take place. What happens at the end of 26 weeks? For this example, we will assume the following:

- The maximum level is 90 items.
- The minimum reorder point is 20 items.
- The lead time to replenish this part from the vendor averages 4 weeks. The average is based on the fact that there are times when this part can deliver faster (3 weeks) and other times it delivers slower (5 weeks).
- Usage of these parts varies by week, but on average is equal to about ten items per week.

Table 6.2 shows the reorder trigger happening when current inventory drops below the minimum amount of 20 items. The first reorder would trigger between weeks 6 and 7, and again between weeks 17 and 18, and again between weeks 25 and 26. During this 26-week period, there would be a total of about 8 weeks of stock-out time. Remember: There is an average of 4 weeks of vendor lead time to replenish this part. This repeating cycle of maximum inventory and stock-outs becomes the norm, and the scenario is repeated time and time again.

Figure 6.3 uses the data from Table 6.2 to graphically display the results of the Min/Max system, and it shows the negative consequences that can occur in this system. If the vendor lead time is not considered as an important reorder variable, then stock-outs will continue to occur. Stock-outs can become a very predictable negative effect in this system.

TABLE 6.2

Simulated Data for the Minimum/Maximum Supply System

Week	Current Inventory	Actual Items Used	End of Week Inventory	Items Added (Replenish)
1	90	10	80	
2	80	15	65	
3	65	15	50	
4	50	15	35	
5	35	5	30	
6	30	15	15	
7	15	15	0	
8	0	0	0	
9	0	0	0	
10	0	0	0	90
11	90	15	75	
12	75	15	60	
13	60	8	52	
14	52	12	40	
15	40	10	30	
16	30	10	20	
17	20	15	5	
18	5	5	0	
19	0	0	0	
20	0	0	0	
21	90	15	75	90
22	75	18	57	
23	57	15	42	
24	42	12	30	
25	30	15	15	
26	15	15	0	

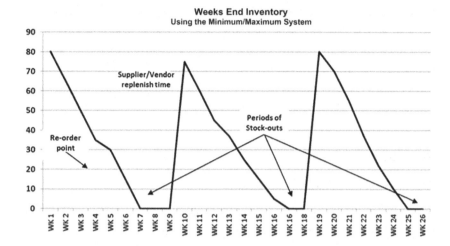

FIGURE 6.3
Consequences of the Minimum/Maximum supply system.

The graph shows the negative consequences of the supply system and demonstrates why supply chain systems using the maximum/minimum concepts will periodically create excessive inventory and stock-out situations. The primary reason this happens is because part lead times are not properly taken into account.

In most cases, the most prominent measures for minimum/maximum systems are focused in cost world (dollars) thinking rather than system needs. If the lead times from the vendors are not considered, then there remains a high probability that stock-outs will continue. The stock-out situation exacerbates itself even further when at the POU a user has experienced a stock-out situation in the past. In that situation, the users will often try to protect themselves against stock-outs by taking more than is needed. In other words, they become hoarders.

It is also possible that some companies will preorder inventory based on some type of forecast for the coming year. This strategy exacerbates the problem even more. At best, it is extremely difficult to forecast what a consumer may or may not buy. This problem is encountered at the manufacturing level and the retail level. Manufacturers will produce excess finished good inventory that must be stored at a great cost or sold to retailers at a discounted price. Because of the flaws in their forecasting methods, some stores are left with large amounts of inventory when new models or products are released. This becomes most visible when stores offer "year-end clearance sales" or "inventory liquidation" events. They guessed wrong with the forecast and have much more inventory than they can sell. In many cases, because stores couldn't get enough of the hot-selling product, they missed out on sales. Now they must sell any remaining inventory, sometimes at bargain prices, to generate enough cash to buy more inventories for the coming year. This cycle of too much and too little repeats itself year after year.

THE ROBUST SUPPLY SYSTEM

One of the primary operating functions of the supply chain system is to build and hold inventory at the lowest possible distribution level. This assumption is both correct and incorrect. The correct inventory should be held at the POU location, but not based on minimum/maximum amounts. Instead, the necessary inventory should be based on the vendor lead times to replenish and maintain sufficient inventory to buffer the variations that exist in lead time. The Theory of Constraints Distribution and Replenishment Model is a robust parts replenishment system that allows the user to be proactive in managing the supply chain system. It's also a system based on usage, either daily or weekly, but not the minimum amount. Some parts/inventory will require much more vigilance in day-to-day management.

Table 6.3 defines the suggested criteria required to implement a TOC Distribution and Replenishment Model in a supply chain system. The TOC Distribution and Replenishment Model argues that the majority of the inventory should be held at a higher level in the distribution system (supply

TABLE 6.3

Criteria for the TOC Distribution and Replenishment Model

---

1. The system reorder amount needs to be based on daily or weekly usage and part lead time to replenish.
2. The system needs to allow for multiple replenish orders, if required.
3. Orders are triggered based on buffer requirements, with possible daily actions, as required.
4. *All* parts/inventory must be available when needed.
5. Parts inventory is held at a higher level, preferably at central supply locations, or comes directly from the supplier/vendor.
6. Part buffer determined by usage rate and replenish supplier/vendor lead time. Baseline buffer should be equal to 1.5. If lead time is 1 week, buffer is set at 1.5 weeks. Adjust as required, based on historical data.

---

chain) and not at the lowest level. It is still important to keep what is needed at the lowest levels, but don't try to hold the total inventory at that location. The TOC model is based on the characteristics of a "V" plant distribution model. The "V" plant model assumes that distribution is fractal from a single location which in this case is either a central supply location or a supplier/vendor location (the base of the "V"), and distribution is made to different locations (the arms of the "V"). The "V" plant concept is not unlike any supply chain distribution methodology. However, using a "V" plant method has some negative consequences, especially when working under Min/Max rules (as shown in Figure 6.3). If one is not careful to understand these consequences, the system can suffer dramatically.

One of the major negative consequences of "V" distribution is distributing items too early and sending them down the wrong path to the wrong location. In other words, inventory is released too early and possibly to the wrong destination. This is especially likely to happen when the same type of inventory or part is used in several locations.

Has it ever happened that at one location you have a stock-out situation, and one of the rapid response criteria for finding the part is to check another production line within a company or call back to the distribution center? If this is the case, then parts/inventory distribution has taken place too early in the system. Sometimes, it's not that the system does not have the right parts/inventory, it's just that they are in the wrong location. Distribution from a higher level in the chain has been completed too quickly.

The TOC Distribution and Replenishment Model also argues that the use of minimum/maximum amounts should be abolished. Instead, the inventory should be monitored based on daily or weekly usage, with replenishment occurring at a minimum weekly and possibly daily for highly used items. The end result of these actions will be sufficient inventory in the right location at the right time, with zero or minimal stock-outs to support production activity. Instead of using the minimum amount to trigger the reorder process, it should be triggered by daily usage and vendor lead time to replenish.

As an example, suppose we apply the TOC Distribution and Replenishment Model rules to exactly the same criteria discussed earlier. We will use the same part simulation, and the same period of time, with the same usage numbers. In this simulation, the difference will be that we will change the rules to fit the TOC Distribution and Replenishment Model, based on usage amount and vendor lead time rather than minimum and maximum amount.

Table 6.4 presents the simulated data for a random reorder scenario using the TOC Distribution and Replenishment Model. In this example, we will assume the following:

- Maximum level is 90 items. (This is the start point for the current inventory.)
- There is no minimum reorder point, but rather reorder is based on usage and vendor lead time.
- Lead time to replenish is still 4 weeks.
- Average usage of the part is about ten per week.

TABLE 6.4

TOC Distribution and Replenishment Model

Week	Current Inventory	Actual Items Used	End of Week Inventory	Items Added (Replenish)
1	90	10	80	
2	80	15	65	
3	65	15	50	
4	50	15	35	10
5	45	5	40	15
6	55	15	40	15
7	55	15	40	15
8	55	10	45	5
9	50	10	40	15
10	55	15	40	15
11	55	15	40	10
12	50	15	35	10
13	45	8	37	15
14	52	12	40	15
15	55	10	45	15
16	60	10	50	8
17	58	5	53	12
18	65	10	55	10
19	65	10	55	10
20	65	10	55	5
21	60	15	45	10
22	55	18	37	10
23	47	15	32	10
24	42	12	30	15
25	45	10	35	18
26	53	15	38	15

The data in Table 6.4 also assumes that no parts inventory is held at the next higher level and that the parts replenishment has to come from the vendor and consumes the allotted vendor lead time. However, if the parts/ inventory were held at a higher level in the distribution chain (central supply or a distribution point), and replenish happened daily and/or weekly, then the total inventory required could go even lower than the data suggests. This could happen because distribution is completed weekly rather than waiting the full 4 weeks for delivery. The part usage rates are exactly the same as the previous run and the starting inventory is equal to 90 parts. This also assumes we have a weekly parts/inventory replenish after the initial 4 weeks of lead time has expired. In other words, every week we have delivered what was ordered 4 weeks ago. In the TOC scenario, the reorder point is at the end of each week based on usage. The total number of parts used is the same number of parts that should be reordered.

Figure 6.4 shows the effects of using the TOC Distribution and Replenishment Model. What is most notable is that total inventory required through time has decreased from 90 items to approximately 42 items. In essence, the required inventory has been cut in half. Also notable is the fact that there are no stock-out situations present.

When the TOC Distribution and Replenishment Model is used to manage the supply chain there is always sufficient parts inventory to continue production work. The total inventory is also much more stable through time, without the large gaps and gyrations from zero inventories

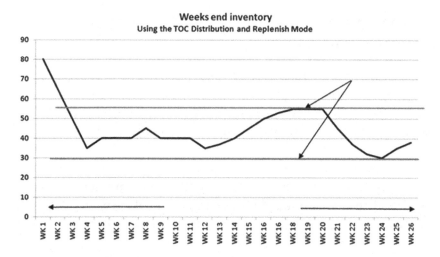

FIGURE 6.4
Overall effect of the TOC method.

available to maximum inventory as noted on the first run (Figure 6.3) using the Min/Max system.

Perhaps the best way to explain the TOC Distribution and Replenishment Model is with an easy example. Consider a soda vending machine. When the supplier (the soda vendor) opens the door on a vending machine, it is very easy to calculate the distribution of products sold, or the point-of-use consumption. The soda person knows immediately which inventory has to be replaced and to what level to replace it. The soda person is holding the inventory at the next highest level, which is on the soda truck, so it's easy to make the required distribution when needed. He doesn't leave 6 cases of soda when only 20 cans are needed. If he were to do that, when he got to the next vending machine he might have run out of the necessary soda because he made distribution too early at the last stop. After completing the required daily distribution to the vending machines, the soda person returns to the warehouse or distribution point to replenish the supply on the soda truck and get ready for the next day's distribution. When the warehouse makes distribution to the soda truck, they move up one level in the chain and replenish from their supplier. This type of system does require discipline to gain the most benefits. It assumes that regular and needed checks are taking place at the inventory locations to determine the replenishment needs. If these points are not checked on a regular basis, it is possible for the system to experience stock-out situations.

CONCLUSIONS

The distinct contrast in results between simulated data runs using the Minimum/Maximum supply system and the TOC Distribution and Replenishment Model are undeniable. The true benefits of a TOC-based parts replenishment system are many, but the most significant impact is realized in these two areas.

The first benefit is the reduction of total inventory required to manage and maintain the total supply chain system. This inventory reduction could lead to a significant dollar savings in total inventory required, perhaps thousands of dollars. In many cases, you can expect to see an inventory reduction in the neighborhood of 50 percent!

The second benefit is the elimination of stock-out situations. Without a doubt, not having parts available is an expensive situation for companies because it slows throughput through the production system. Production lines sit idle just waiting for parts to become available. Or worse yet, they just start making products that aren't needed simply because parts are available, and everyone needs to be kept busy. Stock-out situations increase frustration, not only in not being able to complete the work but also in the time spent waiting for parts to become available. When this happens, orders will be delivered late, and customers will be frustrated and orders will decline.

Looking for parts and experiencing part shortages are a continuing problem in most supply chain systems. These problems are not caused by the production people, but by the negative effects of the supply chain system and the way it is being used. If the current supply system is maintained, then the output from that system cannot be expected to change much, if at all. However, if new levels of output are required from the system now and in the future, then new thinking must be applied to solve the parts supply system issues. The concepts and methodologies of the TOC Distribution and Replenishment Model can positively impact the ability to produce products on time and in the correct quantity.

7

A Case Study on the Theory of Constraints

As discussed in Chapter 1, the Theory of Constraints is all about being able to identify the limiting factor in a system or process that controls the rate of units through it. You then focus your improvement efforts on this limiting factor in order to leverage the potential gains to be made. I've been using this methodology since the 1990s and it has provided significant improvements each and every time. What you're about to read is a true story related to my first experience with the Theory of Constraints and all that it has to offer.

One of my former bosses had called me and wanted me to come to work for him. When I asked him what kind of position he wanted me to take, he explained that he had become the CEO of a new company and that he had a manufacturing facility in Kentucky that he wanted me to run. I was very excited to have been chosen to run a manufacturing facility because I had never been in charge of one before. I agreed to meet him there several weeks later.

When I arrived at this manufacturing facility, we met to discuss this business behind closed doors. One of my first questions was, "Why he wanted me?" and he replied that he really liked my people skills and my quality ethic. I then asked him if he had a specific way that he wanted me to run this business and to my surprise, he just smiled and said that he actually wanted me to close the doors and shut it down. I totally thought he was joking, but I soon found out he wasn't. I pushed back hard and told him that he owed me a chance to try and turn this facility around, rather than shut it down. He explained that they had put their "best plant manager" in charge and he was unable to make a difference. I pushed back even harder and he finally agreed to at least let me try with one stipulation. I had 3 months to make it profitable, but after 3 months, if it wasn't profitable, I had no choice but to shut it down. Reluctantly, I agreed.

So, there I was. I had just been hired to facilitate either a best-case turnaround or a worst-case closure of this manufacturing facility. This particular manufacturing plant produced fiberglass hard tops on one side of the plant and convertible tops on the other side with approximately 250 employees working at the location. When I arrived to start at this site, I found it virtually in shambles. It had just missed being unionized by five votes, so the workforce was pretty much split down the middle in terms of "camps," with one camp being pro-management and wanting to turn this plant around, while the other camp, those who had voted to unionize the facility, having a very negative view of leadership. From a financial perspective, the facility was on credit hold with some of its key suppliers and overtime was very high.

On further investigation, I discovered that customers were threatening to pull their business because of poor quality and terrible on-time delivery. Absenteeism was high, and morale was in the tank. Sound like a fun place to work? Add to this my background had been almost exclusively Quality and Engineering with virtually zero operations experience. I was definitely going down a new path.

This company was using a form of Enterprise Resource Planning (ERP) to schedule their production, but they weren't very successful using it. ERP systems are supposed to help a business by providing a common set of tools that can be used across an enterprise to both plan for and control the execution of actions at each resource. Scheduling in an ERP system begins with an order due date and then attempts to start as late as possible while still meeting the date or it starts with today and tries to complete the work as soon as possible, which often times is well before the due date. Typically, scheduling through a manufacturing plant uses production rates and times or units of production capacities to schedule each resource. I mention this point early on because we modified this company's ERP system to merge with another scheduling mechanism known as Drum-Buffer-Rope from the Theory of Constraints. We will cover this merger later in the chapter.

When I arrived at this manufacturing plant, there were two operations managers already in place. One had been there for 20 years and the other had just been hired. Because I had no real operations management experience, I thought I could rely on at least one of my two operations managers to help me learn the ropes. But I found out quite early on, that wasn't such a good strategy. Neither of them could offer any real vision for what we had to do to effectuate a turnaround. I was starting to panic!

On my first day on the job, I spent all three shifts within the four walls of the factory out on the production floor introducing myself to the employees and trying to get some sense of the true state of the business. What I found that the first day caused a great deal of anxiety for me personally because they were all looking to me to help save their jobs. The next morning in desperation, I visited the local library to find something, anything, on operations management to read (i.e. back then there was no internet to search like today). That visit turned out to be a good move for me because in that library I discovered a small, partially hidden, paper-back book that would change the course of history at this plant in Kentucky. This book would become my blueprint for a complete transformation of not only this manufacturing facility but for me personally and professionally. The name of this book was *The Goal: A Process of Ongoing Improvement* by Eliyahu Goldratt and Jeff Cox [1].

For those of you not familiar with the Theory of Constraints (TOC), the basis behind TOC is that manufacturing output is dictated by the slowest operation. It's like following the cadence of a drum beat. I'll discuss this concept in more detail later in this chapter. Meanwhile, back to my case study.

I spent the remainder of my second day in my office and most of the night reading this manufacturing masterpiece. There were concepts within this book that I had never heard of before. I was so excited to get started applying these concepts, but I knew my team had to understand the teachings within this book before we could truly begin our transformation. I found a local book store, purchased copies of *The Goal* for all of my direct reports and supervisors to read. I overnighted them in and mandated to all of my direct reports to have read this book within 2 days. We had round-table discussions about the key teachings within this book on a daily basis and within a week we were ready to begin.

One of the first things we did was to establish a morning "Herbie Hunt" to search for and find the system constraint. (For those of you who have never read *The Goal*, Herbie was an overweight boy scout with an overloaded backpack who controlled the pace of a boy scout's overnight hike.) He was constraining the rate of progress of the boy scout troop. The troop finally figured out that if they could reduce the weight of Herbie's backpack, the troop could increase the amount of distance covered on their hike. This was how the authors of *The Goal*, Eliyahu Goldratt and Jeff Cox, chose to introduce the concept of the constraint.

Because we were losing so much money on the hardtop side of the business, we decided we would start our improvement effort on this side of the business. We would walk the process until we came upon a backlog of partially finished hardtops. Once we found it, we then stopped and asked the operator why he or she felt that the process was blocked at their station. We also asked this same person what they thought should be done to alleviate the backlog. This technique turned out to have multiple effects.

First, we were able to identify the constraint (aka bottleneck) and then decide how to exploit it or make the most of it. In the early going, it was clear that we had to subordinate the rest of the process to the pace of the constraint. This was a difficult decision because our corporate office tracked our overall efficiency and by asking the non-constraints to slow down, the overall efficiency took a nosedive. However, we did track the efficiency of our bottleneck operation because we knew that the constraint was the only process step that it made sense using.

Perhaps the most important effect of our daily Herbie Hunt was the true involvement of the hourly workforce in our improvement effort. They were amazed that someone was actually listening to them and that we not only solicited their ideas, but we implemented them exactly as stated, as long as no safety, company, or customer rules and regulations were violated! I remember one operator telling me that nobody had ever listened to the workforce before. And so, our total company improvement effort had begun.

One of the first constraints or bottlenecks our team discovered was when it was time to mount the hardtop on the chassis of a very popular German sports car. Along the hardtop mounting surface, there were 48 control points that had to be within the specification limits provided by this German manufacturer. To our amazement, 36 of these points failed to conform to the specification limits. Many of the points were above the spec limits and could be repaired, but many times they were below the limits, so the hard top had to be scrapped. In fact, approximately 20 percent of all of the tops fell into this category, which caused deep financial pain for our plant.

I also discovered that the hardtop was 4 months late coming to market. We formed a team of hourly employees and our one, lone engineer to solve this problem which turned out to be an alignment issue within our bonding process. The team determined the root cause of the mismatch in surfaces, implemented a Statistical Process Control (SPC) initiative, and the scrap level fell to almost zero, which immediately improved both our on-time delivery metric, the customer's perception of our quality, but more importantly, our bottom line. We celebrated this success with a pizza party which brought our two distinct "camps" much closer together. In addition, the morale of the workforce as a whole jettisoned upward.

One of the problems I haven't mentioned was the quality of materials being received from our suppliers. I remember on at least two occasions scrapping an entire batch of resin used in our hardtop molding process. We also had supplier delivery issues from the standpoint of on-time delivery. Part of this was due to our inability to pay our bills on time and part of it was due to the poor processes that some of our suppliers had. As some of you might have guessed, the previous leadership, in an attempt to improve profitability, chose the lowest cost suppliers, which in some cases had the poorest quality and on-time delivery rates.

One of our hourly employees suggested that we have a Supplier Appreciation Day and invite all of our suppliers into our plant. He reasoned that if they could see how their products were used and talk about the problems we were seeing with their products, there would be an immediate improvement in both quality and on-time delivery. Another employee suggested that we pay all of our bills within 30 days as an incentive for suppliers to improve their delivery performance. Guess what … both ideas worked!! Within a matter of weeks, our supplier performance improved dramatically and because we were paying within 30 days, we were able to negotiate significant early pay cost reductions which also helped our bottom line.

I mentioned earlier that when we subordinated the rest of our process to the constraint, our efficiencies took a hit. The reason being that we ran all other process steps at the same speed as our constraint. I remember our corporate office sending a team down to our plant to determine the cause of our deterioration in efficiencies. They came unannounced, just sort of showed up at our front door. I invited them into our conference room and they made a presentation demonstrating on a run chart the sudden decrease in efficiencies.

I let them finish their presentation and asked them if they had looked at any other performance metrics? Of course, they hadn't! I had anticipated a visit from corporate at some point, so I had prepared a brief presentation of my own for when they arrived. The very first slide said it all. It was a plot of weekly on-time delivery and I think it shocked them. When I had arrived, the plant's on-time delivery was just under 60 percent, while the efficiencies were around 80 percent, which was still too low for the corporate "experts." When they saw our data, they didn't believe it because even though the efficiency had dropped to around 65 percent, the on-time delivery now stood at 88 percent (which was still not good enough for me). Actually, the most current week which had not yet been plotted now stood at 94 percent!!

I asked the "experts" if they would like to see how it was possible to improve on-time delivery while reducing our process efficiencies. I went through my traditional drawings of the piping system and simple four-step process and explained the concept of a physical constraint. But for those of you who haven't read about the concept of the constraint, here are the two drawings I used.

In this first drawing (Figure 7.1), I explained that this was a simple gravity fed piping system used to transport water. I then asked the corporate "experts" what they would do if additional water was needed to flow through the piping system. They answered the question correctly in that it would be necessary to increase the diameter of Section E. I also

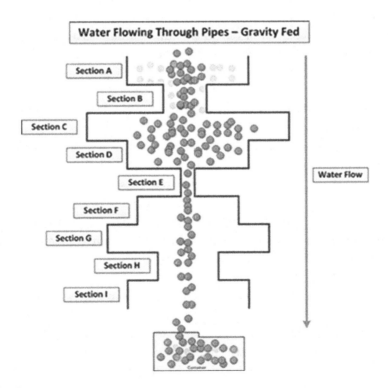

FIGURE 7.1
Gravity-fed piping system for delivering water.

asked them if increasing the diameter of any other section would increase the flow of water through this system and again, they answered correctly by saying no, only Section E. This exercise was intended to implant the concept of the system constraint firmly in their minds.

I then inserted a second drawing (Figure 7.2) which depicted the condition where Section E's diameter had been enlarged and the constraint had moved to Section B of the piping system as demonstrated in the drawing. These two drawings had a positive impact on the demeanor of the meeting.

I then laid out the five basic steps of the Theory of Constraints process of on-going improvement as follows:

1. Identify the system constraint (i.e. Section E in the first drawing).
2. Exploit the system constraint (i.e. enlarge the diameter of Section E).
3. Subordinate everything else to the constraint (i.e. run at the same speed as the constraint).
4. If necessary, elevate the system constraint (i.e. this was done when we opened Section E's diameter).
5. When the constraint is broken, return to Step 1 (i.e. when we enlarged Section E's diameter, the constraint moved to Section B in the second drawing).

Identifying the system constraint, in its simplest form, means to find the bottleneck within your process or system or that point that is limiting production. Exploiting the constraint simply means making improvements in order to get the most out of your constraint. In our plant, exploiting the constraint meant that we needed to reduce the processing time of our constraint, which we did. Subordinating our constraint meant that our non-constraint process steps should never out-pace our constraint. Elevating the constraint meant that we might have to spend money on more resources or equipment if we still weren't producing at a fast-enough rate. Fortunately, in the short term, we did not have to perform this step as well as the final step simply because our constraint was supplying enough throughput to meet the needs of our customers.

I then inserted another drawing (Figure 7.3) of a simple four-step process for manufacturing something and asked them where they believed the constraint was in this process. Without exception, everyone agreed that Step 4, because it had the longest cycle time at 5 minutes, was the system constraint.

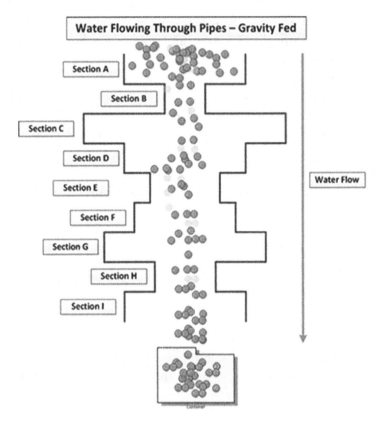

FIGURE 7.2
Piping system with new constraint.

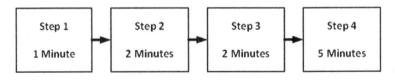

FIGURE 7.3
Simple four-step process.

I repeated the same questions I had asked about the piping system and they answered each one correctly. I then asked them to tell me what would happen if I were to run every process step as fast as I could to increase efficiency like they wanted? One of the "brighter" corporate folks got a smile on his face and said that you would end up with two piles of inventory, one in front of Step 2 and another one in front of Step 4. When I asked him to explain, he said that because of the differences in capacities, it would be a natural effect. Since Step 1 could produce at double the rate of Step 2, the Work-In-Process (WIP) in front of Step 2 would build up at a rate of one extra part per minute or 240 parts in 8 hours. The pile of WIP in front of Step 4 would be 144 parts in 8 hours (see Figure 7.4). Once again, these simple drawings had a very positive impact on how the corporate group approached the issue of efficiencies at our manufacturing facility.

I then asked this same man to tell me the rate at which I should run the current process and he correctly stated one part every 5 minutes to match the rate of the constraint. Everyone had just experienced that concept of slowing down in order to speed up and that attempting to drive efficiencies upward could have a negative impact on on-time delivery. Before the corporate group left, I wanted to make sure they had a complete understanding of why all of this mattered in terms of our plant's profitability.

One of the key things I learned by reading *The Goal* [1] was the whole idea of Throughput Accounting (TA). I had never been introduced to TA, so it was an eye-opening experience for me. Actually, I had never been responsible for a company's financials before and had difficulty understanding some of the "rules" of cost accounting. I was being held accountable to traditional Cost Accounting and quite frankly some of the rules made no sense at all to me, so I was questioning things. For example, how could excess inventory be viewed as an asset? Isn't inventory tying up cash? And as I explained earlier, running all process steps to the maximum capacity only served to drive WIP inventory higher. And since we had discovered that there was a direct correlation between having excess WIP and elongated cycle times, it made no sense to do so. But those were the rules of engagement that I was being judged on.

When I read *The Goal*, I had an epiphany of sorts. Goldratt introduced the world to a new way of looking at profitability through a completely

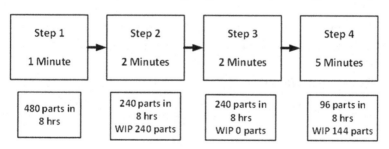

FIGURE 7.4
Simple process with WIP.

different spectrum. While Cost Accounting preaches their sermon of profitability through saving money, Goldratt argued that rather than trying to save money, companies should be focused on trying to make money and as I would soon discover, the two approaches are drastically different!

One of the principle lessons within *The Goal* is that the goal of for-profit companies is to make money now and in the future. He analogized that just like a chain having a weakest link, so too does a company. And this weakest link controls how much money a company will make. Goldratt also explained that attempts to strengthen any other part of the chain (or company) will do nothing to drive profitability higher. From an organizational perspective, this simply means that every decision or action taken must be considered based upon its impact on the goal of making money. If the action or decision doesn't get you closer to the goal, then don't take that action. Goldratt further explained that if you want to know if you're moving in the right direction in terms of profitability, you should ask yourself three simple questions:

- Does your action or decision result in more Throughput (T)?
- Does your action or decision result in more Inventory (I)?
- Does your action or decision result in more Operating Expense (OE)?

If you answered yes to the first question, then it's a good action or decision. If you answered yes to either question two or three, then it might not be a good thing to do. The optimum conditions for maximizing profitability are to have Throughput increasing while Inventory and Operating Expenses are decreasing or remaining constant. Notice I used the word "optimum" in terms of maximizing profitability. It is certainly plausible to have OE increasing to drive T higher, it just won't result in optimum profitability. Let's take a look at the definitions of these three components of profitability.

- Throughput (T): The rate that the organization generates new money primarily through sales. Goldratt provided this formula for Throughput as:
  Throughput = Revenue (R) $ minus Totally Variable Costs (TVC) or,

$$T = R - TVC$$

TVC includes things that vary with the sale of a single unit of product such as the cost of raw materials, sales commissions, shipping costs, etc.

- Inventory (I): The money that an organization invests in items that it intends to sell. This category would include inventory of all kinds (i.e. WIP and Finished Goods).
- Operating Expense (OE): The money an organization spends to turn (I) into (T) which includes ALL labor costs, raw materials, office supplies, employee benefits, utility bills, etc.

Goldratt expanded his TA definitions still further by defining net profit, return on investment, productivity, and inventory turns and he based them all on the three simple measures T, I, and OE. So, with these simple definitions, our team was able to not only take actions and make decisions in real time, but we were sure they would positively impact our bottom line. Here are Goldratt's other definitions:

- Net Profit (NP) equals Throughput minus Operating Expense or NP = T – OE
- Return on Investment (ROI) equals T minus OE divided by I or ROI = T – OE/I
- Productivity (P) equals T divided by OE or P = T/OE
- Inventory Turns (IT) equals T divided by I or IT = T/I

Our team went against the company culture when we decided to use Throughput Accounting, but believe me, it worked. And because of the simplicity of the definitions for each, we were able to teach our workforce how to use them as well. Yes, we had to continue using Cost Accounting to satisfy GAAP reporting requirements, but for daily decision-making, we found Throughput Accounting to be vastly superior to Cost Accounting. After hearing what I had to say about Throughput Accounting, the team from corporate was clearly impressed, packed up and went home.

Earlier, I presented a brief explanation of ERP systems and how they are supposed to function. I explained that scheduling in an ERP begins with a due date for an order and tries to start as late as possible, but still meet the due date. TOC uses a simpler approach as it begins by identifying the constraint and then schedules the other resources around the pace of the constraint. With a simple change of scheduling production around the pace of the constraint, we were able to maximize our ERP system. In other words, we used ERP to schedule production in our plant but used the "drum beat" of the constraint to ensure it was never starved for work. All other resources worked at the same pace as the constraint (i.e. subordinated) and this new system worked extremely well.

In the TOC world, this form of scheduling is known as Drum-Buffer-Rope with the drum being the pace of the constraint. We also established buffers upstream from the constraint so that it would never run out of materials to process. The buffer can be inventory (in ERP, it is referred to as Safety Stock) or it can also be reserve resources. We used a combination of the two with the goal being to never starve the constraint. The rope is an artificial mechanism, or a signal tied to all upstream resources so that they never fall behind the constraint or create excessive WIP inventory.

One of the pleasures of being a part of a turnaround is seeing the transformation of the systems, people, product, and customer. On this last point, the customer, I want to relate an event that took place about 5 months after we began our transformation. This event was a visit we had from one of the purchasing executives from the German car manufacturer. Since we had improved so rapidly, he decided to pay us a visit to see firsthand just what we had done to improve our quality and on-time delivery rates.

Remember earlier, I explained that there were 48 measurement points to determine how well the hard top mounted to the vehicle. We greeted the executive team that had accompanied the purchasing executive, exchanging pleasantries and getting to know each other until he announced that he was going to our manufacturing area and that he would randomly select a completed hard top and have it mounted on their vehicle. He further stated that his quality manager would inspect all 48 control points for conformance to specs. The quality manager took his time, inspected each point, and concluded that all points met their specs. The purchasing executive's eyebrows rose in disbelief and with a very heavy German accent said, "Mr. Sproull, the measurements are only part of what we expect." He then said, "Mr. Sproull, you will drive me on the Interstate at a high rate of speed and I will listen for air entering into the vehicle."

He and I drove to the Interstate and he instructed me to accelerate until he told me to hold at 65 mph, which I did. His ear was pressed close to the hardtop mounting area as he listened for the slightest sound of air passing under the hardtop. At 65 mph there was no sound, so he instructed me to accelerate again up to 75 mph, but still no air entering the vehicle. He had a very disappointed look on his face so, on my own, I continued to accelerate to 90 mph, then one 100 mph, and finally, to 105 mph. He looked at me with a fearful look on his face and instructed me to return to our facility. We had passed his functionality test with flying colors!!

When we returned, he explained that he wanted to mount a black hardtop on his vehicle so that he could compare our paint job with his. Painting at our facility was something we now took pride in, but not so in the beginning. When I had arrived at the Kentucky plant, I saw firsthand just how bad our paint jobs were. We had a very old paint booth which was apparently full of dust particles that ended up on the surface of our vehicles. I put together a team of maintenance mechanics and explained that since our corporate office would never approve a new paint booth, we needed to figure out a way to keep our paint booth free of particles and that I needed some good ideas. To make a long story short, one of the maintenance mechanics had a side business for lawn sprinklers. He had this bright idea that if we mounted such a system in the paint booth, we could actually clean the air between paintings by emitting a fine mist of water. We tried it and it worked like a champ!

The purchasing executive randomly selected a completed black top and we mounted it on his vehicle. We parked it in a highly lighted area and he scrutinized it for a good 30 minutes. When he was finished, he summoned me to the vehicle, looked me in the eye and said, "Mr. Sproull, we have a serious problem!" I asked him what the problem was, and he told me that our paint job did not match the paint job on his vehicle. I was shocked because I knew our painting was now the best in the industry. When I asked him, what was wrong with our hardtop's paint job, he sneered at me and said absolutely nothing! The problem was with his own vehicle. There was a large amount of orange peel on his vehicle's surface. My response to him was, "Would you like us to add orange peel to our hardtop's surface?" He looked at me and simply said, "I don't find any humor in that remark!"

Yes, this day was one of our great days for our plant. All of the hard work and dedication of our employees had paid off as the purchasing executive from Germany told us that he wished all of his suppliers were as good as we were. I asked him to speak to my employees and let them know his feelings which he did. That day was clearly a turning point for our plant, both in our reputation and the morale of our workforce. They had pride for the first time in years and I've always believed that "people who feel good about themselves, produce great results."

Just for the record, the first month that I took over this failing facility we lost about $600,000, but within two and a half months we were making roughly $500,000 per month. It was such a joy to see this wonderful team of people doing so well. I was so proud of every single employee for it was them that made it all happen!! One of the things the management team learned, and something I insisted upon, was that all improvement ideas would be considered on their merit and would be implemented, as long as they didn't violate company rules, safety policies, or customer requirements. I can honestly say that 95 percent of all of the solutions came directly from the shop floor workers, the true subject matter experts. Since that fateful turnaround, I have successfully used this basic idea, what I refer to as *active listening*. It worked for me then as a General Manager and it continued to work for me as a consultant.

Like most companies who manufacture parts, before my arrival at this facility, those in charge purchased numerous Stock Keeping Units (SKUs) that were needed to fabricate their products. So, to make sure they had enough of each part, they used the Min/Max system to replenish their supplies. For those of you not familiar with the Min/Max system, there are several "rules" as follows:

1. Determine the Minimum and Maximum levels for each SKU.
2. When reordering, never exceed the maximum level for any SKU.
3. Never reorder until you go below the minimum level defined for that SKU.
4. Total part inventory is held at the lowest level of distribution (usually at point-of-use).
5. Parts are inventoried once or twice a week and order placed, as required (i.e. when less than the minimum target).

Leadership religiously followed these rules, but it seemed as though no matter how diligent they were, they still had stock-outs. And when they did, they "stupidly" raised their maximum reorder quantity. I say stupidly because all they were doing was needlessly tying up excessive amounts of cash on parts they didn't need. In the first couple weeks I was there, I think our part's inventory increased something like 40 percent, yet we still suffered from stock-outs. I wondered what we could possibly be doing wrong.

The assumptions driving the five "rules" are based in cost world thinking. This thinking believes that in order to save money and minimize the cash you tie up in inventory you must minimize the amount of money you spend for these items by never buying more than the maximum amount and not spending any money until it's absolutely necessary (i.e. order parts only when they reach the minimum level). As I said, we scrutinized our purchases and lived by these rules, but at the end of the day, we still had numerous stock-outs which were beginning to impact our on-time delivery gains and we simply couldn't let that happen.

One day, one of our hourly supply guys (Jimmie) said he wanted to talk to me about an idea he had to reduce these stock-outs and asked for a one-on-one meeting with me in my office. I asked him why he wanted this kind of meeting and he told me that everyone thought his idea was silly and that he didn't want his co-workers to know he had suggested it. I smiled and invited him into my office and shut the door. He asked me if he could use my board to draw while he talked and of course I obliged. Jimmie and I talked for over 2 hours and I was convinced that his idea would work because it was all based upon common sense.

Jimmie suggested that we go away from the Min/Max system and replace it with a system that is completely based upon part's usage. What he really pushed for was ordering more frequently based upon what we had used. He told me that he got the idea from watching canned goods at a grocery store where he observed as one can is purchased, a replacement can is ordered using their bar code system and they never seem to have stock-outs.

He further explained that the grocery store keeps a minimum amount of stock in their stock room to replenish what was used that day, but they frequently reorder two to three times per week to replenish their stock room. I thought the idea was fantastic and asked Jimmie if he would lead the effort. He was hesitant at first but then agreed to do so. We tried it, and over the course of the next 6 months, we reduced our total inventory by nearly 50 percent while virtually eliminating stock-outs. It wasn't all smooth sailing, but as we ran into problems, Jimmie always found a way to fix it. What I didn't know was that Jimmie had worked for a grocery store as a stock-boy and had obviously paid attention to his surroundings. I later promoted Jimmie to the new job title of Logistics Manager. It was such a proud day for Jimmie, but he had earned it!!

What Jimmie had suggested was a form of TOC's Parts Replenishment System which, as Jimmie had suggested, uses the concept of replenishment based upon usage. That is, rather than using the traditional Min/Max system which replenishes based upon minimum and maximum quantities, replenishing based on usage.

One of our other customers operated a facility situated within 2 miles of our plant. Even though we were in close proximity, we really didn't produce much for them and when I arrived there, I wondered why we didn't. I decided that it was time to make an unscheduled visit to see if I could get to the bottom of why this was the case. As I drove that short distance to the facility, I kept imagining to myself why they didn't use us as a major supplier. I knew we had experienced quality problems in the past, so I thought maybe that was the major reason.

When I pulled into their manufacturing plant's parking lot there was a line of their sleek, sporty vehicles parked in a line in most of the executive's parking slots. I got out of my car and started walking past each one, but their allure made me stop and admire each one. I had always wanted one of these sports cars but could never afford to buy one. I had never even driven one before.

As I continued stopping and looking at each one, I heard a voice behind me say, "You like these?" I responded immediately without looking back, "You bet I do!" He then floored me and asked, "Would you like to drive one?" I immediately turned and looked him in the eye and smiled. He said, "I'm serious, would you like to drive one?" Knowing he was serious, I said, "Sure, but who are you?" He said, "I'm the plant manager at this facility." I told him that I was actually coming to meet him and chat a bit about my plant's lack of business with his company. He said, "Let's chat while we drive," and with that he opened the driver's side door for me and then walked around to the passenger side and crawled in.

This facility had a mile-long test track built around it, so off we went. The ride was so fast, smooth and the handling was excellent. I was driving about 65 mph when he said, "Do you always drive this slow?" With that, I punched it, and soon we were at 110 mph, and it felt so good and natural. He eventually asked me what I wanted to talk with him about, so there we were traveling at 100 plus miles per hour talking shop. I had trouble concentrating going at these speeds, but he seemed perfectly comfortable as though he had all of his business meetings like this. I got right to the point and asked him what my plant had to do in order to do more business with his plant. He went on to explain parts of the sorted history between the two facilities. It seems as though even though we were the closest of all supplier plants, we were unable to ship anything on time. And when we did, our quality wasn't always stellar.

As I was driving and listening to him, I was thinking about what kind of an offer I would have to make to him that he simply couldn't refuse. "It would have to include a guaranteed on-time delivery provision," I thought. "It would also have to include a provision for a high enough quality level that would differentiate us from his other suppliers," I continued. I didn't know it at the time, back then, but what I was considering was something in the TOC world referred to as a Mafia Offer. He told me that he would love to do business with us again, if we could show him that our facility was capable of being a reliable supplier. With that, I invited him to come visit our plant to which he agreed.

As I drove back to my plant, I had a vision of an offer that I wanted to make to him. It had to be something that he could not refuse. If he would give us exclusive business for specific fiberglass parts, I would offer him 100 percent on-time delivery or the order would be free. I also decided that our quality levels we would offer would be based upon a running average that must be greater than 98 percent compliant to specs. I knew we had excess capacity because of all the throughput improvements we had made, so I was confident in our ability to assure flawless delivery of parts. And since we had a very well defined SPC initiative in place, I felt confident that we could meet the quality requirements as well.

My next thought was about the price of our products that we would offer. I decided that we would match our competitor's price, minus 10 percent. Since we had excess capacity in our fiberglass process, I knew that as long as we covered the totally variable costs, which were now quite low, nearly all of what we charged would flow directly to the bottom line. I knew this because we would not be adding any additional operating expenses beyond what we already had. The beauty of Throughput Accounting is how easy it is to make real-time financial decisions. Since we had set his visit for 2 days from our meeting, I had plenty of time to create my Mafia Offer.

Right on schedule, the plant manager showed up on our doorstep. Because we had done multiple 5S events, he was quite impressed with not only the cleanliness of our plant but also with how organized it was. He told me that the last time he was in my plant there was inventory everywhere, but since we had applied TOC to our facility, there were no longer any piles of WIP like before. We had also done a lot of work with our ERP system, visual buffer management, and Drum-Buffer-Rope concepts and techniques, so that we knew at a glance the status of all of our orders. He was clearly impressed! What amazed him the most was how little our raw material and finished goods inventories we had at our site. But the one thing that impressed him the most, or should I say the biggest difference to him, was the obvious uptick in the morale of our workforce.

When he had seen enough of our improvements, he simply said, "Let's go to your office and talk." He told me how impressed he was with all of the changes since his last visit here, but that he wasn't sure if we could do business. He told me that he thought it would take a while for me to generate an offer that would turn heads at his corporate offices in Detroit. With that, I handed him my single page Mafia Offer which told him that we would generate a specific SKU at 100-percent on-time delivery, at best cost minus 10 percent, with a greater than or equal to quality level of 98 percent or the entire order would be free! He asked me if this was a real offer or simply one to make me laugh. I assured him that it was genuine and that if he was in agreement, that my accountant could contact his accountant that day and we could deliver our first shipment within 24 hours. He was flabbergasted to say the least and said that in all of his years he had never seen an offer like this and that he simply couldn't refuse it!

The next day we delivered our first order and after a lengthy inspection, it was deemed 100-percent compliant. A week passed by with the same results every time. And then 1 month and 6 months with the same results each time. In fact, the only quality issues we experienced in that time period were labeling issues. Our plant's revenue and profitability skyrocketed as did our orders from his company and our other customers. We even added new customers for body and quarter panels to our mix of products. We continued our improvement efforts to our entire plant and the results were amazing! It was an exciting time for our plant and our plant which had been scheduled to be shut down when I assumed leadership of it, ended up becoming the model for our entire corporation. We had numerous visits from other plants within the same company. The bottom line was that by integrating the Theory of Constraints, with both Lean and Six Sigma, amazing things will happen!

REFERENCE

1. Eliyahu M. Goldratt and Jeff Cox, *The Goal: A Process of Ongoing Improvement*, North River Press, Great Barrington, MA, 1984.

8

A Case Study on Helicopter Maintenance, Repair, and Overhaul

INTRODUCTION

In early 2012, an improvement team was dispatched to an organization that specialized in contract Maintenance, Repair, and Overhaul (MRO) of military aircraft. This contractor provided maintenance services for a fleet of rotary wing aircraft (i.e. helicopters) owned and operated by one of the Department of Defense (DoD) entities and was intended to provide training for new pilots.

Because training was the mission at this location, it was imperative that flyable helicopters were available on a timely basis. Per the contract with this DoD agency, this contractor was required to have "x" flyable aircraft per day available for student pilot training and if "x" was not met, significant financial penalties were assessed on this contractor. There had been significant problems meeting this requirement on a consistent basis for a variety of reasons, but the improvement team believed that the real problem was the absence of a clearly defined flow path and synchronization of helicopters into and out of the unscheduled maintenance hangars. In fact, when the improvement team arrived, this MRO Contractor had been averaging five flyable aircraft less than the contract called for each day.

The financial penalty for not supplying the contracted number of flyable aircraft to this military customer was $600 for each aircraft under the contracted number. Based upon the daily average deficit of five flyable helicopters, the daily financial penalty to this MRO Contractor was $3,000 per day with no signs of relief for this contractor. On an annual basis, the total penalties being assessed on this contractor were in excess of $1 million per year.

In an attempt to satisfy the contracted number of flyable aircraft, the MRO Contractor had elected to use excessive amounts of overtime (i.e. mandatory 12-hour shifts for all key hourly labor positions). And while the contractor had hoped that this action would reduce the deficit of flyable helicopters, in reality it did not work. In fact, the excessive use of overtime only served to decrease worker morale, increase the number of call-ins for sick days, and create a very tired workforce without any significant improvement in the number of flyable aircraft. When our improvement team arrived, this mandatory overtime policy had been in effect for about 2 months and was costing over $3 million on an annual basis. Based upon the penalties assessed for missing the contracted number of aircraft and the amount of money being spent on overtime, this contractor was on pace to lose $4 million just for these two issues.

Our methodology combines the focusing power of the Theory of Constraints, the waste reduction actions of Lean, and the variation reduction of Six Sigma into an improvement methodology we refer to as the Ultimate Improvement Cycle (UIC). This methodology is used to answer five basic questions:

1. Why should we change?
2. What should we change?
3. What should change to?
4. How should we cause the change to happen?
5. How can we sustain the gains?

Figure 8.1 (developed by Bob Sproull and introduced in his book, *The Ultimate Improvement Cycle: Maximizing Profits Through the Integration of Lean, Six Sigma, and the Theory of Constraints*) is the improvement roadmap that we use which incorporates the Theory of Constraints, Lean, and Six Sigma into a powerful and synergistic improvement methodology and serves to answer all of these five vital questions. Figure 8.1 demonstrates our integrated approach with three concentric rings demonstrating the milestones for each of the three improvement methods.

In this case study, we used the Theory of Constraints to identify the system constraint which is the leverage point in any process or system. By identifying and exploiting the leverage point, we were able to maximize throughput by focusing both Lean and Six Sigma efforts directly on it. We used Lean to simplify the processes, eliminate waste, and increase the velocity or speed of products through the process and Six Sigma to

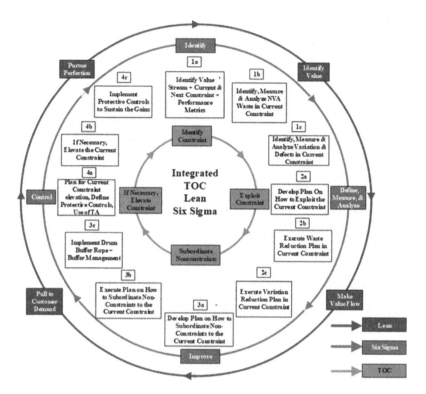

FIGURE 8.1
The integrated TOC, Lean, and Six Sigma methodology.

reduce and control the system variation and defects as well as sustaining the gains we made. It is important to understand that variation can never be completely eliminated, but it can be reduced and controlled. This integrated approach has proven to be the preeminent improvement methodology available today.

In this case study, we used a wide array of tools and actions to achieve improvement as is depicted in Figure 8.2. These tools and actions include things like process maps to better understand the flow of helicopters through the MRO process and to identify the system constraint. Once the value stream and the constraint within it are identified, positive things began to happen almost immediately, and this was the case with the improvement effort at this MRO Contractor's site.

In Figure 8.3, the deliverables are listed that you should end up with if you follow the first two roadmaps.

I begin most improvement initiatives with a full system's assessment and analysis of the organization requiring my services. In this assessment,

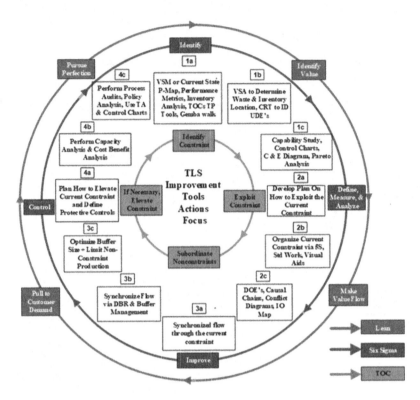

FIGURE 8.2
Improvement tools and actions.

I first seek to understand the system so that I am able to align my improvement strategy with the needs of the organization. This system analysis includes identifying the key value stream(s), the current and next constraint, and the key performance metrics being used by the organization to assess and track their performance. I have found that one of the keys to understanding an organization's current state performance is a focused look at the performance metrics being utilized. It is my belief that performance metrics motivate and drive the predominant behaviors being observed throughout any organization.

Once the system assessment is complete, I typically assemble the true Subject Matter Experts (SMEs), who are the people doing the real work within the organization in order to develop an Intermediate Objectives Map (a.k.a. Goal Tree). The Intermediate Objectives Map (IO Map) or Goal Tree is intended to help assess the status of the current state, as well as identify actions that must be taken to achieve the goal of the organization. In the case of this MRO Contractor, the Leadership Team

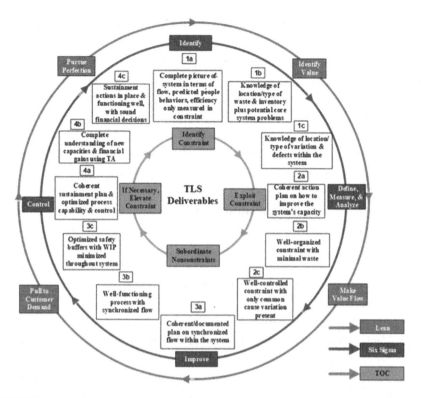

FIGURE 8.3
Deliverables.

elected to not have the SMEs construct the IO Map, but rather to have the SMEs examine and review what the Leadership Team had developed. The MRO Contractor wanted to have their SMEs continue working on their MRO work.

The IO Map is a necessity-based logic hierarchical structure that uses the syntax, "In order to have 'x' we must have 'y.'" The intended Goal sits at the top of this structure, while directly beneath it are three to five entities referred to as Critical Success Factor (CSFs). These CSFs must be in place and functioning if the Goal is to be achieved. Both the Goal and CSFs are written as terminal outcomes as though they are already in place and functioning. Directly beneath each of the CSFs are entities referred to as Necessary Conditions (NCs) that must be in place to achieve each of the individual CSFs. Unlike the Goal and CSFs, which are written as terminal outcomes, the NCs are stated more as activities and form the basis for the organization's improvement plan. This organization's IO Map will be presented later on in this case study.

Our team began the initial assessment by submitting a series of questions to be answered by the client's Leadership Team prior to our arrival. The answers to these questions provided valuable insight into key value drivers and provided our team with a starting point as to what to expect when we arrived at the MRO Contractor's site. Several of the key responses and the potential impact included:

1. Only first shift does a shift tie-in or hand-off meeting. If there is not an effective hand-off from shift-to-shift, there is a high potential for multi-tasking.
2. A Min/Max parts replenishment system was in place indicating high potential for part shortages and higher than required inventory levels of parts and materials.
3. One Lean event was held about 8 years prior to our arrival indicating significant waste existed in the process.
4. There was a problem having to wait for inspectors to inspect and sign-off maintenance work completed.
5. Very experienced workforce, especially with mechanics indicating potentially good knowledge exists to work on the aircraft.
6. No "full-kitting" was in place indicating the potential for multi-tasking and the potential for excessive wait times due to waiting for needed repair parts and supplies.

One of the first activities was to create a project charter with the following objectives and estimated completion dates identified:

1. Reduce number of daily aircraft availability misses (Misses) from five misses/day to <1.0 miss/day.
2. Reduce lost revenue due to "misses" by 90 percent.
3. Reduce overtime rate by 50 percent.
4. Position MRO Contractor for contract re-compete award.

The Leadership Team was given a series of mini-workshops which included the basics of the UIC. This first workshop established the foundation for the improvement effort that was about to begin and why it was so important to (1) identify and exploit the system constraint and (2) subordinate everything else to the system constraint. One of the key learning tools in this mini-workshop was the presentation of a simple piping diagram as seen in Figure 8.4 to demonstrate the existence of a constraint, but also the

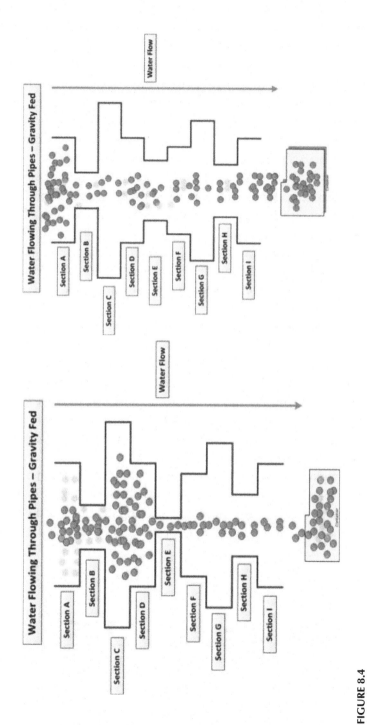

FIGURE 8.4
Before and after exploiting the constraint.

importance of focusing our improvement efforts on the system constraint. This simple diagram demonstrates what can happen to the throughput of the system when the constraint is identified and exploited.

The key learning for the Leadership Team was that because the system constraint controls the throughput of the system, improvements in any other part of the system will not increase the system throughput. This simple exercise demonstrated to the Leadership Team that only by focusing the improvement efforts on the system constraint will meaningful improvements in aircraft availability be achieved.

One of the first activities that our team facilitated was the development of a Process Map. This exercise was completed using the Leadership Team to better understand their inherent knowledge and understanding of their own MRO process. The full process map was reviewed and approved by an hourly core team to validate its accuracy. After much discussion and the development of a high-level Process Map, the conclusion of the SMEs and Leadership was that the system constraint was the time waiting to begin repairs on the aircraft as depicted in Figure 8.5.

The MRO Contractor had an internal policy that required all of the necessary paperwork with corresponding approvals to be in the hands of the mechanics charged with repairing the downed aircraft before beginning any repairs on the aircraft. Estimates on how long this approval process was taking typically ranged between 2 and 4 hours. Because of this delay, it was apparent to everyone that this delay had to be rectified before moving to Section B (i.e. the actual aircraft repair) and then on to Section C (i.e. Aircraft Release to Customer).

Our team employed the Five Focusing Steps of the Theory of Constraints (TOC) popularized by Dr. Goldratt but also added two additional focusing steps a la Boaz Ronen. The two additional focusing steps included stating the system goal and defining global performance measures. In fact, our

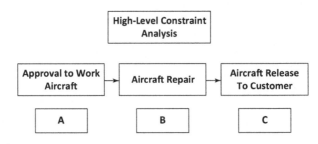

FIGURE 8.5
High-Level Process Map.

team expanded upon Ronen's first step and restated it as, "State the goal, critical success factors and necessary conditions of the system." The seven focusing steps were:

1. State the system Goal, Critical Success Factors, and Necessary Conditions.
2. Define the system boundaries, span of control, and sphere of influence.
3. Identify the system constraint.
4. Decide how to exploit the system constraint.
5. Subordinate non-constraints to the system constraint.
6. If necessary, elevate the system constraint.
7. When the current constraint is broken, return to Step 3 and identify the new system constraint.

In order to satisfy Step 1 of 7, our team facilitated the creation of a Strategic IO Map with the MRO Contractor's Leadership Team to identify the Goal of the organization plus Critical Success Factors and Necessary Conditions required to be in place if the Goal was to be achieved. Because the overwhelming number of flyable aircraft originated from the MRO Contractor's Unscheduled Maintenance area (i.e. greater than 96 percent daily), the MRO Contractor insisted that the IO Map be constructed around the contractor's Unscheduled Maintenance effort rather than the total system for delivering flyable aircraft.

Figure 8.6 is the Unscheduled Maintenance IO Map. Because of the decision to focus on Unscheduled Maintenance, no effort was made to change the contractor's Scheduled Maintenance process.

The keys to getting started with the development of an IO Map are to provide a clear definition of both the system and its boundaries, a consensus on the Goal of the system, a determination of the CSFs that must be in place to achieve the consensus Goal and the NCs which must be completed to achieve each of the CSFs. In other words, the IO Map should be a clear articulation of what should be happening within the system if the consensus Goal is to be achieved. The other important attribute of the IO Map is that it acts as a focusing tool to keep everyone's eye on what's really important. The system and its boundaries were therefore all processes impacting the successful completion of Unscheduled Maintenance aircraft.

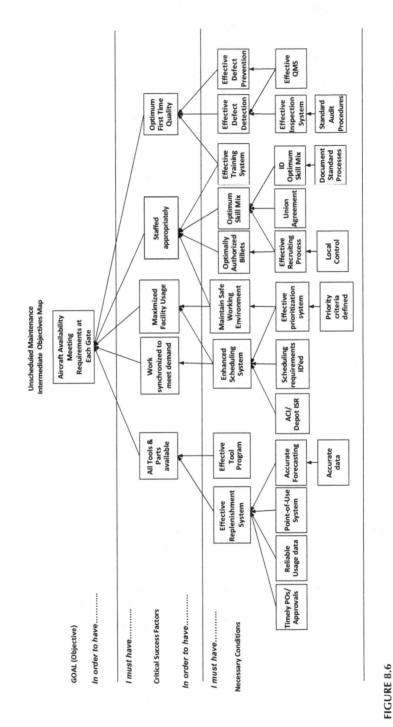

FIGURE 8.6
Unscheduled maintenance IO Map.

When developing an IO Map, it's very important to define those items that are within your span of control and those that are included within your sphere of influence. The span of control items are those aspects of your system in which you have unilateral change authority over, while your sphere of influence items are, as the name implies, those things that you can influence, but not necessarily control. For example, at the MRO Contractor, the Leadership Team might be able to influence the procurement of parts, but they do not have control over how they are procured.

The Goal was selected to be "Aircraft Availability Meeting Requirements at Each Gate." There were four different periods (gates) per day when the maintained helicopters must be available for the Naval flight students with the total "must haves" for the day being 92 flyable aircraft. The team selected five CSFs and numerous NCs as depicted in Figure 8.6.

Upon completion of this IO Map, our improvement team then facilitated a discussion on the state of each CSF and NC. Each CSF and NC was color-coded as either medium gray (no work required), light gray (in place but work required), or dark gray (not in place or not functioning). Those CSFs and NCs shaded in dark gray were considered the highest priority and would form the key focal points within the MRO Contractor Improvement Plan. The entities shaded in light gray were also candidates for improvement. Both the light gray and dark gray shaded entities in the IO Map are considered Undesirable Effects (UDEs in TOC's Thinking Process Tool Set) and form the basis of a Current Reality Tree (CRT). Because of time limitations, our improvement team elected not to create a CRT, but rather a simple improvement plan. Figure 8.7 is the Intermediate Objectives Map after each of the boxed entities were evaluated using the above assessment criteria (i.e. light, medium, or dark gray).

One of the most effective tools to reduce waste within the constraint is a little-known and little-used tool referred to as the Interference Diagram (ID). The principle behind the effective use of the ID is that obstacles exist within the system that are preventing you from achieving more of something you want. To that end, our team then facilitated a simple workshop with the Leadership Team on how to construct and use an ID.

One of the keys to success for the MRO Contractor was convincing the Leadership Team that unless the general workforce was part of the improvement effort, shop floor change would be difficult, if not impossible. To that end, we facilitated the formation of a Core Team comprised solely of hourly SMEs. The team consisted of hourly employees from all disciplines

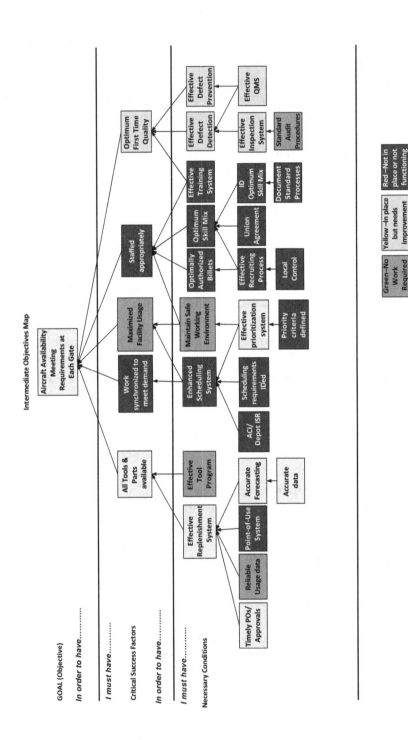

FIGURE 8.7
IO Map improvement assessment.

such as mechanics, logistics personnel, avionics techs, flight line plane captains, inspectors, and maintenance control specialists. We provided strict guidelines as to the make-up of this core team which included the following four demonstrated behaviors and/or qualities required of each of the potential team members:

1. Must be an informal leader from their perspective discipline
2. Must be outspoken
3. Must be an experienced employee in their discipline
4. Must volunteer to be on the team

We explained that the structure of the Core Team meetings should be such that the hourly workers should bring problems and solutions to these problems and other ideas for process improvement to the meeting. The meetings were to be run by the Maintenance Manager with assistance from our improvement team and the Site Leader and that all ideas, etc. should be clearly heard, recorded, but more importantly, implemented. That is, as long as no safety or company policies or contractual obligations were violated, we would implement the solutions from the core team. I refer to this method as Active Listening. We then scheduled a meeting for the following week to kick-off this Hourly Core Team.

As scheduled, the hourly core team held its first meeting during the following week and basic team training was provided on the basics of the Theory of Constraints, using the same piping diagram provided to the Leadership Team, plus the basics of Lean and Six Sigma. The team then reviewed the original Process Map and the three-step, higher level process map that the Leadership Team had constructed earlier. The Core Team agreed with the process map layouts and the conclusion of the Leadership Team on where the system constraint resided—the time spent waiting for approval to begin work on the aircraft.

Our improvement team then delivered a brief workshop on how to create and effectively utilize an ID which was intended to identify the existing barriers or interferences that were delaying the start of work on the aircraft. The ID was seen by the team as an excellent tool to be used during the exploitation step of the seven focusing steps. Figure 8.8 is the Interference Diagram created by the Hourly Core Team as well as their "best guess" on how much time was lost for each identified interference.

Upon completion of the Interference Diagram, the Hourly Core Team discussed each of the interferences and concluded that one of the key

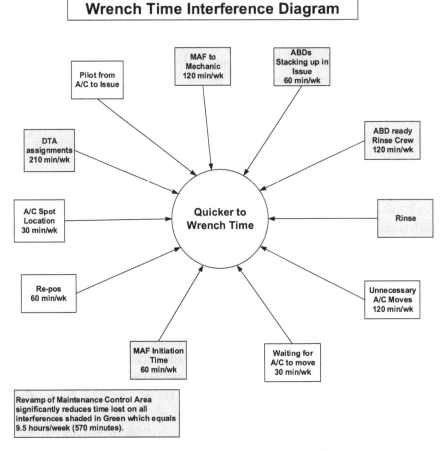

FIGURE 8.8
Interference diagram. ABD: Aero Basic Design.

initiatives needed was a revamp of the Maintenance Control (MC) area. In particular, one of the problems identified within MC was the workload placed on the Aircraft Issuer during issue times was too excessive. The team believed that if the work within MC was spread more evenly across the MC employees, then the wait time associated with the creation of the MAFs could be significantly reduced. In fact, the areas shaded in medium gray in the ID (Figure 8.8) could be alleviated with a revamp of MC. (An MAF is a document which requires signatures before work can begin on the aircraft.)

One significant event that happened as a result of the ID training was that the Plane Captain, who was part of the Core Team, was so captivated by the potential power of the Interference Diagram, that she facilitated the creation of a lower-level ID without any direction from our improvement team or the contractor's Leadership Team. This Plane Captain facilitated the creation of an ID on one of the interferences (Rinse) identified by the Core Team as depicted in Figure 8.8. This was a significant event for us because we knew that in doing this, without any direction, the hourly workforce had embraced our improvement methodology.

Not only did this Plane Captain develop this second ID on her own, she facilitated the development of "fixes" for each of the interferences highlighted in light gray on Figure 8.9. The solutions that were developed, as a result of this Plane Captain's resourcefulness, were simple and very easy to implement, and resulted in immediate improvement to the flow of helicopters through the Unscheduled Maintenance process.

As mentioned, our improvement team viewed this as a breakthrough in the acceptance by the shop floor employees of this improvement initiative and the new methods that they had learned. It is my belief that, unless and until SMEs truly embrace any improvement efforts, improvement

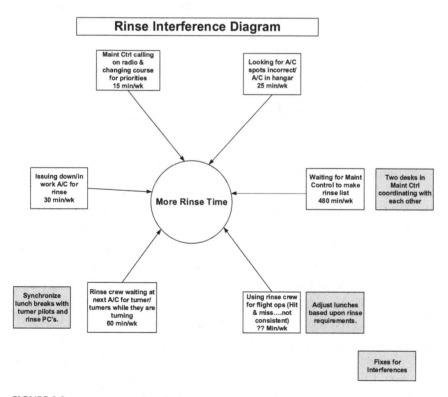

FIGURE 8.9
Plane Captain Interference Diagram with fixes.

will either not be achieved or will come very slowly. I also believe that it is critical to listen to the SMEs, relative to problems and solutions and then implement their solutions as stated. That is, as long as the intended solutions do not violate any safety and company policies, or contractual obligations, they should be implemented. One of the keys to improvement is ownership of solutions by the front-line employees and by implementing their own solutions, ownership is facilitated.

Since that initial Hourly Core Team meeting, there were countless new ideas and suggestions on how to streamline this process and reduce the time waiting to begin aircraft repairs. As we discussed, with these ideas and suggestions it became apparent that many of the interferences being experienced were the direct result of outdated actions taken in conjunction with Corrective Action Requests (CARs). CARs are required when either the internal Quality Group or the Customer (the U.S. Navy) discovers deficiencies on the shop floor such as not following established repair guidelines. When the CAR was written as a result of an internal inspection, sometimes the actions become internal Policy Constraints.

POLICY CONSTRAINTS

Throughout this engagement, we encountered numerous policy-related constraints that were addressed and resolved by the Hourly Core Team with support from the Leadership Team. As previously mentioned, many of these policy constraints were created as a result of responses to internal CARs that had been put in place in the past, but no longer served any useful purpose. Some of these constraints were simply on-going procedures that had been in effect for years. Even though many of these policy constraints seemed trivial on the surface, the negative, cumulative effect on the process throughput was evident once the teams understood these types of constraints. Several of the more notable policy constraints that were uncovered as a result of this improvement initiative included:

1. The practice of requiring an inspector's stamp on daily cards thus resulting in wasted time before an aircraft could be repaired.
2. The practice of an aircraft being shut down after a training mission, rather than having a Trouble Shooter inspect it for potential problems

later in the day, which required the time-consuming restart of the aircraft.

3. Holding of daily cards and delivering them to Maintenance Control in batches. Much time was saved when the Plane Captains went to single-piece-flow of the daily cards, whereby upon completion of a set of cards for an individual aircraft, they were immediately delivered to MC.

ARTIFICIAL CONSTRAINTS

In addition to the numerous policy constraints uncovered during this engagement, there were also constraints referred to as artificial or dummy constraints. A dummy constraint is defined as a situation where the system bottleneck is a relatively cheap resource, compared with other resources in the system. One such example was the purchase of a new torque wrench so that mechanics didn't have to wait until one became available to use. There were numerous examples of such constraints that required little or no investment to be made to eliminate them.

THE RESULTS

The performance metric chosen to be tracked as an indicator of improved performance was the number of daily misses. A miss occurs when the MRO Contractor fails to deliver their full contractual requirement of 92 aircraft per day. You will recall, when a miss occurs, the MRO Contractor is assessed a penalty of $600 for each missed aircraft.

When this engagement began in early March, the data indicated that between March 1 and March 19, 2012, the average number of misses per day was five, which translated into an assessment penalty of $3,000 per day of lost revenue. If we annualize this loss, assuming 240 flying days, the total loss of revenue for aircraft misses would be approximately $720,000. It is important to note that the actual number of misses was higher than five, but because the causes for these misses were not completely documented, it forced our improvement team to discard them. In reality, we believe that the actual number of misses per day was closer to ten, which would mean a saving of almost $1.5 million.

Figure 8.10 is a run chart depicting the average number of misses per day by month for which the MRO Contractor was assessed $600 per missed aircraft. (Note: This graphic does not include the discarded misses due to incomplete documentation.) When the improvement initiative began, conservatively, the average number of misses was five per day. In April, the average number of misses per day had been reduced by 60 percent, down to two per day. This reduction was due to the focused improvement effort being driven in large part by the SMEs. By the time our improvement team left the contractor's site, the average number of misses per day had dropped by over 99 percent to an average of 0.01 misses per day for the month of August.

In addition, the MRO Contractor had been on mandatory overtime for the two previous months (i.e. January and February and part of March) which was seriously impeding their profit margins. Figure 8.11 represents a run chart of the penalty dollars being charged to this MRO Contractor by the U.S. Navy. When our team arrived, the penalty dollar amount was approximately $63,000 for the month of March. In April, the amount of penalty dollars had been reduced to $24,000 and when our team departed, the total penalty amount was less than $600 per month!

In addition to the gain in revenue due to aircraft misses, another substantial change occurred which resulted in a significant improvement to the MRO Contractor's bottom line. Effective May 4, 2012, the use of mandatory overtime was ceased. The financial impact of this change was an immediate reduction in overtime dollars spent (see Table 8.1). In fact, the pay period immediately following the elimination of mandatory overtime,

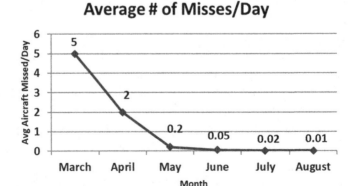

FIGURE 8.10
Average misses per day.

FIGURE 8.11
Penalty by month.

the number of "double time" hours fell from 310 hours to 33 hours while the level of straight overtime fell from 1,773 hours to 1,344 hours. Only considering this time period, the net annualized financial gain was approximately $778,000.

In subsequent conversations with the Site Leader of this facility, we were informed that the reduction in overtime hours continued to decline, and at last report, the number of overtime hours had decreased to under 500 hours per month, which translates into well over $1,000,000 in savings!

There are many reasons why this improved performance had occurred, but I believe that the key reason was due to the MRO Contractor's new focus on the system constraint and a new, highly motivated workforce that has willingly and passionately developed and implemented solutions. In my opinion, the general workforce drove this improvement effort, and because the Leadership Team used Active Listening and acted upon ideas

TABLE 8.1

Overtime Reduction $ Impact

Overtime Reduction $ Impact		
	D	D
April	310.5	1773.1
May	33.5	1344.4
Diff.	277	428.7
$ Impact	13850	16076.25
Total $/2 Wks.		29926.3
Annualized $ Reduction		$778,084

and solutions initiated by the Core Team, rapid improvement was achieved and has been continued since our departure.

Prior to our improvement team's departure, several other key activities were completed, including:

- Development and implementation of an effective shift tie-in procedure to ensure multi-tasking and re-working aircraft already repaired were significantly minimized.
- Development of a TOC-based parts replenishment system based upon usage to prevent the stock-out of MRO parts and supplies while significantly reducing the overall dollar value of the inventory (i.e. approximately 30-percent reduction).
- Bench stock (i.e. commonly used items like standard nuts, bolts, washers, etc.) was moved from the warehouse to the shop floor to reduce the walk and wait times for mechanics who previously had to go to supply to retrieve bench stock.
- Addition of a designated person to "run errands" for the mechanics to retrieve needed items like parts and/or equipment.
- Implementation of "full kits" whereby no aircraft would be brought into the hangar until all parts, supplies, paperwork, etc. were available as a package and delivered to the hangar bay to prevent wait times for said items.
- Implementation of point-of-use tool storage racks in close proximity to the aircraft to reduce time spent searching for required tools.
- Establishment of an inspector notification system to reduce the wait times associated with inspection and sign-off or work completed.

These improvements, along with all of the others mentioned in the body of this case study helped to reduce the protracted cycle times in the unscheduled maintenance area. The other significant event that occurred since our team departed was in the area of contract renewal. Because of this contractor's excellent performance results in supplying aircraft, this contractor was awarded a new, 5-year re-compete contract thus securing their future.

Once again, the combination of the Theory of Constraints, Lean, and Six Sigma has delivered exceptional results!

9

Healthcare Case Study

![INTRODUCTION bar]

INTRODUCTION

In this chapter, we're going discuss a case study from the healthcare field. We will discuss a Process Value Stream Analysis (PVSA) project at a hospital located in the midwestern United States. The focus of this PVSA was on this facility's Emergency and Cardiology Departments, where they wanted to improve one of their key performance metrics, Door to Balloon (D2B) time. For those of you (like me before I started this engagement) who don't have a clue as to what D2B time is, let me fill you in. Door to Balloon is a time measurement in Emergency Cardiac Care (ECC), specifically in the treatment of ST Segment Elevation Myocardial Infarction (or simply, a STEMI heart attack).

The interval starts with the patient's arrival in the Emergency Department and ends when a catheter guide-wire crosses the culprit lesion in the Cardiac Cath lab. In everyday language, this just means that a balloon is inflated inside one of the heart's primary blood vessels to allow unimpeded blood flow through the heart. The clock starts ticking either as a walk-in to the Emergency Department or in the field where a patient is being attended to by medical personnel. This metric is enormously important to patients simply because the longer this procedure is delayed, the more damage occurs to the heart muscle due to a lack of oxygen to the heart muscle. It's damaged because the cause of this problem is typically due to a blockage within the heart that prevents oxygen from being supplied to the heart, and without proper amounts of oxygen, muscle damage results. The inflated balloon "unclogs" the blood vessel. Graphically, to D2B might look like Figure 9.1.

I started this event with a training session for the team members focusing on how to use an integrated Theory of Constraints, Lean Six

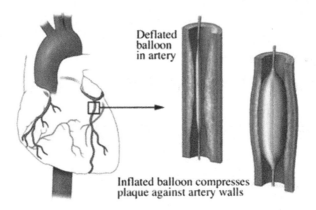

Deflated balloon in artery

Inflated balloon compresses plaque against artery walls

FIGURE 9.1
Door to Balloon (D2B) time graphic.

Sigma improvement methodology. I have seen a lot of PVSAs where waste is identified throughout the process, and then the team works to either reduce it or eliminate *all of it*. It has been my experience that, when attempting to reduce the time it takes to process something through a process such as this one by attacking the entire process for waste reduction, teams frequently miss the opportunity to reduce the cycle time much more quickly than they otherwise could have. This is where the Theory of Constraints (TOC) and its Five Focusing Steps offers a much quicker solution to this type of project. Just to review, TOC's Five Focusing Steps, first introduced by the late Dr. Eli Goldratt, are:

1. *Identify the system constraint*: In a physical process with numerous processing steps, the constraint is the step with the smallest amount of capacity. Or another way of stating this is the step with the longest processing time.
2. *Decide how to exploit the system constraint*: Once the constraint has been identified, this step instructs you to focus your efforts on it and use improvement tools of Lean and Six Sigma to reduce waste and variation but focus your efforts mostly on the constraint. This does not mean that you can ignore non-constraints, but your primary focus should be on the constraint.
3. *Subordinate everything else to the constraint*: In layman's terms, this simply means don't overproduce on non-constraints, and never let the constraint be starved. In a process like the Door to Balloon time, it would make no sense to push patients into this process, since

they would be forced to wait excessively. But of course, the hospital cannot predict when patients with heart attacks will show up needing medical attention. But by constantly trying to reduce the constraint's time, the wait time should be continuously reduced.

4. *If necessary, elevate the constraint*: This simply means that if you have done everything you can to increase the capacity of the constraint in Step 2, and it's still not enough to satisfy the demand placed on it, then you might have to spend money by hiring additional people, purchasing additional equipment, etc. That is, anything that would reduce the time in the constraint.

5. *Return to Step 1, but don't let inertia create a new constraint*: Once the constraint's required capacity has been achieved, the system constraint could move to a new location within the process. When this happens, it is necessary to move your improvement efforts to the new constraint if further improvement is needed. What is the thing about inertia? What Goldratt meant by that was to make sure things you have put in place to break the original constraint (procedures, policies, etc.) are not limiting the throughput of the process. If necessary, you may need to remove them.

There was also a review of the basics of both Lean and Six Sigma and how to combine these three methodologies into a single methodology. Figure 9.2 is a basic look at how these methods can be used together to generate improvements to any process or system being studied. Remember, the Theory of Constraints identifies the focal point for improvement, while Lean works to reduce waste and Six Sigma reduces and controls the variation within the process.

For whatever reason, the agency that developed this universal metric used the *median* rather than the *mean*. The current median standard for D2B time had been set at 90 minutes, and this hospital was actually doing quite well against this standard with a median score of 66 minutes. However, because this hospital was anticipating the standard would be changing to 60 minutes in the future, they decided to be proactive by putting together a team of subject matter experts to look for ways to achieve this future target, before it was mandated to do so. In addition to this new time benefitting the patient (i.e. much less heart muscle damage), there was also a financial incentive for the hospital, in that reimbursement rates for Medicare and Medicaid patients are tied to completing the D2B time below the standard median time (Figure 9.3).

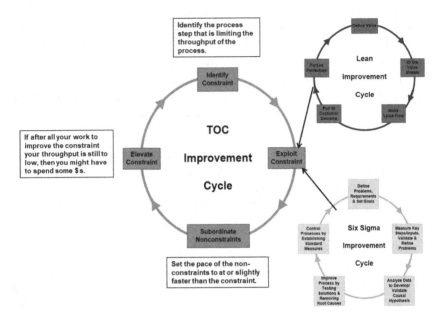

FIGURE 9.2
Integrated TOC, Lean, and Six Sigma.

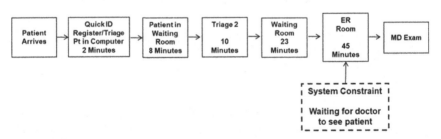

FIGURE 9.3
Door to Doctor estimated time.

After completing the training session, the team was instructed to "Walk the Gemba" by going to both the Emergency Department and Cardiology Department to observe what happens during this process and to have conversations with employees from both departments about problems they might encounter. This was a fact-finding mission aimed at understanding how patients are managed through this treatment process. The team collected many observations during this walk, most of which would be used to construct their Current State Process Map, which will be displayed shortly. Figure 9.4 is a high-level summary of part of their Gemba walk for Door to Doctor.

The team then developed the following problem statement: *Hospital's current state cycle time is 66 minutes (median) for Door to Balloon Time when patients arrive at the Emergency Department and are classified as a STEMI candidate. The Hospital's goal is less than 60 minutes (median) 100% of the time.* In addition, the team set two primary performance goals as follow:

1. Hospital's median Door to Balloon time below 60 minutes or below.
2. Decreased Door to Balloon time will improve patient outcomes as measured by quality metrics. Additionally, these quality metrics are tied to the hospital's reimbursement based on the result of those outcomes.

Next, the team developed a business case for the efforts: *In addition to the quality and reimbursement benefits, this project will help in the marketing of the hospital's Cardiology services. Improved performance in quality metrics will lead to awards and preferred provider status. Examples include: Chest Pain Accreditation, Top 100 Heart Hospital, Blue Cross Distinction for Cardiac Care.*

As a final step before their improvement work began, the team developed their performance metrics to be used to judge the final impact of their improvement efforts. These metrics are shown in Table 9.1.

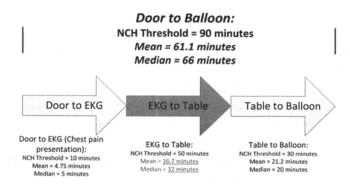

FIGURE 9.4
Door to Balloon (D2B) summary.

TABLE 9.1

Performance Metrics

Metric/Unit:	Baseline:	Goal: Future	Future Estimated
Complete cycle time in Median Minutes	Median = 66 Min	Median = ≤60 Min	Median = 53 Min

The team had access to D2B time data that had been collected on previous patients passing through this process. The team analyzed the data to better understand what was happening on previous D2B events and to determine the location of the constraint within this process. Figure 9.4 is a summary of this analysis before any improvements were initiated for three phases, which were Door to EKG, EKG to Table, and Table to Balloon.

The time data that had been collected was broken down into three separate phases of the D2B process: Door to EKG, EKG to Table, and Table to Balloon. This was extremely helpful for the team in their efforts to identify the system constraint. As you can see in Figure 9.4, the EKG to Table phase, with a mean value of 36.7 minutes, is clearly the part of the process requiring the most time and was designated by the team to be the *system constraint*. Table to Balloon time, at 21.2 minutes on average, also consumed a significant amount of time, while Door to EKG only required 4.75 minutes to complete. It is important to remember that this metric (D2B Time) was developed to capture median times rather than mean times, so hospitals are judged (and reimbursed) by a median time and are reported as such. The difference between the median and mean times for EKG to Table (i.e. median = 32 minutes and mean = 36.7 minutes) indicates that the data might be somewhat skewed and not perfectly normally distributed. This, of course, means that there are outliers that must be investigated for cause.

After collecting and analyzing this data, the team was instructed to create two Interference Diagrams (IDs), one for Phase 2 (EKG to Table) and one for Phase 3 (Table to Balloon). You may recall from an earlier chapter that the purpose of the ID is to identify any barriers or obstacles (i.e. interferences) that stand in the way of achieving a goal or objective. In the cases for Phases 2 and 3, the goal was identified as reducing the time required to complete each phase. Figure 9.5 is the Interference Diagram created by this team for EKG to Table.

The photo of the Interference Diagram was created for the EKG to Table phase and is presented here only to depict what an Interference Diagram looks like for those of you who may never have used one before (Figure 9.6).

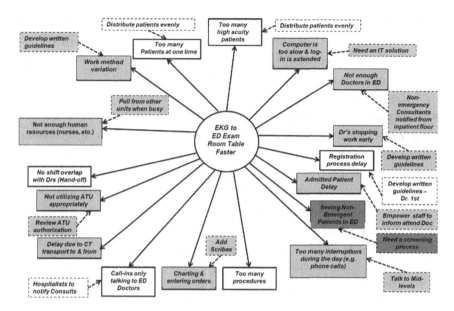

FIGURE 9.5
EKG to Table Interference Diagram (ID).

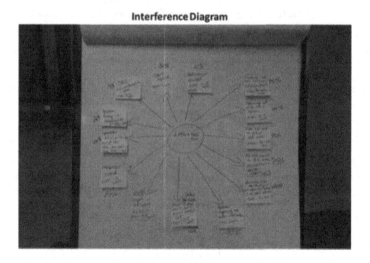

FIGURE 9.6
Interference Diagram EKG to Table.

The post-it notes contain a description of the interference with an estimate of how much time the interference might negatively impact the goal of reducing cycle time. The Interference Diagram can then be used to develop an improvement plan on how to reduce the EKG to Table phase time.

The team then used their fact-finding "walks" (i.e. observations and conversations) and the Interference Diagrams to create a SIPOC as demonstrated in Figure 9.7. The team next developed a current state process map (Figure 9.8) and then completed a value assessment (Figure 9.9) of each step with medium gray being seen as an acceptable process step with no improvement required. Light gray indicates that the step in its current state needs improvement. Dark gray indicates that the step is not adding value and needs to be either removed or improved dramatically!

Figure 9.9 is the Current State Map after completion of the standard value analysis, and as can be seen, the number of total dark gray steps that exist was quite high. The team next developed a future state map that reduced the number of decision points, swim lanes, and hand-offs. This effort resulted in a dramatic reduction in the number of non-value-added (i.e. dark gray) steps (i.e. 27 to 3).

This team did an excellent job of analyzing this important process and was able to remove much of the waste contained within it. But the real improvement came in the overall potential time to complete this procedure, which should have a significantly positive impact on the damage to a patient's heart muscles when their recommendations are implemented, and this was the overriding premise and objective of this event. Figure 9.10 is the final future state map for the door to balloon time,

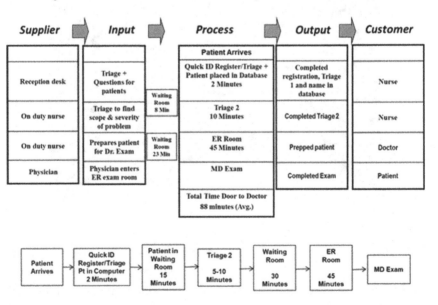

FIGURE 9.7
Supplier Input Process Output Customer (SIPOC) diagram.

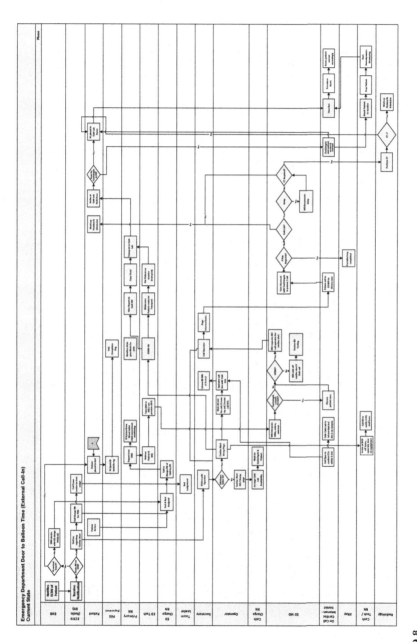

FIGURE 9.8
Current State Map.

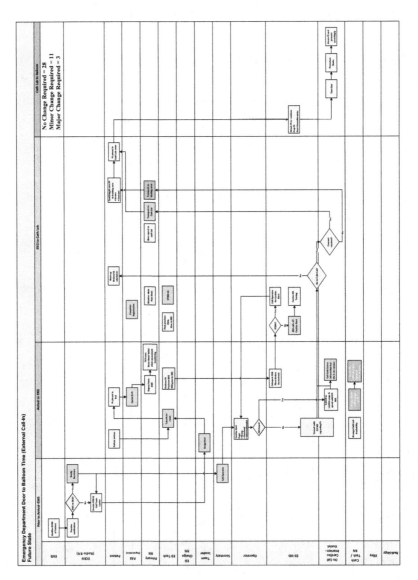

FIGURE 9.9

Current State Map after assessment.

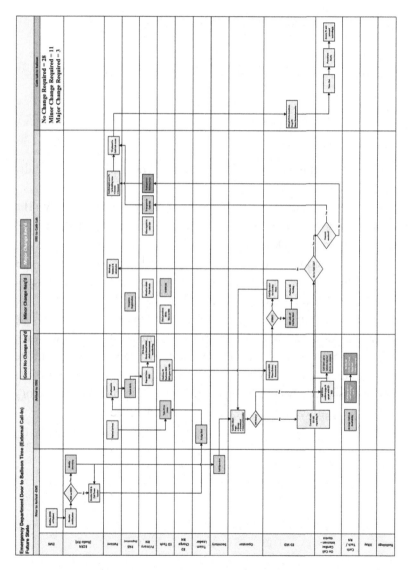

FIGURE 9.10
Final Future State Map.

Metric	Pre-Event	Post-Event	Improvement
Total Number of Steps	69	42	-27
% of Value-Added Steps	38 %	69 %	31 %
# of Swim Lanes	16	15	-1
Cycle Time	66 Min	~53 Min	~-13 Min
# of Decisions	13	6	-7
# of Green Steps	26 (3)	29 (3)	+3 (0)
# of Yellow Steps	16 (3)	10 (4)	-6 (+1)
# of Red Steps	27 (6)	3 (0)	-24 (-6)

FIGURE 9.11
Improvement results summary.

and as you can see, the number of steps in the process was dramatically reduced!

The following is a summary of before and after for this PVSA. The highlighted numbers in Figure 9.11 represent a summary of the actual cycle time reduction for Door to Balloon time, as well as reductions in the number of decision points and total steps in this process, which was a total of 27 steps. Another key element of this effort was a 31 percent improvement in the number of value-added steps.

Although a reduction in D2B time of 13 minutes might not seem like much of an improvement to some of you, you must consider how much less damage to a patient's heart muscle might be avoided. In the healthcare field for procedures such as Door to Balloon time, every minute counts. As you have just observed, by combining Lean and Six Sigma with the Theory of Constraints, significant improvements can be realized.

10

Case Study on a Medical Device Manufacturer

INTRODUCTION/BACKGROUND

Because of the sensitive nature of this case study report, the name of the company in this case study will be withheld and as such will be referred to simply as "manufacturing company." This manufacturing company was founded in 1988 and had been reported to be applying fairly sophisticated, high-volume manufacturing expertise to the Medical Device Market. This company also reports that it is heavily engaged in top-of-the-line technology, quality systems, and engineering expertise to respond quickly to the changing needs of their global customers.

This manufacturing company utilizes equipment such as Computer Numerical Control (CNC) precision turning, milling, cutter grinding, mill/turning, gun drilling, precision grinding, and a host of other machining operations intended to supply precision parts to the medical and surgical communities. Although this company proclaims itself to be one that insists on streamlined "dock to dock" delivery, what I found upon arrival was a manufacturing facility, it had excessive amounts of Work-In-Process (WIP) and finished goods inventory. And because significant amounts of inventory existed, customer due dates were not being met to the satisfaction of the company's CEO or their customer base.

Because I had done consulting work for this CEO in the past, I was called upon to assist the manufacturing facility with a variety of improvement needs. The corporate office acknowledged to me that the labor content (salaried and hourly) used to produce parts at this manufacturing facility was much higher than it should be (i.e. by as much as 50 percent). I agreed to analyze the current manufacturing process and staffing levels, recommend necessary process improvement actions, and develop a future manpower staffing model based upon the improvement actions to be used to produce and ship finished product at this facility.

Prior to my arrival, a significant headcount reduction had been mandated by the CEO which meant that improvements had to occur at lightning speed. After some intense discussions, it was agreed that if the lay-off were to occur, it had to be completed prior to my arrival so as to not relate improvement actions to headcount reductions. It was also agreed that I would focus improvement efforts on the product having the highest demand. The manufacturing facility would then translate the improvements to other parts that they produced. (Note: Throughout this report, I am not using the actual part name, but will refer to it as the "selected part.") In light of this need, I agreed to the following actions and deliverables:

1. Analysis of the current state process flow using the existing process layout and manpower used to produce the selected part.
   - Deliverable: Current State Process Map (or Value Stream Map) with current WIP levels and labor used to create WIP and finished goods.
2. Analysis of the current process flow to identify the current system constraint(s) and opportunities for improved synchronization within the process used to produce the selected part.
   - Deliverable: Identification of the current system constraint(s) and recommendations for a Theory of Constraints (TOC) based pull system (e.g., Drum-Buffer-Rope [DBR] and Buffer Management [BM]).
3. Analysis of a potential future state process using a cellular layout, optimized transfer batch sizes, TOC, and DBR/BM for the selected part.
   - Deliverable: Future State Process Map, WIP, and finished goods projections using the recommended future state process and DBR/BM.
4. Analysis of current changeover methods to better understand why changeovers are taking so long (i.e. days rather than hours).
   - Deliverable: Generally recommended equipment changeover actions to significantly reduce the changeover times on key machines used to produce the selected part.
5. Based upon the proposed future state cellular layout, use of TOC principles, rapid changeovers, DBR, and BM, calculate anticipated future manpower requirements used to produce the selected parts.

- Deliverable: Manpower requirements using recommended future state process.
6. A review of the current Min/Max parts acquisition process to determine potential applicability of TOC's Replenishment model for parts acquisition system for this manufacturing facility.
   - Deliverable: Recommendation of the most cost-effective parts acquisition process for this manufacturing facility.

As discussed in previous chapters, I utilized an integrated Theory of Constraints, Lean, and Six Sigma improvement methodology which I refer to as the Ultimate Improvement Cycle (UIC) or TLS. This methodology is used to answer five critical questions:

- Why should we change?
- What should we change?
- To what should we change to?
- How do we cause the change to happen?
- How do we sustain the gains?

Figure 10.1, which I first presented in my book, *The Ultimate Improvement Cycle: Maximizing Profits Through the Integration of Lean, Six Sigma, and the Theory of Constraints* [1], is my improvement roadmap which combines the Theory of Constraints, Lean, and Six Sigma into a powerful improvement methodology and serves to answer all of these five vital questions.

As I've stated in previous chapters, I use the Theory of Constraints to identify the system constraint which is the leverage point in any process or system. By identifying and exploiting the leverage point, companies are able to maximize throughput by focusing both Lean and Six Sigma tools and efforts directly on it. We use Lean to simplify the processes, eliminate waste, and improve flow of products through the process and Six Sigma to reduce and control the system variation and defects, as well as sustaining the gains we have made. It is important to understand that variation can never be completely eliminated, but it can be reduced and then controlled. This integrated approach has proven to be the preeminent improvement methodology available today. I use a wide array of tools and actions to achieve improvement as is depicted in Figure 10.2.

These tools and actions include things like process maps to better understand the flow through the process and to assist with identifying the

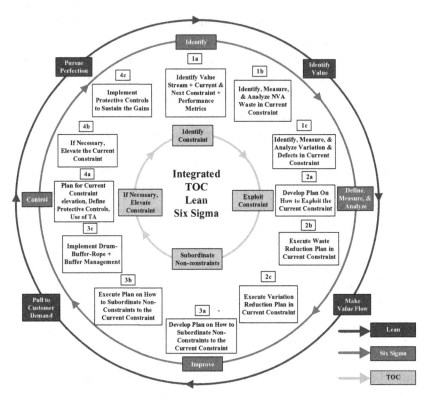

FIGURE 10.1
Integrated Theory of Constraints (TOC), Lean, and Six Sigma.

system constraint. Once the value stream and the constraint within it are identified, positive things begin to happen almost immediately, and this was the case with the improvement effort at this manufacturing company.

Figure 10.3 demonstrates the expected deliverables from each of the individual UIC steps. For example, Step 1a tells us we should achieve a complete picture of the system in terms of flow, predicted people behaviors, and efficiency as measured in the constraint only.

The centerpiece for the UIC improvement methodology is the Theory of Constraints. Specifically, we use TOC's Five Focusing steps to identify and exploit the system constraint. For those of you not familiar with these steps they are:

- Identify the system constraint (i.e. the bottleneck).
- Decide how to exploit the constraint (make the most of it).
- Subordinate non-constraints to the system constraint (never outrun the constraint).

- If in the first three steps, the system constraint is not broken, elevate it to achieve the needed capacity (you may have to spend money to do so).
- Return to Step 1 to identify the new system constraint, but don't let inertia create a new system's constraint (don't become complacent).

I typically begin any improvement initiative with a full system's assessment and analysis of the organization requiring my services. In this assessment, I first seek to understand the system, so that I am able to align my improvement strategy with the needs of the organization. This system analysis includes identifying the key value stream(s), the current and next constraint, and the key performance metrics being used by the organization to assess and track their performance. I have found that one of the keys to understanding an organization's current state performance is a focused look at the performance metrics being utilized. It is my belief

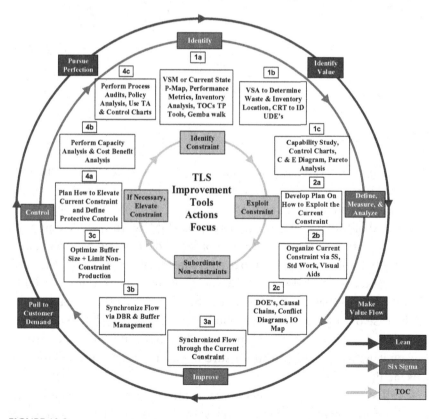

FIGURE 10.2
Tools, actions, and focus.

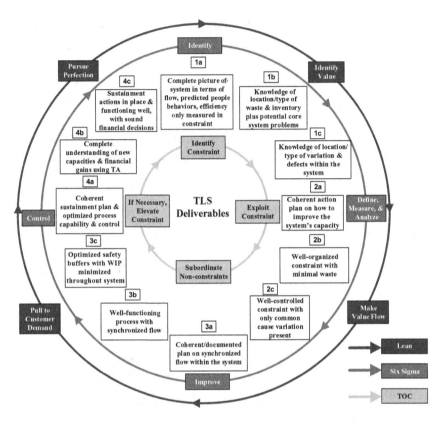

FIGURE 10.3
Deliverables.

that performance metrics motivate and drive the common behaviors observed throughout any organization.

Once the system assessment is complete, I typically assemble a team comprised of the true subject matter experts (SMEs), the people doing the real work within the organization in order to develop a Goal Tree (a.k.a. Intermediate Objectives). The Goal Tree/Intermediate Objectives Map (IO Map) is intended to help assess the status of the current state, as well as identify actions that must be taken to achieve the goal of the organization. In the case of this manufacturing facility, the Leadership Team elected to construct the Goal Tree/IO Map themselves but stated that they would review it with the SMEs to make sure it was a correct representation of this facility.

A full systems analysis is necessary before making recommendations about how this manufacturing facility should be staffed. It is imperative to look at the systems that are in place and how well they are functioning both in isolation and in combination with each other. These systems include things like the current production scheduling system, inventory control methods, the maintenance and quality systems, tooling and materials procurement system, and others. All of these systems and others play a key role in the profitability of any manufacturing operation.

One of the best tools available for performing such an analysis is the IO Map. Bill Dettmer created the IO Map (aka Goal Tree) which is a necessity-based logic structure that uses the syntax, in order to have ... (entity x) ... I must have (entity y) [2]. The hierarchical structure places the organizational Goal at the top of the IO Map with three to five Critical Success Factors (CSFs) directly beneath the Goal. Both the Goal and CSFs are written as terminal outcomes as though they were already in place. Directly beneath each of the CSF are entities referred to as Necessary Conditions (NCs) which must be in place in order to achieve each of the CSFs. Figure 10.4 is the IO Map/Goal Tree for this manufacturing facility.

The owner of the organization is charged with identifying the organizational goal which in the case of this manufacturing facility was defined as Profitability Maximized. There were three CSFs declared as Throughput Maximized, Inventory Minimized, and Operating Expenses Controlled. Beneath each of the CSFs are the Necessary Conditions required to satisfy each of the CSFs.

With the IO Map defined, it was then used to evaluate how the organization was functioning relative to the stated Goal, CSFs, and NCs by coding each entity against the following criteria:

- Medium gray: The entity is in place and is functioning well in this manufacturing facility. It indicates no need for improvement.
- Light gray: The entity is in place, but not functioning well enough in this manufacturing facility. It indicates the need for some level of improvement.
- Dark gray: The entity is either not in place or is in place, but not functioning well in this manufacturing facility. It indicates the need for "significant" improvement.

Figure 10.5 is the coded version of Figure 10.4, and as can be seen by the number of dark and light gray entities, a significant number of improvements are in order if this improvement initiative is to be successful. In fact, aside from having high-quality products and superior customer service, this manufacturer's system is not functioning well at all.

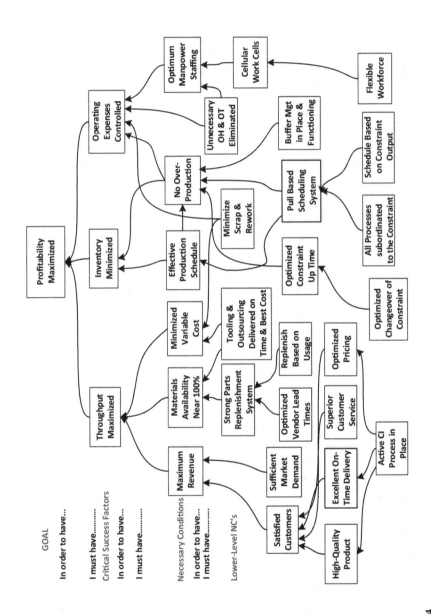

FIGURE 10.4

IO Map.

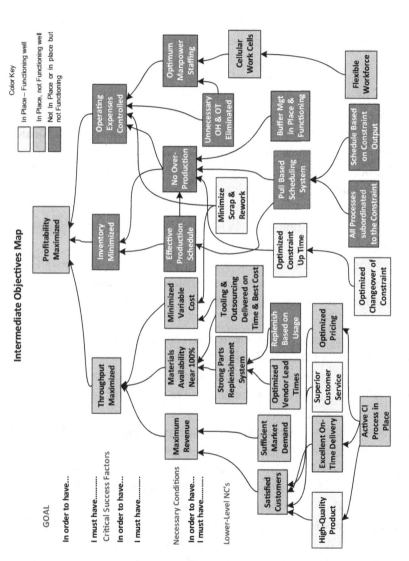

FIGURE 10.5
IO Map after assessment.

ANALYSIS OF CURRENT STATE PROCESS FLOW

Figure 10.6 is a simple Process Flow Map of the current state process for the selected part with the current WIP levels observed and capacities listed in each of the process boxes. It is important to lay out the full fabrication process in order to understand several important factors:

- Determination of the number of steps required to produce the part in question so that estimated manpower requirements can be determined.
- The identification and location of the system constraint, which controls the throughput of parts through the entire process.
- Opportunities to develop recommendations for a cellular arrangement of the manufacturing process to achieve enhanced flow and throughput.
- Location and amount of WIP contained within the fabrication process.
- Method of scheduling the selected part and to better understand the current synchronization of parts through this process.
- Historical equipment downtime.

The fabrication process for the selected part contained a total of 22 discrete process steps as outlined in Figure 10.6. As can be seen, the amount of WIP in some of the process steps was disproportionate and unbalanced, especially when one considers the demand requirements for this part was 17,000 parts per year, or roughly 350 parts per week.

The total number of parts contained within the process stands at 9,569 parts, which includes 884 parts in finished goods. WIP in Operations 125 and 130, E-Hone ID and E-Hone Irr. accounted for a combined total of 2,640 parts while the WIP accumulated in Operation 80, Deburr–Bead Blast had a total of 1,488 parts. Based upon the annual demand for this part, the number of parts in process was equivalent to 56.3 percent of the annual demand or 6.75 months-worth of demand. This level of WIP was clearly too high and was probably one of the primary reasons the CEO believed that this facility was over-staffed. At the time of my visit to this manufacturer, the total dollar value of WIP contained within the selected part process stood at nearly $1,000,000, not including the 884 parts in finished goods.

Shell Assembly Process Flow Map

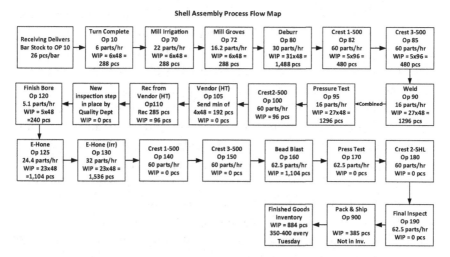

FIGURE 10.6
Shell assembly Flow Map.

Excessive WIP levels in any process only serve to drive apparent cycle times higher and higher with a high probability of negatively impacting on-time deliveries, tying up excessive amounts of cash unnecessarily, and creating the apparent need for more labor than is truly required. In the case of the selected part, the labor requirements appeared to be much higher than was actually needed to produce this part.

If the selected part was representative of the other processes within this manufacturing plant, and there is no reason to believe that it wasn't, then the only conclusion to be made must be that the manpower levels are significantly higher than they should be. Because of the extremely high levels of WIP observed with this part and finished product levels on other parts, the conclusion drawn is that direct labor manpower levels, prior to the large lay-off by the CEO, were probably on the order of 25- to 30-percent higher than actually required to produce and ship parts.

In addition to the cash being tied up by the excessive amount of WIP for this selected part's process, the impact on throughput and timely flow of parts was devastating. In reality, based upon a sampling of product travelers, from beginning to end for the selected part (i.e. Operation 10 through Operation 190), the average length of time for the parts to progress through the total process was roughly 165 days. When one considers the cycle times for each process step, it becomes apparent that the lack of synchronization was having a devastating effect on the overall processing time for this part.

The excessive amount of WIP within the selected part's process was the result of several different factors, with the primary factor being the scheduling system that was in place, which appeared to lack any kind of synchronization. Any schedule or production plan must be productive, consistent, robust, and realistic. Productive in the sense that it must relate to the market demand while contributing to and being measurable against the organization's goal. It must be consistent and robust in that it must reflect the capacity of the resources available and be able to overcome the inevitable disturbances or disruptions (Murphy's Law) that will happen from time to time. It must also be realistic, in that it must not permit over-production and prevent build-up of excessive amounts of WIP.

Based upon the excessive WIP build-up within this process, the current scheduling technique being used in this production facility does not appear to be productive, consistent, robust, or realistic. In fact, the scheduling system being used within this facility appears to be driven by the Site Leader's production meetings held twice a week and not on a documented production schedule. Weekly and monthly needs were received from the customer receiving this part and parts are produced based upon these requests. What I observed was that this facility produced what the leader wanted to produce that day and not necessarily what was needed.

Another factor believed to have led to the build-up of excessive WIP in this process was a corporate mandate to have 1 month's worth of Finished Goods inventory available for shipment. This mandate itself did not cause the WIP explosion, but rather the reaction to the mandate. That is, there appears to be a belief that in order to increase the amount of finished goods, more product must be "pushed" into and through the system which eventually will be completed as finished goods. As a result of this reaction, enormous amounts of WIP were created which effectively "clogged" the system and prevented a synchronized flow.

Another factor leading to the excessive WIP within this process is more of an opinion or observation rather than being based upon fact. It appears as though there is an inherent desire to simply keep employees working, rather than working to meet customer's actual demand requirements. Based upon the capacities of each individual operation, I found it difficult to understand why so many employees were working four 10-hour days (i.e. M–Th) plus one 8-hour day, Friday (F was paid overtime) when capacities would tell us this amount of work was unnecessary. Unwritten policies can often lead to excess manpower within the system with the result being excessive WIP. As further indirect evidence, a review of other parts in this plant demonstrated that the plant lacked a synchronized schedule and was over-producing on virtually every part as well as over-ordering purchased parts.

One of the first actions taken was to stop production of all parts having an excessive amount of WIP within the system. This action was necessary to "un-clog" the processes so that it was possible to improve the flow of parts through each of the various processes. This step was met with much opposition from the Site Leader because of his paradigm of pushing parts into the process and his desire to keep everyone busy producing parts that weren't needed. Because this plant was required to maintain high levels of manpower efficiency and equipment utilization, two common Cost Accounting performance metrics, these two metrics were probably the major reason why WIP levels were so high in this facility.

SCHEDULING USING THE SYSTEM CONSTRAINT

In any plant, there is usually only one (or maybe two) Capacity Constrained Resources (CCRs) that control the rate of throughput within the system. Once the CCR is identified, the various orders that are to be processed through it should be scheduled according to the capacity potential of the CCR and to the market demand. The scheduling system I recommend in most manufacturing environments is referred to as Drum-Buffer-Rope (DBR) with the CCR setting the drum beat or pace for the total process. The essential operational steps of DBR scheduling are as follows:

- Establish the due date requirements for the orders in question
- Identify the CCR in the system, which in the selected part was clearly Operation 10 (see Figure 10.6 above) at six parts per hour.
- Develop a drum-based schedule for the CCR which makes best use of it and is in-line with the market demand. The drum is effectively the master production schedule which establishes the "drum beat" and control for the entire system.
- Protect the throughput of the factory from statistical fluctuations through the use of buffers (both physical and time) at critical locations. Buffers are strategically located to protect the throughput of the entire system and to protect the due dates promised to customers.

- Use a logistical rope tied to the CCR drum schedules for each resource. The rope is a signal sent to the originating process step to begin production.

Figure 10.7 was the current layout of this process when this improvement initiative began. A study of the processing times indicated the presence of dual constraints as indicated in mid-gray on the drawing. If we were to look only at this part in isolation, then we would incorrectly conclude that either Operation 10 or Operation 120 or both would be the system constraints.

I wasn't satisfied that by selecting either of these two operations as the drum (i.e. the constraint), that we would solve this plant's scheduling problems. I reviewed many of the other parts and their process flows and discovered that the true system constraint was the combined operations 125 and 130, E-Hone, as seen in Figure 10.8. In doing so, I discovered that numerous other parts must pass through these two operations, so I declared these operations as the system's constraints. I say these two operations in tandem because both machines are used to remove chips and/or metal shavings from inside the parts and are run by a single operator. We'll return to the scheduling process shortly in this case study report, but for now, I want to turn our attention to TOC's Step 2 of the 5 focusing steps, exploitation of the constraint.

Now that the true CCR has been identified to be the E-Hone Process (i.e. Operations 125 and 130), improvements to the capacity of these two process steps was the next step. In Operation 125, eight parts are placed in a holding fixture and a jellylike substance known as media is passed through each part using high pressure to remove any kind of metal fragments. Prior to implementing any improvements, the starting cycle time for this operation was approximately 30 minutes for the eight parts encased in the part-holding fixture. After the cycle was complete, the operator removed the samples from the fixture and placed them in a sample basket. The operator would then clean the fixture and reload it with eight new samples and run for another 30 minutes. The time between batches to unload parts from the fixture and to clean and reload the fixture was taking roughly seven minutes to complete. Figure 10.8 is a graphic image of how the E-Hone operator was running Operations 125 and 130 before any changes were made.

I asked the E-Hone operator to run a study for me whereby, as soon as he completed the first run of eight parts, he would pass them on to

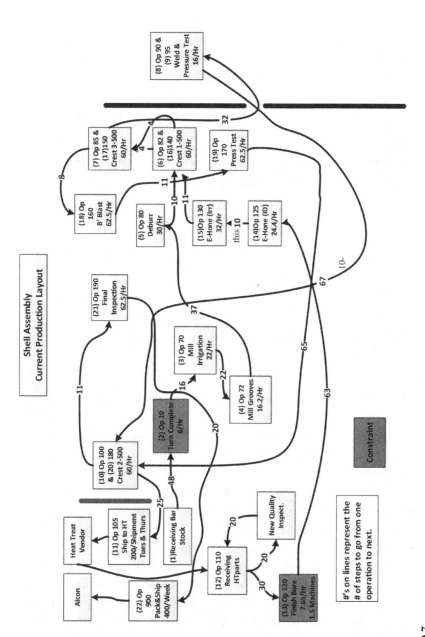

FIGURE 10.7
Current production layout.

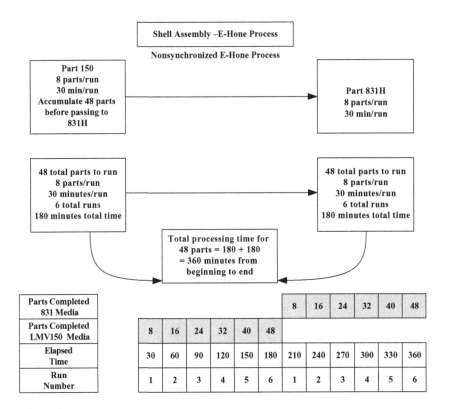

FIGURE 10.8
E-Hone process.

Operation 130. In effect, I was asking him to change his transfer batch size from 48 parts to eight parts. Figure 10.9 demonstrates the results of this brief study. By making this small change to synchronize the flow of parts, the time required to complete all eight fixture runs (i.e. 48 parts) through both Operations 125 and 130 decreased from 360 minutes to 210 minutes without costing this facility any money at all. This simple change to improve synchronization had significantly increased the capacity of this CCR, so we were now moving closer to being able to implement our new scheduling system … Drum-Buffer-Rope.

I asked the machine operator why he waited until the sample basket was full of Operation 125 parts before he passed them on to Operation 130 (i.e. 48 parts)? His response was that it has always been that way and that it was the Kanban rule which he could not violate. Apparently, this facility, as part of an earlier Lean improvement initiative, had established batch sizes on all of their equipment and parts and mandated that nobody was permitted to "violate" the "rules" that had been put in place.

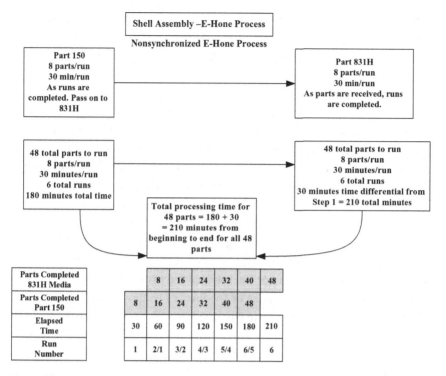

FIGURE 10.9
New E-Hone process.

Once I was satisfied with the synchronization between Operation 125 and 130, it was time to look for other forms of waste, but only within the system constraint. As I was observing the flow of parts in Operation 125, I noticed that a second holding fixture was in a rack nearby. I asked the operator what the fixture was for and he told me it was for a different part number. I then asked him what was different in this fixture compared with the one he was using? He told me that there were no differences. So, the first action we took was to begin using this second identical fixture for the selected part. My thought was that the operator could load this second holding fixture with parts so that it would be ready to immediately load in the machine, rather than having to wait for the cleaning and re-loading of the original fixture. In doing so, using Lean to identify waste, approximately six minutes were saved immediately.

In addition to this change, we made other simple improvements such as re-designing the holding fixture so that it would take less time to fill the sample chamber with media. We also ran studies increasing the temperature of the media to improve its viscosity, so as to speed up the fill rate of the sample chamber. The changes we made at Operation 125 automatically translated to Operation 130 with the net effect being a dramatic reduction in cycle time from 30 minutes for eight parts to approximately 11 minutes for eight parts. This, of course, was an immediate capacity increase for this set of operations.

As indicated earlier in this case study report, Figure 10.7 was the current production layout used to produce the selected part and as you can see, the process appears to be highly fragmented and disjointed with parts of the process spanning much of the factory floor. As a simplistic measure of the degree of fragmentation, the numbers listed on the tracking lines in Figure 10.7, between operations, are the number of footsteps required to move parts from one operation to the next. The approximate distance in feet is the number listed on the tracking lines, times three feet (e.g., Operation 10 to 70, for example, equals 3 feet per step × 16 steps or approximately 48 feet). In fact, the total distance the selected part traveled was 530 steps × 3 ft per step or 1,590 feet. Because of the level of fragmentation, it was clear that this facility needed to create work cells to at least attempt to reduce the distance the part travels. The cellular concept was also necessary because of the CEO's workforce reduction that had taken place prior to my arrival. In order to get complete buy-in for the creation of manufacturing cells from the machine operators, I included them as part of the design team for the new cellular concepts. I knew that if I wanted the SMEs to own the new cellular layout, then it had to be based upon their input.

This first cellular arrangement required that we place a small wash station within the cell, so as to avoid having the operator to walk across the shop to have his parts cleaned in batches. Using Lean tools, this small change made it possible for one operator to run Operations 140 and 150.

Figure 10.10 was the first cell the team put in place and the operators independently concluded that by using this arrangement, a single operator could easily run all three machines.

Figure 10.11 is a graphic of the second cellular arrangement which moved more of the machine operations closer together and significantly reduced the walk time between operations. With the cells now in place, it was my belief that we were now ready to begin our Drum-Buffer-Rope implementation to synchronize the scheduling and flow of parts through this manufacturing facility.

In order for a manufacturing plant, such as this one, to realize the full benefits of synchronization, a logistical control system that is manageable and results in a predicted level of performance is absolutely essential.

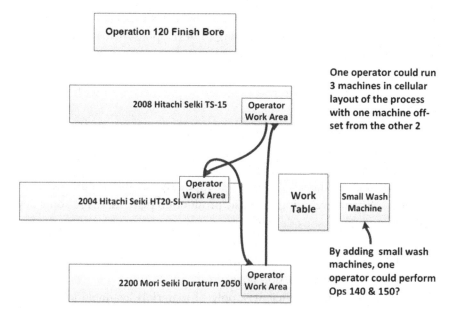

FIGURE 10.10
First cell.

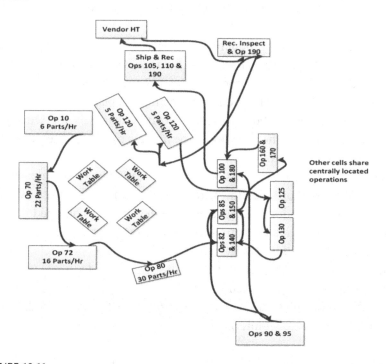

FIGURE 10.11
Second cell.

220 • *Theory of Constraints, Lean, and Six Sigma*

TOC's DBR is such a system. There are two basic concerns that must be addressed and reconciled when trying to develop a synchronized flow of product as follows:

- The ability of the plant to execute the planned product flow over a given period of time.
- The ability to "handle" the impact of the ever-present deviations in the planned flow.

The good news is the DBR approach explicitly considers both of these concerns. When developing the basic production plan, there are some key points that must be considered:

- The production plan quantities should not exceed the expected market demands (i.e. don't overproduce).
- There must be a sufficient supply of materials available to support the plan.
- The proposed product flow required to support the plan must never overload the processing capabilities of the resources.

Once the preliminary production plan has been developed, the next step is to develop a detailed schedule for the CCR, which in this plant's product flow is the E-Hone process (Steps 125 and 130). The CCR schedule can be used to finalize the production plan. This plan, referred to as the Master Production Schedule (MPS), becomes the basis for scheduling actual production on the shop floor. The process used to create the MPS is referred to as the drum.

Because there are always disruptions and variation in any manufacturing process, the actual product flow through the system will deviate from the planned flow of product. Because of these deviations to planned flow, we must create a protective cushion or buffer to protect our customer due dates. Because we don't want excessive amounts of WIP to enter the process, as has been the case in this facility, the buffer we use is primarily time-based rather than actual physical product. For planning purposes, we use the following simple equation to protect our planned product flow (i.e. creating our safety buffer):

Planned lead time = Sum of process and setup times + Time buffer

In other words, the planned lead time for a product is calculated as the longest of the planned lead times for its component parts plus any additional time buffer. In effect, the time buffer increases the planned lead time from the absolute minimum required to machine the products by an amount sufficient to accommodate these disruptions that are likely to occur within the total process.

Buffers provide the timely protection of the CCR from any likely or unexpected disruptions. The rope is the timely release of raw materials into the system at the front end of the process. Buffer Management (BM) provides the means by which the schedule is managed on the shop floor. One other important factor to consider when developing buffer sizes is the downtime history of each piece of equipment. Unfortunately, no historical records existed within this facility to be able to factor in equipment downtime. Because this manufacturing facility is equipment intensive, I highly recommended that downtime (or uptime) histories be established to aid in future planning and scheduling.

DRUM-BUFFER-ROPE

Earlier, I mentioned that one of the major reasons for excessive WIP in the process was the scheduling system used to schedule work in the plant. I further recommended the use of a TOC-based scheduling system referred to as Drum-Buffer-Rope. In production, many different scheduling approaches are used to attempt to manage the capacity of the system and protect the system from the impact of variation (Murphy's Law), so as to deliver the product or services "on time." The difficulty facing operations environments is to find a solution in environments where demand is fluctuating. Murphy strikes frequently, customers change their demand requirements, and conditions rarely remain constant. I was told that the demand fluctuation from the customer using the selected part appears to be an issue for this facility, but with the right scheduling system in place, this issue could be permanently resolved.

DBR is an operations scheduling methodology based on Dr. Eli Goldratt's and Jeff Cox's Theory of Constraints (TOC) and first written about in *The Goal* [3]. Drum-Buffer-Rope is just one part of the TOC Operations solution and is the "machine" that sets the pace for all of the individual operations. The second part of the TOC Operations solution is Buffer Management. Buffer Management is the monitor and control mechanism that ensures the machine is running well in execution.

Drum-Buffer-Rope enhances and protects the weakest link in the system, and therefore the system as a whole, against process dependency and variation and thus maximizes the system's overall effectiveness. The outcome is a robust and dependable process that will allow this facility to produce more with less inventory, less rework and fewer defects, and better on-time delivery without tying up huge amounts of cash.

The fundamental view of DBR is to focus on the system as a whole rather than only a single segment of the system. This idea of looking at the global system is a major shift in the way systems have previously been viewed and managed at this facility. A system can be defined as a sequence of steps or operations that are linked together to produce something as an end result. With that definition in mind, it's easy to understand how virtually everything can be linked to some kind of a system.

All systems are restricted, at some point in time, by some type of output limitation. This limitation is usually determined by the presence of some kind of system-capacity limit. No matter how good the system is, there is still only so much it can do. Sooner or later whatever kind of system is being analyzed will reach its maximum system capacity and be unable to produce more. If higher system outputs are required beyond the current capacity, then the system must be changed. All of this was true for this manufacturing facility.

When viewing a system through the eyes of DBR, it becomes apparent very quickly that improving every step in the process is not required, nor will the sum total of all of those discrete system improvements equal an improved overall system. For example, recently at this facility, an improvement was made at Operation 90 Weld that resulted in a faster welding process. The problem with focusing efforts on non-constraints, such as Weld in this case, is that the throughput rate of the entire process does not change by a single part, simply because the throughput is dictated by the capacity of the system constraint, Operations 125 and 130. In essence, the only way to achieve higher levels of throughput is to focus improvement efforts on the system constraint which is what was done at this facility. This is the reasoning behind Goldratt's Step 2, decide how to exploit the constraint.

To ensure that this WIP explosion doesn't happen again in this facility, an artificial rope must be tied to the first (gating) operation of the system. The rope prevents raw materials from entering the process prematurely.

This is calculated by the date the order appears on the Drum Schedule minus the Constraint Buffer time giving a schedule for material release into the system. To ensure the Shipping Schedule is met, after meeting the Drum Schedule, there must be a schedule developed that assures continuous flow of product through the entire process. This facility can no longer permit WIP to accumulate between and within subsequent steps. So, let's take a look at what a DBR system might look like.

Figure 10.12 is a simple generic Drum-Buffer-Rope system. Raw materials enter this process and are processed through the first workstation. Per the guidelines discussed earlier, a time buffer is created just in front of the constraint to assure that the constraint always has product to be worked on because one of the basic premises of TOC is that the constraint can never be idle. Once the material is processed and released by the constraint, a signal (the Rope) is sent back to the raw material release point to begin processing more product. In this way, this facility should be able to minimize the amount of WIP in the system.

If there were no disruptions like machine breakdowns, scrap and repair parts, and so on, the production lead time would simply be the time it takes for the raw materials to be processed into finished parts which would be the sum of the process and set-up times at each of the process steps. Unfortunately, we do have disruptions so that whenever there is a task that is subject to variability, it becomes clear that the actual time to complete the task is going to be different than the planned time. This is where the time buffer enters the picture. Notice from the drawing that the buffer is time-related rather than physical product. The essence of the time buffer is the recognition that the goal of the DBR system is not to make each

Basic DBR System

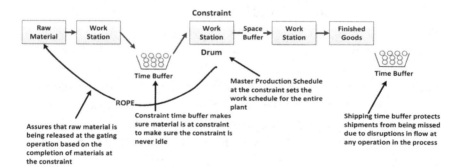

FIGURE 10.12
Basic DBR system.

task finish on time, but rather to make sure that the system is on time. This is what makes the DBR system more reliable compared with a push or Kanban systems. Specifically, a time buffer represents the additional lead time allowed beyond the process and set-up times. The objective then of the time buffers is to protect the throughput of the system from the inevitable disruptions that will always occur. So, the planning relationship between the processing times, set-ups and time buffers can be expressed by the following formula:

$$\text{Production lead time} = \text{Sum of the processing times}$$

$$+ \text{set-up times} + \text{time buffers}$$

Now the question becomes, how do we establish the proper time buffer length? Although this may seem to be a complicated process that might require things like detailed equipment downtime data, scrap and rework data, raw material receipts to schedule, and so on, in reality, it isn't. For DBR, we take a more practical approach to determining the size of the time buffer. It is simply the production lead time defined in the formula above. We can start with the time buffer being one-half of the sum of the processing times plus set-up times. If our calculated time buffer is too large, we will see piles of inventory everywhere. If the calculated buffer is too small, the cumulative disruptions for each process step will quickly consume the time buffers and parts will be late. So, how do we use and track the time buffers?

The way we track the buffer status is by using a simple color scheme assigned to each order. As demonstrated in Figure 10.13, if the lead time remaining for an open work order is less than one-third of its standard production lead time (i.e. in the dark gray zone), then the buffer status is less than 33 percent and it should be flagged for action. This would require the production supervisor (or someone designated to track orders) to investigate where the batch is and expedite it or it will be late. Conversely, if the work order falls into the light gray box, it means that the buffer status is between 33 and 67 percent. In this case, the person responsible for tracking orders should develop a plan to expedite, if necessary, but only implement the plan if the order falls into the dark gray zone. If an order falls into the medium gray zone, then there is still 67 percent (or more) of the buffer remaining and the order should be completed on time. My recommendation is that at the beginning of each shift, the supervisor should review the status of all work orders so that priorities can be

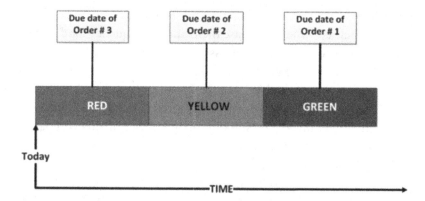

Designation of buffer status by a color. Comparison of time remaining (Due Date of Order to Today) to the planned buffer time to assign a color to a work order. Status and Action:
- Red – Time remaining is less than 1/3 of the buffer, EXPEDITE
- Yellow – Time remaining between 1/3 and 2/3 of the buffer, MONITOR & PLAN
- Green – Time remaining greater than 2/3 of the buffer, DO NOTHING

FIGURE 10.13
Buffer management system.

established. Obviously, the dark gray orders have priority status, then light gray, then medium gray. If the operators are working on a light gray work order, for example, and a dark gray work order is observed, the dark gray moves up to the front of the queue.

Another positive feature of assigning colors is that they provide information about how accurate the lead times are, meaning that if the number of dark gray zone occurrences are too low (e.g., less than 10 percent), then the assumed lead time is larger than it needs to be and can be lowered. This could be a competitive advantage for this manufacturer in that shorter quoted lead times could be given to the customer. If, on the other hand, the number of dark gray zone occurrences are too high (e.g., greater than 15–20 percent), then it probably means that there are disruptions occurring within the process which should be investigated and corrected. It also means that the lead times are too aggressive and should be increased until the causes are determined and corrected.

The final piece of the DBR system is the rope which is a mechanism that is used to control the flow of parts through the entire production system. While the drum has provided us with a master schedule and the time buffers provide a margin of safety to assure parts get completed on time, the rope essentially communicates to the rest of the operations the necessary actions to support the drum. The simplest way to implement the rope is for the raw material release point to be given a list of what raw materials to release, when to release them and the sequence for doing so. If we do this consistently, then unnecessary work won't enter the production system. The net effect of controlling the release of raw materials into the manufacturing system will be that WIP will be controlled because the equipment operators can only work on products that are available to be worked. In simple linear flows, like most processes at this company, by simply controlling the release of materials into the system there should be sufficient control of the entire operation. The bottom line is that if we make sure that a workstation only works on material required to meet a pending customer order, then the days of excessive WIP build-up at this manufacturer should be a remnant of the past.

Figure 10.14 is a simplified version of the actual scheduling system that was developed and put in place at this manufacturing facility, and demonstrates which parts must be made and the order in which they should be processed through the Capacity Constrained Resource (i.e. Operations 125 and 130). With Drum-Buffer-Rope firmly in place and functioning, I now turned my efforts toward improving this facility's extended equipment changeovers.

One of the easiest and most cost-effective ways to improve the capacity at this or any facility was to overhaul the way in which changeovers are accomplished. In this facility, changeovers were taking much too long to complete and with a focused effort, significant time reductions could be achieved. After evaluating the current changeover practices at this facility, the following items were considered as opportunities to significantly reduce the time to complete the changeovers. The words written in italics are intended to be action items to be put in place to improve changeovers.

- There are no documented changeover procedures or checklists in place at this facility. *Use experienced operators, develop consensus, and documented changeover procedures, checklists, and guidelines. When completed, copies should be provided to all operators and supervisors to review for completeness and training of the general workforce.*
- Although set-up kits did exist in a central location, needed changeover items are often missing from the kits. *Review all set-up kits in advance of the changeover to assure needed items are available in advance of the changeover. If possible, assign one person to be responsible for completing this action.*

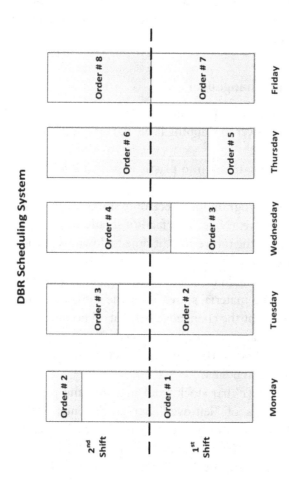

FIGURE 10.14
DBR scheduling system.

- Changeovers at this facility appear to just "happen." That is, there is not much pre-planning prior to the changeover and as a result, significant time is wasted looking for needed parts, tools, etc. *Develop a comprehensive list of needed items and assure availability before the changeover begins.*

The following bullets were developed by the team I put in place that should apply to all changeovers at this facility and will be documented in the final changeover procedure.

Prepare Area for Changeover

Collect completed finished parts and deliver to the holding rack for the next operation or deliver to shipping if the part is completed

- Remove pin sets, insert into plastic cases, and deliver to Gage Lab shelf location
- Download old program into electronic storage device and deliver to supervisor to save. (Note: This facility should be going to a wireless arrangement in the future so wait time to download program should be improved.)
- New materials should be delivered to the operator. Supervisor sends an email to the material's area with the estimated time materials will be needed for the changeover so that all necessary materials are available in advance of the changeover.
- Remove "old" paperwork from area and place it in the Manufacturing Document return holder.
- Remove "left-over" bar stock from machine and place it on a cart. Measure lengths of "left-over" bar stock, enter information on paperwork (tag) and return it to shipping area. Label returned bar stock, insert label in plastic holder and attach it to returned bar stock. **This should all be done by the shipping department.**

Begin Changeover to New Product

- Review "new" paperwork, insert into plastic sleeves, and mount sleeves on machine and workstation.
- Where appropriate, remove "old" tooling from machine and place it inside the plastic kit for this part

Machine Set-up

- This section had to be further developed but should be activity specific. For example:
  - Set-up bar feeder—change collet.
  - Insert/install collet and guide bushing to set path for bar stock.
  - Feed bar stock into housing and adjust tension on bar stock to just the right amount of torque.
  - Install "new" tooling.

Note: Because the second shift operator had no interface with the first shift operator, a significant amount of time was spent trying to determine what had and what had not been completed. There must always be an interface with operators so that there is no question about what stage of the changeover is in.

Notes After Changeover Completed

- Throughout this changeover, there were frequent tool problems requiring the operator to go away from the machine to search for and find necessary tooling. *All required tools should be in place prior to the changeover beginning.*
- It is clear that the majority of time spent on changeovers is due to "dialing-in" the part characteristics. That is, setting up the machine is relatively easy (if all tools and needed items were available), but adjustments to achieve part's spec limits are very time-consuming. *A sheet should be developed at the end of each run indicating what the current machine settings are, so as to reduce the time spent dialing in the adjustments. These setting should be the starting points for the next time this product is run.*

OTHER RECOMMENDATIONS

- In SMED, changeovers are made up of steps that are termed "elements." Internal elements are elements that must be completed while the machine is stopped while external elements are elements that can be completed while the machine is still running. *The key is to first convert as many internal elements as possible to external elements and then shorten the time required to complete the remaining internal elements. Because external elements can be completed while the machine is still running, a plan should be developed to complete them in advance of the changeover.*

- *A team of machine operators should be formed to develop a standardized step-by-step checklist/procedure on how to perform changeovers. This is necessary because each operator has "their own way" of performing changeovers which may or may not be based upon best practices. It was clear that the first operator performing this changeover had to stop and think about what he should do next.*

This variation in set-up methods translates not only into variation in the time required to complete the changeover but also contributes to variation in the finished parts. This checklist/procedure will serve the following benefits for this facility:

1. Significant reduction in operator-to-operator method variation in changeovers which should significantly reduce the elapsed time. This is especially true for less experienced operators not totally familiar with the machine/part. This will also help increase the flexibility of the facility's workforce.
2. Reduction in the average time required to set-up a machine thus providing more time to make parts.
3. Improvement in the consistency of parts produced (i.e. quality and throughput) both in the short term and long term.
4. More effective capacity since run times will increase creating the opportunity to produce more parts between changeovers.
5. Because changeovers take multiple shifts to complete, having a changeover checklist would reduce the time it would take the "relief operator" to determine where in the changeover process the first operator was.
   - Although kits are currently available for machine changeovers, many times items have been "robbed" by someone needing a specific item (e.g., tool) and then did not replace it later. When this occurs, valuable time is lost searching for the needed item. A replacement system needs to be developed and implemented to assure that items removed are replaced in a timely manner. One person should be assigned to reviewing all kits to assure that all needed items are within each kit. This person could also assist

the operator during the changeover process by doing things like cross-checking the first article parts which is currently done by another machine operator. This would eliminate the need to shut down the second operator's machine to check first articles.

- Although Changeover Carts are in place, they should be developed and prepared at least a day in advance of the actual changeover and contain all needed items. The cart should include all necessary documentation, parts, tools, materials, and so on required to successfully complete the changeover.

- All necessary tools should be located at each machine (or at least shared between two machines) to avoid the need to leave the machine and search for them. In addition, when tools such as collets are in a centralized location, they should be organized and clearly identified to eliminate the need to search through the entire stock of tools until the one needed is found. An example observed during this changeover was how different sized collets had been placed in a drawer, but because they are not organized and labeled according to size, the operator on this changeover had to pick up each collet and read the size until the right sized collet was found.

- During this changeover in order to remove the machine tooling, the operator had to remove numerous bolts, remove the existing tool, and then install the new tool. An effort should be made to develop and implement quick disconnect devices to replace the constant unscrewing and screwing of bolts to remove and secure the machine tooling.

- Tools required for changeovers are typically disorganized and there appears to be a shortage of common tools needed on multiple machines. During this changeover, on at least two occasions, a specific machine tool was required, but because the tool was running on another machine a "work-around" was necessary. An effort should be made to define the necessary number of tools for the shop and then purchase them. An example of such a tool needed during this changeover was a Z-axis spindle for end drilling and milling. There were only three such tools available within the shop and all were in use on other machines. This shortfall extended the changeover for several hours until a "work-around" could be determined. All shared tools should be organized and placed near each machine to avoid these lengthy searches.

Changeovers can and should be done flawlessly, but without a person responsible for this, flawless execution will be difficult. In this facility, the average changeover time reduction was approximately 6 hours which translated immediately to 6 hours of additional production capacity.

PARTS REPLENISHMENT

Earlier in this case study, we discussed the need to evaluate and improve the parts replenishment system currently in use at this facility. A complete review of the parts replenishment system and significant changes were made.

Figure 10.15 represents a plot of the average days the selected part had been spending in each of the operations required to produce the part prior to any improvements being made. For example, the average time parts stayed within Operation 70 was 10.3 days before it moved on to Operation 72. It then stayed in Operation 72 for 17.3 days. If we sum the total days spent in each operation, the total days were an incredible 164.8 days.

Figure 10.16 is the plot of the average days in each operation after improvements were made throughout this manufacturing facility. What had been taking a total of 164.8 days to complete, was now taking only 35.5 days. Much of this reduction was due to improved synchronization of the process steps throughout this factory as a result of the new DBR scheduling system and the "burn-off" of the massive amounts of WIP that existed when I first arrived.

Since departing from this facility, on-time delivery had reached record levels, and they were able to operate comfortably with the new level of staffing. One area that the Site Leader elected not to change was the parts replenishment system and after reviewing their current method, I *reluctantly agreed* that this was one area that did not need to change. All other deliverables spelled out at the beginning of this report were met.

This case study resulted in significant reductions in total processing times for this part, but more importantly, the customer satisfaction levels improved beyond what the CEO of this company believed was possible. Some of the most critical actions taken included:

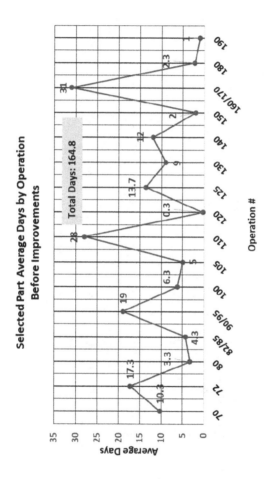

FIGURE 10.15
Part averages before improvements.

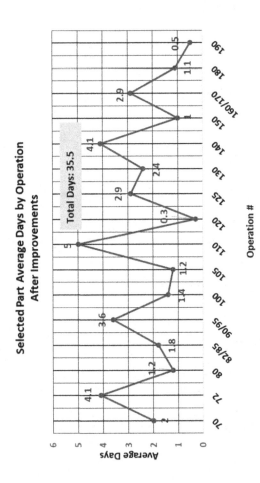

FIGURE 10.16
Part averages after improvements.

- Major reductions in WIP and Finished Goods inventory level.
- Synchronization of parts through the system.
- Significant reduction in the amount of cash tied up within this manufacturing facility.
- The active involvement of the true Subject Matter Experts, the front-line workers.
- Development and implementation of a robust scheduling system (DBR/BM).
- Development and implementation of work cells throughout this facility.
- Significant reduction in equipment changer-over times resulting in major gains in capacity.
- A new mindset of system thinking and the concept of focus and leverage by all members of the management team as well as the SMEs.

As with the other case studies in this book, the integration of the Theory of Constraints, Lean, and Six Sigma continues to produce superior results, no matter what the industry type!

REFERENCES

1. Bob Sproull, Reprinted with permission from *The Ultimate Improvement Cycle: Maximizing Profits through the Integration of Lean, Six Sigma, and the Theory of Constraints*, CRC Press, Taylor & Francis Group, Boca Raton, FL, 2009.
2. H. William Dettmer, *The Logical Thinking Process: A Systems Approach to Complex Problem Solving*, Quality Press, Milwaukee, WI, 2007.
3. Eliyahu M. Goldratt and Jeff Cox, *The Goal: A Process of Ongoing Improvement*, North River Press, Great Barrington, MA, 1984.

11

Case Study on Engine Overhaul

INTRODUCTION/BACKGROUND

This was an unusual case study for me for an assortment of reasons. One of the primary reasons was my absolute lack of experience in engine overhaul technology. Because of this, I spent the first several weeks just analyzing and learning the Engine Overhaul Process at this location. Once I was comfortable with the engine overhaul process, I developed a comprehensive process map, outlining all the required steps for completing this process and then developed a series of causal chains and sub-process maps to better understand why things weren't operating as they should be. Because the engine overhaul process cycle time is much longer than planned:

- Costly rental engines remain on the aircraft much longer than the budgeted time: the estimated loss/OH is ~$10,000.
- Significant parts discounts from DAI cannot be captured: the estimated loss/OH is ~$9,500 for new parts and ~$6,700 for serviceable parts for a total of ~$16,000.

Because the engine overhaul contract is based upon a firm, fixed price basis, the expenses resulting from extended engine overhaul cycle time seriously erode the margins. The reality was that this company was losing a significant amount of money on this complete overhaul process for two primary reasons:

1. Engine rental costs are excessive because of the excessive rental engine hours flown. That is, because it was taking so long.

2. Part's discount costs are less than optimal because the Wing to Wing Turnaround Time (W2WTAT) was excessive (i.e. >80 days).

The hard reality was that this customer was losing between $1,000 to $20,000 on each engine overhaul conducted.

The objectives for this project were as follows:

1. Achieve an average W2WTAT reduction from 144 days to 72 days in order to achieve the maximum parts discount of 30 percent off list for new material.
2. Decrease the average Regular Engine Ship-off Cycle Time (RESCT) by 50 percent from current levels in order to prevent any liquidated damages.
3. Decrease the average Rental Engine Flight Hours (REFH) flown on each rental engine from 248 hours to 124 hours to significantly reduce financial losses against the Firm Fixed Price (FFP) of $64,000 per occurrence overhaul.
4. Improve the per occurrence average profit margin per engine overhaul from a $5,000 loss to a minimum of $5,000 profit in order to eliminate financial losses in the engine management of the contract.
5. Complete implementation activities by said due date.

The first four objectives were tied to this company's ability to reduce the time required for the entire engine overhaul process. That is, if the W2WTAT was significantly reduced (i.e. by ~50 percent), objective numbers 2, 3, and 4 would be achieved.

Figure 11.1 is the process map developed to describe the individual process steps in the engine overhaul process.

Like any process improvement effort, the key to reducing the turnaround time for the total engine overhaul process was to identify the system constraint and then focus the improvement efforts directly on it. Figure 11.2 is a high-level process flow map developed by sampling eight randomly selected engines and determining the average cycle time for each.

The constraint's analysis determined that there were, in fact, dual constraints that must be considered for improvement. They were considered dual constraints simply because of the closeness of their cycle times. The customer's response time to the Over and Above Authorization to Proceed (O&AATP) at 28.5 days is one constraint, while the other constraint is the

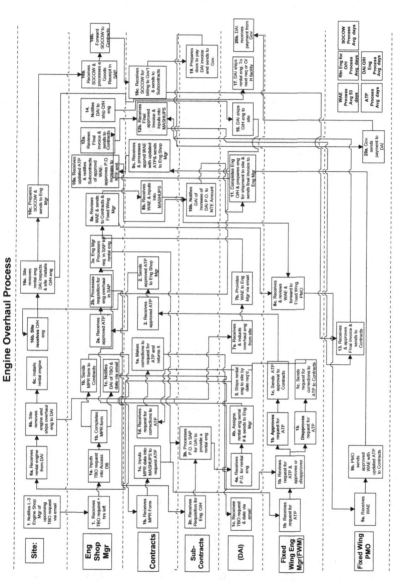

FIGURE 11.1

Process map of the Engine Overhaul Process.

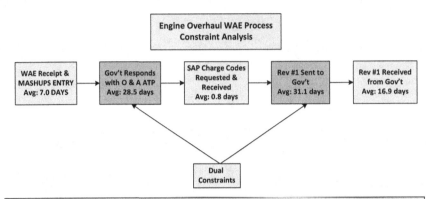

FIGURE 11.2

High-level process flow map.

amount of time for this company to supply corrected information to the customer within 31.1 days. If these two constraints could be improved by 50 percent, then this company could realize a net gain of approximately 30 days in W2WTAT and therefore a 30-day reduction in rental engine charges.

One of the significant costs to this company was the cost incurred as a result of the rental engine remaining on the aircraft for greater than the budgeted 120 hours. My analysis of the rental engine hours and associated costs for the first 9 months of the year, based upon Option Year 1 rates, was approximately $450K as displayed in Table 11.1, which when annualized was approximately $600,000.

My next step in this improvement effort was to create an Engine Overhaul Strategic Intermediate Objectives Map (IO Map) to determine how best to maximize the profitability of the total engine overhaul process for this company. Figure 11.3 is the IO Map that was developed.

As can be seen in Figure 11.3, the Goal was stated as "Maximum Profit on Engine Overhaul." In order to realize this goal, four Critical Success Factors (CFSs) were stated in the format, "In order to maximize profits on the engine overhaul process, I must have CSF1, Increased Margins per Engine; CSF2, Reduced Unfunded O & A Work; CSF3, Increased Parts Discount from DAI; and CSF4, Decreased Days Sales Outstanding." If we could realize all four CSFs, then we believed our goal would be achieved.

TABLE 11.1

Costs for Nine Months

Engine Type	Option Yr. $1/ Hr.	# in Fleet	Avg YTD Hrs./AC	Average Hours Above 120 Hrs.	YTD # of A/C Flown	$s Above 120 Hrs.
A	97.85	58	131.4	11.4	6	6,692.94
B	97.85	204	247.7	127.7	33	412,349.7
C	128.75	4	0			0
D	128.75	64	166.9	46.9	4	24,153.5
E	128.75	2	0			0
F	154.5	40	0			0
G	180.25	16	152.7	32.7	1	5,894.175
Total		388				$449,090.32

We then developed Necessary Conditions to realize each of the Critical Success Factors, with the primary Necessary Condition being NC2-2, Reduce W2WTAT of the Engine Overhaul Process. We then developed five Level 2 Necessary Conditions all aimed at satisfying this primary Necessary Condition. While all five of these Necessary Conditions were important, it was clear to me that NC2-2, Reduce the WAE Cycle Time was

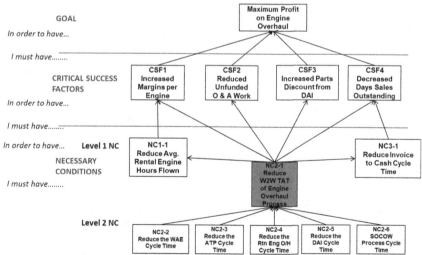

The IO Map is read as follows: In order to have *Maximum Profit* (The Goal), I must have CSFs 1-4. In order to have increased margins per engine, I must *reduce average rental engines flown* (Level 1 NC). In order to reduce average rental engine flown, I must reduce the W2W TAT (Level 2 NC). Action plans are developed and executed at the lowest levels, and then roll upward to satisfy each of the above NCs, CSFs and finally, the Goal.

FIGURE 11.3

Engine overhaul strategic Intermediate Objectives Map.

critical to the achievement of reducing W2WTAT of the Engine Overhaul Process.

My next step was to perform root cause analyses, using primarily causal chains (aka Why-Why? Analysis) on W2WTAT and the WAE process. If we could find the key root causes of the failure of these two process steps, then we were convinced that we could achieve the overall goal in the Strategic Intermediate Objectives Map as laid out in Figure 11.3.

Figures 11.4 and 11.5 are these two causal chains and as can be seen in Figure 11.4, the major constraint in this process was the delay in the approval process. That is, rather than batching the O&AATP, perhaps a simple solution was to move toward single-piece flow. And as it turned out, this simple solution did resolve this problem.

The analysis revealed that for both the W2WTAT and the WAE Approval Process, the dual constraints, the impact on each could be significantly reduced by having this company supply a data entry assistant to support the engine manager. Because of the workload on the engine manager, all three of the ATPs (i.e. Initial ATP, WAE ATP, and Final (O&AATP) were being batched instead of using one-piece-flow concepts. This batching effect extends the approval process throughout the entire process flow. That is, because of his workload, the engine manager was not always

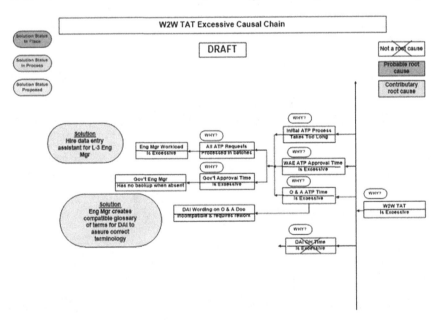

FIGURE 11.4
W2WTAT excessive causal chain.

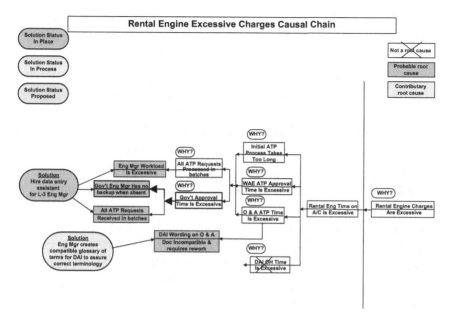

FIGURE 11.5
WAE approval process causal chain.

available to process the Initial ATP requests as they arrive and as such, they could actually sit in his email inbox for several days. And when he did receive the requests, it was not unusual to process them in batches that were typically 8–12 at a time. These batches of requests were received by Contracts who then batched them into MASHUPS. The Engine Manager then received the requests in batches from Contracts.

The effect of the initial batching was passed on throughout the process and valuable time was being lost. And while this time was being lost, the rental engine hours continued to accumulate. The causal chain for the excessive loss was due to extended W2WTAT, which resulted in the rental engine staying on the airplane too long which in turn caused rental engine flying hours to be approximately double the budgeted hours on the rental engine.

The question that needed to be answered was, if there was a way to enter the requests as they arrived (i.e. using single-piece-flow concepts) rather than batching, would the flow time for each request be significantly reduced? This same batching scenario applies to WAE ATPs and Final ATPs which also extended the overall engine overhaul process. This batching concept was best characterized by the "Pig in a Python" effect, whereby the pig moves through the python at a much slower pace than if the python had taken smaller bites.

There was a very simple solution to this problem as is articulated on both of the causal chains. If there was a data entry person working for the engine manager, who could enter the initial, WAE and final ATPs, rather than having the engine manager do so, the problem could be resolved. In so doing, the aforementioned parts discount issue would also be resolved, since the W2WTAT would be significantly reduced. This company was only receiving a 20-percent discount on parts whereas if the W2WTAT could be reduced to under 80 days, this company would receive an additional discount of 10 percent. By applying these simple fixes to this problem, the profit improvement for this customer was approximately $1.4 million!

Once again, by using an integrated Theory of Constraints, Lean, and Six Sigma improvement effort, significant improvements in profitability were achieved. The improvement all starts by first identifying the system constraint(s) and then applying the tools of both Lean and Six Sigma in a strategic way. And when this process is followed to the ultimate end, improvement is always realized.

12

A Case Study on Project Management

If yours is an organization that relies on project completions as their source of revenue and you're like many other project-based organizations, then the results of multiple surveys by the Standish Group [1] and others might be of concern to you. In 1994, the Standish Group conducted a landmark study of nearly 10,000 IT projects across America and found that 52 percent of projects ended up costing greater than 189 percent of the original budget, 31 percent were canceled, and only 16 percent of the projects were completed on time and on budget. The cost of these failures and overruns are just the tip of the proverbial iceberg. The lost opportunity costs are probably not measurable but could easily be in the trillions of dollars. Pretty scary figures if project execution is your business model.

In 2002, the Public Accounts Committee [2] reported that the English government had 100 major IT projects underway, with a total value of roughly £10 billion. The Spending Review of 2002 allocated ~£6 billion over 3 years to government electronic service delivery [3]. However, *Computing* magazine calculated that the cost of canceled or over-budget government IT projects over the last 6 years is greater than £1.5 billion [4].

In 2006, the new Chaos Report [5] revealed that only 19 percent of projects begun were considered outright failures, compared with the 31 percent reported in 1994. In addition, 35 percent of software projects started in 2006 can be categorized as successful, meaning they were completed on time, on budget, and met user requirements. Although this is a marked improvement from their initial groundbreaking report, it's safe to say that these statistics still aren't acceptable or at least where they need to be! The point is, project failure rates appear to be a universal problem, spanning virtually all industry types and although the success rates are improving, they still don't rise to an acceptable level. So, the question I pose to you is this. What if there was a way to demonstrate a method that would push your projects successful completion rate from where it is now to over 90 percent? Would you be interested in hearing about it?

Ninety percent of the Project Managers around the world are using a project management methodology known as the Critical Path Method (CPM) and have been doing so for many years. If you ask a typical project manager about what factors delayed a completed project, most will tell you that something they didn't expect or even had no control over cropped up in some of the tasks and delayed them. In other words, uncertainty or the Murphy bug bit them! Every project from virtually every environment has uncertainty associated with it and how this uncertainty is dealt with determines the ultimate success or failure of the project. So, in order for a project to be successful, there must be a way to protect it from uncertainty. Let's take a look at how traditional project management (CPM) attempts to protect a project from inevitable uncertainty.

CPM does so by using a "fudge factor." When developing the project plan, durations for each individual task are estimated by the resources responsible for executing them and then a safety factor is added to each task by the resource responsible for completing it. For example, suppose the realistic estimate of time for an individual task is 1 week. Is 1 week what the resource actually tells his or her project manager? Typically, the resource will add a safety factor of their own to guard against "things" that might happen that would delay completion of the task. So, it's not unusual for the original 1 week to be quoted as 2 weeks. Resources react this way because they know from experience that as soon as they give the project manager an estimate, it automatically becomes a commitment!

A typical project manager will then add up all of the individual, inflated time estimates and then add his or her own safety factor. Why is this done? Project Managers know that at some point in the project Murphy will strike and some of the tasks will be delayed, so they add a safety factor to protect the project from being late. Keep in mind that every resource inflates every task, so it's not uncommon for the estimated duration to be 50-percent greater than it takes to actually complete the task. So, with all of this built-in safety, the project should be completed on time ... right? So it would seem, but the statistics on project completions paint a different picture. The reasons for this lack of success will be explained later.

In traditional project management tracking (i.e. CPM), the progress of the project is typically done so by calculating the percentage of individual tasks completed and then comparing that percentage against the due date. Sounds reasonable, but is this the right way to track progress? The problem with using percentage of tasks completed is that not all tasks have equal duration estimates. That is, comparing a task that has an estimate of 1 day to a task that should take 1 week is not a valid comparison. Compounding this problem is the mistaken belief that the best way to ensure that a project will finish on time is to try to make every individual task finish on time. This too sounds reasonable, but later on, we'll show you why this just isn't so.

So the question remains that if individual project tasks have so much extra time imbedded in them, then why are so many projects coming in late? We think that this is partially explained by two common human behaviors. Resources know that they have built "safety" into their tasks, so they often delay work on the task until much later than they had originally planned. Think back to your high school days. When you were given a due date for a paper for Thursday, when did you start working on it? How about Wednesday? Eli Goldratt coined the term, Student Syndrome, to explain one of the reasons why the apparent built-in safety gets wasted. When the task start is delayed and Murphy strikes, the task will typically be late because the built-in safety was wasted through procrastination.

The other human behavior that lengthens projects is referred to as Parkinson's Law. Resources intuitively know that if they finish a task in less time than they estimated, the next time they have the same or a similar task to complete, they will be expected to finish it early. So, to protect against this, even when a task is finished early, the resource doesn't notify the project manager that it is finished until the original due date is reached. After all, we're talking about personal credibility here, so to protect it, early finishes aren't reported. Parkinson's Law states that work expands to fill the available time so if the resource has 1 week to finish a task, the entire week is taken to finish it. The key effect on projects of these two behaviors is that delays are passed on, but early finishes aren't. So, is it any wonder that projects are late?

While these two behaviors negatively impact project schedules, there are other reasons why projects are late. Many organizations today have multiple projects going on at the same time and it's not unusual for projects to share resources. In fact, many project managers tend to "fight over" shared resources because they believe their project is the one that has the highest priority. Another significant problem is that in many project-based companies, leadership initiates projects without considering the capacity of the organization to complete the work. Leadership also mistakenly assumes that the sooner a project is initiated, the sooner it will be completed. As a result, perhaps the most devastating problem of all associated with project completion occurs ... bad multitasking! But wait a minute ... I thought we'd all been taught for years that multitasking is a good thing? Good multitasking is good, but bad multitasking is not.

Bad multitasking happens when resources are forced to work on multiple project activities at the same time. Like we've always said, humans aren't very good at rubbing their tummy and patting their heads at the same time. Many people believe (especially in leadership positions) that multitasking is a good thing because it increases efficiency since everyone is "busy" all of the time. If you've ever to read *The Goal* by Eli Goldratt (if you haven't, you should), you might remember how focusing on local activities actually damaged the overall system performance.

You may also recall how Goldratt used his robot example whereby running the robots continuously, efficiency did improve, but at the expense of creating mountains of excess inventory. The negative impact of bad multitasking in a project management environment is much, much worse. Let's look at an example. Suppose you have three projects (see Figure 12.1) that you are assigned to and in each project, you have estimated that you have 2 weeks (10 days) of work on each project for the tasks assigned to you. Assuming Murphy didn't strike, if you started and finished Project 1 without stopping or working on any other project, it would be done in 10 days. Ten days because that's what you told everyone it would take (Parkinson's Law). But having laid it out like this, if all three projects were scheduled to start on the same day, then Project 1 would be on time at 10 days, Project 2 would be done in 20 days, but would be 10 days late, and Project 3 would be done in 30 days, but would be 20 days late. Likewise, for Projects 2 and 3, assuming no other interruptions, each would take 10 days to complete for a total time to complete the three

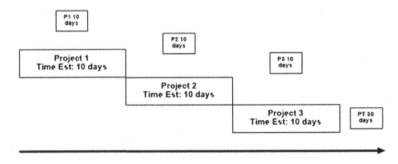

FIGURE 12.1
Three projects.

projects of 30 days. But CPM doesn't usually work like this in a multi-project environment.

Because there are probably three different project managers, each one is most likely telling you (or maybe even screaming at you) that they need you to show progress on their project (remember, projects are typically measured by percentage of tasks complete versus due date). You want to satisfy all three managers, so you decide to split your time between the three projects (i.e. you're guilty of bad multitasking). So, as is demonstrated in Figure 12.2, you start with Project 1 and work on it for 3 days. On the fourth working day, you begin Project 2 and work on only it for 3 days. You repeat this sequence until all projects are completed.

By using bad multitasking, look what's happened to the time to complete each individual project. Without bad multi-tasking, each project took only 10 days to complete and 30 days to complete all three. With bad multitasking, Project 1 took 28 days, Project 2 took 29 days, and Project 3 took 30 days, again with all of them finished in 30 days. Both methods completed all three projects in 30 days, but which set of results do you think your leadership would prefer? Having two projects done in 20 days and the third one at the 30-day mark or the results of bad multitasking? Keep in mind also, that when you are guilty of bad multitasking, there is also time required to get re-acquainted with each project, so the multitasking times

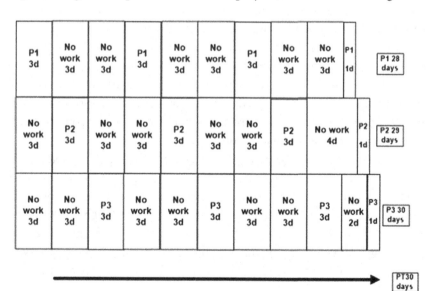

FIGURE 12.2
Splitting time between three projects.

will actually be considerably longer. In fact, some studies have shown that tasks often take two to three times their estimated duration when multitasking occurs.

So, let's summarize what we've learned before we move on. We've learned that task time estimates for tasks are artificially lengthened as a protective measure against Murphy and all of the negative baggage he brings to the party. We've learned that even though this safety is built in, it is wasted because of the Student Syndrome and Parkinson's Law. With the Student Syndrome, we put off work until the last minute, while Parkinson's Law says that if we're given ten days to complete a task, that's how long it will take, even if it is completed earlier. And finally, we've learned how devastating bad multitasking can be to the completion rate of projects and if we could eliminate it, we know our on-time completion rate will improve. Although eliminating bad multitasking improves our on-time completion rate, are there other things that can be done to improve these rates even more? Let's take a look.

As we've seen in CPM, task durations are inflated to protect against Murphy. What if we could significantly reduce these imbedded safety buffers and still provide the protection that we need? In our example from Figure 12.2, suppose we were able to reduce the estimated duration by 50 percent and still protect against Murphy. In other words, if we could complete the tasks in 5 days instead of 10 days, wouldn't this be a quantum leap in project completion time reduction?

Figure 12.3 depicts the 50-percent reduction in duration of each project. We have just reduced the time to complete these three projects from 30 days to 15 days, but can we do this and safely guard against the uncertainty introduced by Murphy? The answer is yes, we can! But before we explain how to do this, we want to introduce (or re-introduce to some of you) something called the Theory of Constraints (TOC).

TOC came on the scene in the mid-1980s through its creator, Eli Goldratt. Goldratt taught the world that every organization has at least one (and usually only one) constraint that prevents an organization from coming closer to its goal. And for most companies, the goal is to make money now and in the future. In fact, Goldratt analogized this concept to the strength of a chain being dictated by its weakest link. The best way to understand TOC is to envision a simple, piping system diagram as seen in Figure 12.4.

Figure 12.4 is a diagram of a simple piping system used to transport water from Section A through the remaining sections until the water

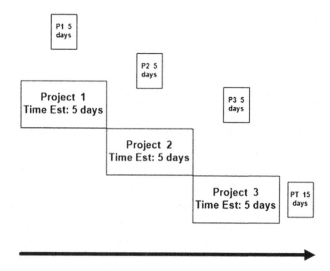

FIGURE 12.3
Reduced task times.

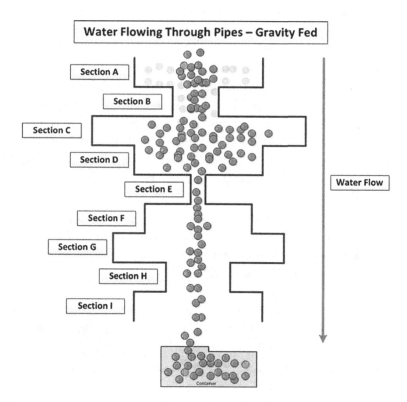

FIGURE 12.4
Simple piping system diagram.

exits through Section I. From a purely physical perspective, it should be obvious that the rate of flow of water through this system is limited by the diameter of Section E because it is the smallest diameter in the system. Equally obvious is the notion that the only way to increase the flow of water through this system is by increasing the diameter of Section E. Section E is referred to as the system bottleneck or system constraint. Increasing any other section's diameter would not result in any additional water exiting Section I. The question of how much larger Section E's diameter must be increased is completely dependent upon how much more water is needed.

With this simple piping structure in mind, let's now transfer these thoughts to a simple four-step manufacturing process shown in Figure 12.5. This process consists of five individual processing steps with the individual processing times for each step listed in each box. Step 1 requires, on average, 2 days to complete, while Steps 2, 3, 4, and 5 require 3, 7, 2, and 3 days on average to complete, respectively. The system constraint in this process is Step 3 simply because the total process throughput is limited by the slowest step in the process ... the system constraint. If this process was being initiated for the first time, the total cycle days for this process to deliver its first part would be the sum of the individual process steps or 17 days. Once this process is up and running, that is, the process is fully loaded, the fastest product can flow through this process shrinks to 7 days, meaning that we would produce one part every 7 days. Like the piping system, the system throughput is dictated by the system constraint.

TOC identifies Step 3 as our constraint and tells us that if we want to improve throughput, then we must focus our improvement efforts on this step. There are two key points that are made here:

1. Attempts to reduce the cycle times of non-constraint process steps that either feed or receive the output of the constraint do nothing to improve the overall output of the total process or system. Only improvements to the constraint positively impact the output of the process.
2. The focus must be on protecting the constraint from starvation because any time lost at the constraint is lost to the entire process.

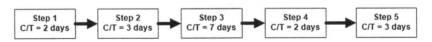

FIGURE 12.5
Simple five-step process.

The Theory of Constraint's five-step process of on-going improvement is as follows:

1. Identify the system constraint.
2. Decide how to exploit the constraint.
3. Subordinate everything else to the constraint.
4. If necessary, elevate the constraint.
5. Return to Step 1, but don't let inertia create a new constraint.

By using TOC to identify your company's leverage point (the constraint) and then focusing your improvement efforts on it, your company's bottom line can increase significantly. And if your constraint is external (i.e. lack of sales), the improvements made can become market differentiators to stimulate additional sales. So, let's get back to how TOC and Critical Chain Project Management (CCPM) positively impact project management.

Earlier we demonstrated how by simply eliminating bad multi-tasking, significant gains can be made in project completion rates, but we still have to address the impact of the Student Syndrome and Parkinson's Law. We know that both of these behaviors work to lengthen the time required to complete projects. Remember how excess safety is imbedded into traditional project management plans? Resources estimate task times and add in their own protection against disruptions caused primarily by Murphy. Knowing that this safety exists, resources then delay starting work on their tasks until the due date is close. Even if the resources don't delay the task starts and finish early, these early finishes are not reported or passed on to the next resource. So how does CCPM deal with these two behaviors?

While CPM relies on individual task durations as well as scheduled start and completion dates, CCPM does not. The focus is no longer on finishing individual tasks on time, but rather starting and completing these tasks as soon as possible and this is a major difference. So how does this work? Like CPM, CCPM still gathers estimates on individual tasks and identifies its own version of the Critical Path. Unlike CPM, CCPM considers competing resources (i.e. the same resource has to work on different tasks) and makes them a part of the critical path. Let's look at an example of how CPM and CCPM identify the critical path.

CPM defines the critical path as the longest path of dependent tasks within a project. That is, tasks are dependent when the completion of one task isn't possible until completion of a preceding task. The critical path is important because any delay on the critical path will delay the project correspondingly. Figure 12.6 is an example of a series of tasks which must be completed in a project with the critical path highlighted in gray. Traditional project management determines the critical path by looking at the task dependencies within the project. For example, Task A2 can only be initiated after A1 is completed. Task B3 can only be performed after completion of B1 and B2. Task D1 can only be performed after completion of A2, B3, and C2. Using CPPM, the critical path would have been identified as C1–C2–D1 (i.e. the longest path of dependent tasks) and the project completion estimate would have been 29 days (i.e. 8d + 12d + 9d).

In addition to task dependencies, there are also resource dependencies that CPM fails to recognize. What if, in our example, tasks A2 and B3 are performed by the same resource? Is the critical path different? In Figure 12.7, we see the new critical path that includes a provision for resource dependencies and as you can see the new critical path is A1–A2–B3–D1 or 5d + 10d + 10d + 9d equals 34 days. So, the minimum time to complete this project is now 34 days. In our opinion, the failure to consider resource dependencies is one of the key reasons why project completion rates are so dreadful. The simple implication of incorrectly identifying the critical path, which we will now refer to as critical chain, is that the project team will never be able to complete their project on time without heroic efforts, adding additional resources, overtime, or a combination of all three. The practical implication of incorrectly identifying the real critical chain is that the focus will be on the wrong tasks. Is this any different than focusing on non-constraints in our earlier discussion on TOC?

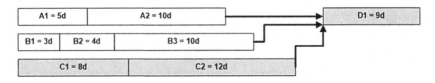

FIGURE 12.6
Series of tasks with the critical path highlighted.

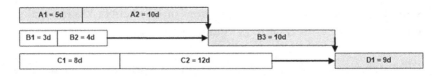

FIGURE 12.7
The new critical path.

Incidentally, this thing we call the critical chain is our system constraint, so by focusing on the constraint, we can maximize the throughput of projects in your organization.

We said earlier that safety is imbedded within each task as a way to guard against the uncertainties of Murphy. Critical Chain takes a completely different approach by assuming that Murphy's uncertainty will happen in every project. Unlike CPM, CCPM removes these safety buffers within each task and pools them at the end of the project plan to protect the only date that really matters, the project completion date. There are many references that explain the details of how CCPM does this, but here's a simple example to explain it.

By simply removing all of the protection from individual task estimates, the estimate is 50 percent of the original estimate. Figure 12.8 demonstrates the removal of this safety. So now, the length of the critical chain is no longer 34 days, but rather 17 days. But instead of just eliminating the safety buffer, we want to place it where it will do the most good … at the end of the project to protect the due date. This isn't exactly how this works, but for presentation purposes to demonstrate the theory behind CCPM, it will suffice.

Figure 12.9 is this same process, but this time the safeties that we removed are added to the end of the project to act as a cushion to Murphy's inevitable delays. Actually, we have added only 50 percent of the safety time

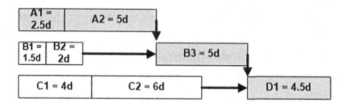

FIGURE 12.8
Removal of safety.

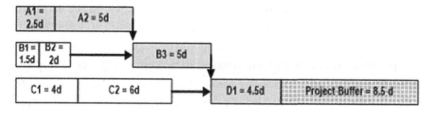

FIGURE 12.9
With safety buffer added.

removed to create the project buffer. So the question now becomes, how do we utilize this buffer and how does it improve the on-time completion of the project?

Suppose task A2 takes 7 days instead of the 5 days that are in the plan? In a traditional project management environment, this would be cause for panic. In a CCPM environment, we simply "borrow" two days from the project buffer and we're still on schedule. Suppose now, for task B3, we only take 3 days instead of the planned 5 days. We simply deposit the gain of 2 days back into the project buffer. In traditional CPM, delays accumulate while any gains are lost, but not so with CCPM. This is a significant difference! The project buffer protects us from delays. For non-critical chain tasks, or subordinate chains such as C1–C2 from our example, we also can add feeding buffers to assure that they are completed prior to negatively impacting/delaying the critical chain. That is, in our example, as long as C2 is completed prior to the start of D1, then the critical chain will not be delayed.

One of the key differences between CPM and CCPM is what happens at the task level. In traditional project management, we said earlier that each task has a scheduled start and completion date. CCPM eliminates the times and dates from the schedule and instead focuses on passing on tasks as soon as they are completed. This function serves to eliminate the negative effects of both the Student Syndrome and Parkinson's Law from the equation and permits on-time and early finishes for projects. In order for this to work effectively, there must be a way to alert the next resource to get ready in time to begin the next task. This is equivalent to a relay race where the baton is handed off from one runner to the next. Since the receiving runner begins running before the baton is handed off, very little time is wasted.

Earlier, we explained that in traditional project management we track the progress of the project by calculating the percentage of individual tasks completed and then comparing that percentage against the due date. The problem with this method is because we aren't considering the estimated durations that are left to complete, it is nearly impossible to know exactly how much time is remaining to complete the project. Using this method to track progress, it's not uncommon to see 90 percent of a project completed relatively quickly only to see the remaining 10 percent take just as long. In fact, looking at the number or percentage of tasks completed instead of how much of the critical path has been completed only serves to give a false sense of conformance to the schedule.

CCPM measures the progress of a project much differently and in so doing allows the project to make valuable use of early finishes. Critical chain uses something called a Fever Chart which is simply a run chart of Percent of Critical Chain Complete versus Percent of Project Buffer consumed. Figure 12.10 is an example of such a chart. In this chart, we see that approximately 55 percent of the critical chain has been completed while only 40 percent of the project buffer has been consumed, thus indicating that this project is actually a bit ahead of schedule.

The medium, light, and dark gray areas of the fever chart are visual indicators of how the project is progressing. If the data point falls within the medium gray area of the chart, the project is progressing well and may even finish early. If the data point falls into the light gray zone, there is cause for concern and plans should be developed to take action, but not yet implemented. Vertical rises such as that demonstrated in Figure 12.10 (Day 3) indicate that buffer is being consumed at too fast a rate relative to how the project is progressing. If a data point falls into the dark gray zone, then the plan we developed should now be executed. But even if the entire amount of project buffer is consumed at the completion of the project, the project is still on time and not late.

In addition to using the fever chart, we also recommend calculating a project index by dividing the percent of critical chain completed into the

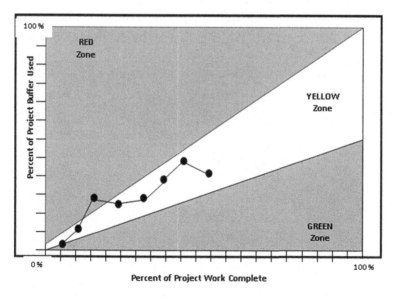

FIGURE 12.10
Fever chart.

percent of the project buffer consumed. As long as this ratio is 1.0 or less, then the project will come in on-time or early. In our example, this ratio would be 40 percent divided by 55 percent or 0.727. This ratio says that this project is progressing nicely with no concern for the project being late.

With most CCPM software, we can also see a portfolio view of the fever chart that tells us the real-time status of all projects in the system. Figure 12.11 is an example of this view and one can see at a glance that four of the projects (Projects 1, 4, 5, and 6) need immediate attention (they are in the dark gray zone), two projects (Projects 3 and 8) need a plan developed to reduce the rate of buffer consumption (light gray zone), and two projects (Projects 2 and 7) are progressing nicely (in the medium gray zone). Having this view enables the Project Manager to see at a glance where to focus his or her efforts. It is important to understand that just because a project enters the dark gray zone, it does not mean that the project will automatically be late. It only means that if expeditious action isn't taken to reduce the buffer consumption rate, the project could be late.

The net effect of CCPM will always result in a significant decrease in cycle time with a corresponding increase in the throughput rate of completed projects using the same level of resources. In fact, it is not unusual for project cycle times to be reduced by as much as 40 to 50 percent! These cycle time reductions and throughput increases translate directly into improved on-time delivery of projects as well as significant revenue increases.

The key to success using CCPM revolves around utilization of the true subject matter experts (SMEs). That is, by developing a core team

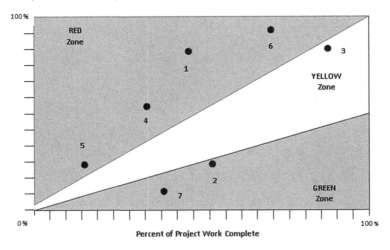

FIGURE 12.11
Portfolio view of fever chart.

comprised of 70–80 percent of employees actually executing projects (i.e. SMEs), and permitting them to develop the ultimate design solution, the resulting implementation will be owned by the people performing the work. This ownership translates directly into making sure the solution will work. Without this level of involvement and approval authority to develop the applied action plans, CCPM will simply not be as successful as it could or should be.

Another key to successful project management application is a series of regular meetings intended to escalate and resolve any problems that surface during the project execution. These include daily "walk-arounds" by the Project Manager with the SMEs to determine the progress of the project so that problems can be surfaced and escalated if the Project Manager cannot resolve them him or herself. In addition, I also recommend that each week or two there must be what is referred to as an Operations Review in which each individual project is reviewed for progress by the leadership team. Again, if problems and issues need to be escalated to keep the project on schedule, leadership must play this vital role.

Clearly, Critical Chain Project Management has demonstrated its superiority over the predominant Critical Path Project Management in a variety of industry settings with reported cycle time improvements in the neighborhood of 40 to 50 percent. And with project completion rates above 90 percent, it is no wonder that organizations that rely on project completions as their revenue source are flocking to CCPM. Organizations like the Department of Defense (DoD), where rapid maintenance of aircraft and other military vehicles is paramount to success, and software development companies have had incredible success using CCPM versus CPM. So, if your organization is a project-based one, CCPM will take you to a new level of success.

PROJECT MANAGEMENT CASE STUDY SUMMARY

My first experience with CCPM came when I was working at a military base responsible for training future helicopter pilots. I worked for a maintenance contractor and was in charge of Continuous Improvement at the base. One day I came across a white paper on the benefits of CCPM, and in this paper, there were claims of 40- to 50-percent reduction in cycle times. I was curious to see if this might apply to our aircraft maintenance activities, so I contacted the software company making these claims. After much discussion, the company agreed to visit our site and discuss potential work.

At this military base, there were numerous helicopter airframes that required scheduled preventive maintenance after completing "x" number of hours of flight time. After much discussion with this software provider, as a group we elected to use their services in the area of scheduled maintenance. We selected our most important fleet of helicopters to "test out" this group's software. And with this agreement in place, we began our journey.

Phase 1: Analysis and Consensus

This phase involves some data collection and analysis by the Software Company. This is then followed by two critical workshops. The first workshop is the leadership workshop, followed by a workshop for the core team. The objective of this workshop was to build consensus on the rules of Critical Chain, as well as to build a high-level solution of how Critical Chain will be applied to the helicopter fleets.

The deliverables of this phase were:

- The leadership team is in full agreement to implement the rules of Critical Chain.
- A "high level" solution of how the Critical Chain rules will be applied to the helicopter line(s) has been understood and agreed upon by the leadership team as well as the core team.
- A detailed implementation plan for the next phase will have been created.

This phase was expected to take about 2 to 3 weeks and is detailed in Table 12.1.

The Phase 1 plan was successfully implemented with all activities completed on time and as described in Table 12.1. With this successful completion, our team then moved on to Phase 2 of our implementation.

Phase 2: Solution Design and Setup

This phase involves detailing the Critical Chain solution, building the production network, building the pipelining model, setting up of the Critical

TABLE 12.1

Phase 1 Plan

Step	Description	Duration	Attendees
1	*Data Collection and Analysis*: In this phase, the software company team will understand the helicopter line operations. This team will have several one-on-one meetings with various levels of site management to understand the current operations, challenges, current processes, etc. Following this, the software company team will analyze the data and prepare for the next step	2 days	As required for one-on-one 1-hr. meetings.
2	*Leadership/Top Management Workshop*: In this workshop, the top management will understand the rules the rules of Critical Chain and discuss how to apply the rules to the helicopter line. The management team will then set a target for cycle time reduction and also form the Implementation Core Team. The agenda is as follows: • Improvement potential • Rules of Critical Chain • Software walkthrough • High level solution (policies, processes, and practices) • Implementation targets • Formation of core team	1.5 days	Top Management of helicopter line Software Co. Implementer
3	*Solution Design Workshop*: In this workshop, the core team will understand the rules of Critical Chain and create the next level of detail of the solution. The Agenda is as follows: • Planning and execution challenges • Uncertainties and their impact • Vicious cycle in projects and its impact • Rules of Critical Chain • Software Overview • Applying the solution to the helicopter line	3 days	Core team Software Co. Implementer

(Continued)

TABLE 12.1   (CONTINUED)

Phase 1 Plan

Step	Description	Duration	Attendees
6	*Implementation Planning for Phase 2*: The Software Co. implementer and the core team will create a detailed implementation plan for the next phase. The agenda: • Implementation goals and obstacles • Implementation tasks and checklists • Implementation roles and responsibilities • Implementation management/review process	1 day	Core team Software Co. Implementer
7	*Presentation to Leadership and Decision*: The core team will present the following to the leadership: • TOC solution as applied to the aircraft line • Phase 2 implementation plan	0.5 day	Core team, Leadership, Software Co. Implementer
	BUFFER	1 week	
	TOTAL	2–3 weeks	

Chain software, and training all the users on the software and Critical Chain concepts and then "going live" with the new process and software.

The deliverables for Phase 2 were:

- The production network template created and Critical Chain analysis completed on the template.
- The "pipeline" model created which means:
    - The production network has been customized for each helicopter and loaded in the Critical Chain Software.
    - The capacity model has been created and loaded in the Critical Chain Software.
    - A Work-in-Process (WIP) reduction strategy has been formulated and put in place.
    - The solution design completed which means:
        - Management processes have been defined.
        - Roles and responsibilities have been defined.
        - The performance metrics have been defined.
- Critical Chain software (server and clients) is installed.
- All managers and users have been trained in the concepts, the new processes, and Critical Chain software.

- GO-LIVE. The milestone of this phase was GO-LIVE which was expected to happen about 8 to 12 weeks from the start of this phase. At the GO-LIVE point, the entire aircraft line will be managed using the critical chain solution.

All Phase 2 activities were completed and all deliverables were met. We were now ready for Phase 3.

Phase 3: Stabilization

After "Go Live," there is a period of stabilization, where coaching and hand-holding is provided to the managers so that they can get used to the new way of managing. Periodic analysis and course corrections will be made as required. This phase was expected to last 8 to 12 weeks and was completed on time.

TRAINING

The most important part of this CCPM implementation was the training for both the executives and the core team. It was imperative that both groups completely understood their roles in this important initiative. The executives within the organization were the first to receive their training with three critical rules as seen in Figure 12.12.

Rule 1, Pipelining/Low WIP, explains that we must stagger the project starts and limit the number of projects in execution. The projects were seen as each individual helicopter having scheduled maintenance completed. Rule 2, Buffering/Reducing Cycle Time, means that we should never turn task estimates into commitments and that we should create aggressive plans with 50-percent buffers. Rule 3, Buffer Management, tells us that we must prevent wastage of buffers in execution and that we should strictly follow task priorities. Both groups were then presented with their roles and responsibilities as outlined in Figure 12.13.

All Supervisors/CSP manager and the Assistant Airfield Manager were then instructed to conduct at least two walk-arounds per shift. During these walk-arounds, it was explained that they will focus on ensuring tasks are being completed in order of priorities, and no issues remain pending. Figure 12.14 is a summary of what should happen during the daily production management meetings.

THE THREE RULES

RULE 1: PIPELINING/LOW WIP
- Stagger project starts
- Limit the number of projects in execution

RULE 2: BUFFERING/REDUCING CYCLE TIME
- Don't turn task estimates into commitments
- Create aggressive plans with 50% buffers

RULE 3: BUFFER MANAGEMENT
- Prevent wastage of buffers in execution
- Strictly follow task priorities

FIGURE 12.12
The three rules.

General Roles	Maintenance Contractor Roles	Responsibilities
Task Manager	1. CSP Lead/Supervisor 2. Sheet Metal Lead/Supervisor 3. Avionics Lead/Supervisor 4. Test Flight	1. Assign resource based on task priorities 2. Update tasks and checklist 3. Resolve issues 4. Shift-to-shift tie-in
Project Manager	1. CSP Manager	1. Customize tail number from template 2. Maintain template 3. Walk-arounds 4. Assign surge crew
Helicopter Portfolio Mgr.	1. Airfield Manager/Deputy Manager	1. Resolve issues 2. Assign surge crew 3. Monitor resource bottlenecks 4. Release control 5. Walk-arounds
Contract Executives	1. Customer Executive 2. Maintenance Executives	1. Monitor performance 2. Address manpower and policy type issues

FIGURE 12.13
Roles and responsibilities.

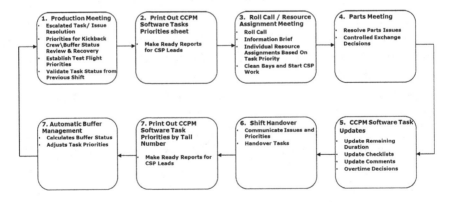

FIGURE 12.14
Daily production management meeting structure.

With all of the necessary training completed, we were now ready to begin our journey into "our unknown" world of project management, according to the rules of Critical Chain Project Management.

THE RESULTS

The first line of helicopters worked on was the largest fleet. Prior to CCPM, we had been using a modified version of CPM. Our average turnaround time to complete scheduled maintenance on this fleet of helicopters was approximately 75 days per helicopter, with little to no improvement observed over the past year. Much to our surprise, within 2 weeks, our scheduled maintenance time had been reduced from 75 days down to 50 days! But we weren't finished yet. We identified the system constraint, applied Lean and Six Sigma, and continued our time reduction effort with still more amazing results. In the next 2 weeks, our scheduled maintenance time decreased from 50 days down to a remarkable 30 days! Our team kept working on removing waste and variation in our scheduled maintenance process and were actually able to reduce the time down to a remarkable 20 days! Imagine going from 75 days to 20 days in less than 6 weeks!

As excited as we were, there was a problem that arose as a result of our dramatic improvement in scheduled maintenance time. Because the time had been shortened so much, we found ourselves working on helicopters which still has flight hours left on them before scheduled maintenance was required. After studying the flow of helicopters into and out of the maintenance hangar, we calculated the optimal time, in terms of flow, and it turned out to be 25 days. We involved the maintenance workers and asked them if they could slow down by 5 days. They agreed, but the level of pride they had was clearly evident for all of us to see.

We then moved on to other helicopter frames applying CCPM and achieved the same kind of results on each helicopter fleet. In fact, our average percent reduction in scheduled maintenance time across all helicopter fleets was approximately 55 percent! Needless to say, our airfield complex became the model for many other locations and the rest, shall we say, is history!

I want to finish this chapter with a Summary Table of Differences between Critical Chain Project Management and Traditional Project Management published by Process Quality Associates Inc. [6], and as you will see, the difference is truly revealing! (Table 12.2).

TABLE 12.2

Summary of Differences Between CCPM and CPM

Critical Path Project Mgt (CPM)	Critical Chain Project Mgt (CCPM)	Benefits Obtained from CCPM
1. Schedules worst-case task durations.	Schedules average task durations.	Task times do not collect safety time "fudge factors." Risk, stress, and effort are shared equally among all tasks and resources. People start to think differently than before. "Sacred cow" schedules are avoided. People can see what's really consuming the elapsed time. Management can manage, project durations are cut, people can go faster with less stress. Everybody and every resource are treated fairly and by the same rules. Ineffective hierarchies are broken down.
2. Protects individual tasks with safety time.	Protects overall project completion with buffers.	Safety time is not hoarded by individual tasks and people, but shared by everyone. Safety time is conserved and used most wisely over the entire project. Focus is placed on what is most important to the customer: speedy deliverables.
3. Emphasizes task progress.	Emphasizes project progress.	Everybody sees the "Big Picture." Micromanagement is avoided. Project Managers have a consistent outlook through the entire project. Events that slow the project are constantly in the schedule spotlight. People stay focused on the problems. Problems get identified more quickly and get solved sooner.
4. Starts gating tasks ASAP.	Starts gating tasks when they need to start.	Critical and limited resources are not plugged up with non-critical tasks which block and slow critical tasks. This is similar to Fire Lanes and sirens on emergency vehicles. Non-critical traffic stays off the roads until the emergency vehicles have passed. Use of bottleneck resources is based on priority, not "first come, first served." Projects get completed faster.

(Continued)

TABLE 12.2 (CONTINUED)

Summary of Differences Between CCPM and CPM

Critical Path Project Mgt (CPM)	Critical Chain Project Mgt (CCPM)	Benefits Obtained from CCPM
5. Starts and finishes tasks at scheduled start and finish times.	Starts tasks as soon as predecessors are done, finishes tasks as quickly as possible.	Project is managed and implemented like a relay race. The baton always goes around the track at maximum speed. Runners pace themselves for hand-offs, so the baton never stops nor slows down. If you are carrying the baton, just finished carrying, or getting ready to carry it next, your activities are tightly monitored, controlled, and managed; all others are of lesser priority and have freedom to self-manage. People focus better, and projects get done faster and cheaper.
6. Makes resource contention a PM "fact of life."	Resolves resource contentions explicitly.	Bottleneck resource is identified by the CCPM schedule. All users of the critical resource are identified up-front and conflicts resolved. Project Managers only watch the critical resource; constantly focusing on what's important and preventing problems from occurring. Constraints are managed.
7. Makes multi-tasking a PM "fact of life."	Minimizes multi-tasking by setting priorities.	The terrible cost of multi-tasking is exposed. All personnel are trained on "bad multi-tasking." People hunt down and eliminate their own multi-tasking, multi-tasking forced on them by others, and multi-tasking done by others. This alone can cut project schedules elapsed time by up to 40 percent.
8. Reacts to uncertainty by changing priorities, expediting, and creating a new schedule.	Manages uncertainty by monitoring impact of events on buffer consumption.	Project schedules and their priorities stay consistent. People don't get confused, nor lost as readily. The impact of one project on all other projects is minimized. The entire organization stabilizes into busy and productive status quo activities, rather than chaos. People feel benefits from CCPM; they are more productive, less frustrated, involved. Their contributions and efforts matter. Morale climbs.

(Continued)

TABLE 12.2 (CONTINUED)

Summary of Differences Between CCPM and CPM

Critical Path Project Mgt (CPM)	Critical Chain Project Mgt (CCPM)	Benefits Obtained from CCPM
9. Makes task linkages and constraints reflect *ad hoc* or habitual scheduling decisions.	Makes task linkages and constraints reflect only physical scheduling requirements.	"Sacred cows" like "we've always done it that way" get challenged. People innovate. Opportunities are identified automatically. Historical systems are re-designed and changed to take advantage of theoretical opportunities; making these opportunities reality. Rate of learning in the organization and adaptability are maximized. Competitors are left behind with their old, non-competitive paradigms. You become a world-leader in your industry.

REFERENCES

1. The Standish Group Report © The Standish Group 1995. Reprinted here for sole academic purposes with written permission from The Standish Group. CHAOS.
2. Improving Public Services through e-Government, Public Accounts Committee, HC845, August 2002.
3. UK Online Annual report, Office of the e-envoy, November 2002.
4. POST Government IT problems since 1997, *Computing*, 13 March 2003.
5. The Standish Group Report © The Standish Group 2007.
6. Process Quality Associates, Differences between Critical Chain (CCPM) and Traditional Project Management.

13

Mafia Offers and Viable Vision

If you are an owner of a business, then you are probably always looking for ways to make more money now and in the future, doing whatever it is that your company does. You might be thinking that the one surefire way to do this is by simply beating your competitor's prices for your products or services. But what if there was a different way to do this? Would you be interested in finding out how this was possible?

What if I told you that rather than focusing on offering your product or service at a cheaper price, you might want to increase the value of your product or service to a level that your customers would have a hard time refusing your offer? This is the essence of a Mafia Offer. Remember in Chapter 7 when I explained how I developed my own Mafia Offer? And in my last book, I dedicated an entire chapter to Mafia Offers.

In this chapter, I am going to present the basics of how you can develop your own Mafia Offer. Things like giving more of your product or service at the same, or even an increased price, than you do now. Mafia Offers rely on offering a proposal to each and every customer that they absolutely would having trouble refusing and by doing so, you would ensure your profits would jettison upward. Mafia Offers work and are on the cutting-edge of an improvement method known as the Theory of Constraints, or TOC. TOC is the backbone of the Mafia Offer, and in this chapter, I want to demonstrate just how to create one.

Dr. Eli Goldratt first introduced the concept of a Mafia Offer in his book *It's Not Luck* [1], but he later defined it as "an offer too good to be refused." Dr. Lisa Lang defines a Mafia Offer as, "An offer so good that your customers can't refuse it and your competition can't or won't offer the same" [2]. Dr. Lang tells us that the first question that must be answered is, "Do you have a Market Constraint?" A market constraint simply means that you have more capacity than you do orders. So, if I asked you this same question, how would your company answer it? Dr. Lang also asks the question, "If I could show you how to increase your sales tomorrow by twenty percent, could you handle this increase while being 100 percent on time, to your very first commitment, without going into a fire-fighting mode, and still maintain a competitive lead time?"

And finally, Dr. Lang tells us that if the only way you could handle the increase is to increase your lead times, work overtime, or maybe even miss due dates, then you have an internal operational constraint [2]. In other words, you don't have a market constraint. On the other hand, if you can answer yes, and you could take a 20-percent increase in sales, and not have any negative effects, then you do have a market constraint or perhaps a sales process constraint.

DO YOU HAVE A DECISIVE COMPETITIVE EDGE?

So, what should be your next step if your answer is: "Yes, I have a market constraint"? You will need to consider the operational improvements required for a Mafia Offer, also referred to by Dr. Lang as the decisive competitive edge, operational advantage, or competitive advantage.

To help you create a Mafia Offer, Dr. Lang tells you to answer two very important questions

- "Why should customers buy from you?"
- "Why should customers choose you over the other suppliers?"

So, before you read any further, take a few minutes now to answer these two questions [2].

THE ANSWERS

Dr. Lang tells us that most people answer the two questions above as follows [2]:

- Because we have outstanding quality and it's better than the competition.
- Because we have a great reputation in our industry.

- Because we get good results for our customers.
- Because we have very knowledgeable employees with very low turnover.
- Because we're very responsive to our customer's needs.
- Because we're very innovative and we help our customers to …
- Because you can trust us.

Did you write some version of these same responses on your list or did you write different ones?

The key point here is that if you're just saying the same thing as your competition, then you're not really providing any compelling reasons why your customers should buy from you. The fact is, if you and your competitors are saying the same things, then why shouldn't your customers just choose their suppliers based upon the lowest purchase price? The other key point here is that if you want customers and prospects to buy from you, then you must give them a compelling reason to do so! In other words, you must have some kind of competitive edge that makes your product superior to your competitions.

Therefore, if you want your sales revenue to increase, you need to start by creating a good Mafia Offer because a good Mafia Offer delivered correctly is the solution to the market constraint. So, the real question that must be answered is, how do we create a good Mafia Offer? Before going any further, I would encourage all readers of this book to read Dr. Lang's book [2], Dr. Goldratt's book [1], and finally, Gerald Kendall's book entitled *Viable Vision: Transforming Total Sales into Net Profits* [3].

If you are a typical business owner or manager, you are always looking for ways to become much more profitable. Ensuring that your business is successful is not simply a matter of beating your competition's prices or services. Instead of focusing on offering a less expensive product (or service) to your customers and prospects, what you really should be doing is working on increasing the value of your product or service to a level that they cannot refuse your offer? This is the heart of a good Mafia Offer.

A Mafia Offer is an offer that can be crafted for any and all businesses with the net result being a customer or prospect order closure rate of 80 percent or more. Think about that for a minute. Eight out of ten offers being closed by all customers and prospects who review your products or services offerings. Sound too good to be true? The truth is, if a Mafia Offer is put together the right way, it is entirely possible to achieve an 80-percent closure rate! If customers and prospects say yes to 80 percent of your offers, imagine what would happen to your profits!

The foundation for a good Mafia Offer is based upon using and capitalizing on the lessons from the Theory of Constraints (TOC). You are very much aware that the concept of supply and demand is behind every instance of buying and selling. The bottom line is that even if it costs you near nothing to produce a product, if the demand is high, then you will be rewarded with a high market price. Market price and value are functions of supply and demand.

What if you could develop a way to significantly increase the demand for your products that was well above your competitors? Doesn't this translate into your company's products being able to be sold for a much higher price than your competitor will? A good Mafia Offer is an offer that is so good that it would be illogical for your customers and prospects to turn it down. In other words, it would be illogical for your customers and prospects to buy that product or service from anyone but you.

Dr. Lang explains that "the Theory of Constraints tells us that in any business, there is always an internal or external constraint that limits the system's performance relative to its goal" [2]. This means that in terms of profitability, profits will not be improved until the constraint is first identified and then exploited. The Mafia Offer builds on this fact and has as its basis, focusing on constantly improving the output of the constraint and then constructing an offer that is so good that customers and prospects will actually pay more for your products because of their perception of value for your products or service.

EXAMPLES OF SIMPLE MAFIA OFFERS

Perhaps the best way to truly understand what a basic Mafia Offer might look like is to see some common examples that you have probably seen on television or the internet.

1. Hyundai, which made this offer at the beginning of our country's last recession. In their advertisement they let the general public know that if their customers happened to get laid off during a two-year period, they would buy back your new car.

2. Domino's Pizza told the general public that they deliver fresh, hot pizza in 30 minutes or less—or you eat it for free! When this ad appeared, it was somewhat of a turning point in pizza delivery. Prior to this, no pizza company had ever presented an offer quite like this one.

3. Amazon Prime might be one of the best examples of a Mafia Offer, especially for such a giant in the online world of eCommerce. Their mafia offer tells customers that for $99 per year, customers get free shipping on all Amazon Prime products, a 30-day free trial for risk reversal, unlimited music streaming, and tons of other bonuses.

4. Netflix presents a Mafia Offer, which might be why they became so popular, so quickly. Their offer is a free one-month trial, and it offers customers the chance to watch shows and films from anywhere in the world, as well as the option to cancel their subscription at any time.

DEVELOPING A STRONG MAFIA OFFER?

Dr. Lang tells us that in order to develop a good Mafia Offer, there are three general questions that you must answer honestly [2]:

1. What are your capabilities? That is, what are they and what could they be, compared with your competition. Your capabilities are how you deliver your product or service and include things like:

   - How's your lead time from the time you take the order until the order is delivered? Is your lead time better, worse, or the same as your competitors?

   - How's your due date performance compared with your competitors? Are you mostly always on time or are you sometimes late?

   - How's the delivered quality of your products compared with your competition? Is your customer delivery quality up near 100 percent or are you much lower? Are you better or worse than your competitors?

   - How's your responsiveness to your customer's needs? Do your customers ask for your help and do you respond quickly and effectively?

274 • *Theory of Constraints, Lean, and Six Sigma*

Your answers to these questions (and others) represent your capabilities and it is these capabilities that you will use to develop your Mafia Offer. Think about it, if you aren't able to differentiate your company from your competitions, then you can't expect to generate significantly more sales.

2. How do you and your competitors sell your products? The second thing to look at to develop your Mafia Offer is how your industry sells their products. There are many questions that will fit your specific industry, but here are some examples that might apply to your company:
   • Is it industry practice to use a price/quantity curve or is there another way you determine your selling price?
   • Is your selling price the same as your competitors or are you higher or lower?
   • How do you and your competitors typically charge for your products?
   • Do you charge by the piece or by some lot size? By the project (which includes time and materials)? Or do you or your competitors charge a flat rate?
   • Who pays for shipping costs of your products? Is it you or is it your customers? How do you compare with your competitors?
   • Are you paid at the start, at the end, or are progress payments used?
3. How are your specific customers impacted by your capabilities and how your industry sells its products or services?

The key is to understand how your industry interacts, in the selling and delivering of your products/services, to your typical prospects and customers. How are your customers impacted by your industry's typical capabilities and how your industry sells? Since your customers are the only real judge of your Mafia Offer, you need to understand how good your current capabilities are compared with your competitors, how the companies in your target market view them compared with your competitions, and how your customers and prospects are affected by the way you sell them.

It is in these interactions and interfaces that could be causing negative effects for your customers and prospects. By understanding these potential negative effects can lead you to uncover your core problem relative to doing business within your industry. Look closely at these three general questions and answer them honestly as they apply to your industry and your company.

In the *Theory of Constraints Handbook*, Chapter 22, Dr. Lisa Lang provides numerous examples of what a good Mafia Offer looks like for a variety of industries [2]. One of the things we know from the first law of forecasting is that forecasts are always wrong. The second law of forecasting tells us that the further into the future you go, forecasts become even more wrong.

If the forecast is too low, then production lines go down and throughput and revenue go down. In addition, when the product is eventually received, companies are forced to work overtime to play catch-up. In addition, because companies are forced to expedite shipments, profits erode even more.

If the forecast is too high, then carrying costs increase and cash is tied up in unnecessary inventory. In addition, damage and obsolescence increases which also eats into profits. So, if forecasting isn't a good way to order future products, what's a company to do? Here is a detailed example of a Mafia Offer which address these issues [2]. (Note: This example has been modified from Dr. Lang's Chapter 22 of the *TOC Handbook* to reflect a generic product.)

> Mr. Customer, don't give me orders based upon forecasts of how many pieces of product you need because forecasts are typically always wrong. Instead, tell us every day how many pieces of product you use, and we can guarantee on the one hand, that you won't have to hold more than two weeks-worth of our products. And you know that your marketing department was complaining that they can't make the changes they want because you have six months-worth of inventory? Well, now you will only have two weeks. On the other, at the same time we will guarantee that we will never have stock-outs. And if we ever do stock you out, we will pay you xxx$'s [sic] per day per part. We offer you all of this at the same competitive price you pay today and of course you will have a lot less cash tied up.

Take some time to analyze this Mafia Offer and imagine how you would react to it if one of your suppliers made you this offer. Look closely at the benefits and guarantees and ask yourself, "How could I possibly turn down this offer?" Think about what it would mean if you only had to hold two weeks-worth of your supplier's products without any worries of stock-outs. And if you did have a stock-out, this supplier would pay you xxx$s per day per part. Think about what happens to your cash on hand.

Here's another example of a mafia offer that addresses lead times.

> Mr. Customer, we know that everyone quotes a 4-week lead time but rarely does anyone ever deliver in 4 weeks. This causes you to juggle your schedule or sometimes your lines go down. So, we are going to give a 4-week lead time at our current competitive pricing, but we are going to back it up with a penalty. For each day that we ship late, we will deduct 10 percent per day off your order. And if we are 10 days late (which presently happens all of the time), your order is free. In addition, we know that sometimes your needs change because your customer has made changes, so we can also offer a 2-week lead time for 2 times price, but if we ship a day late we deduct 50 percent per day. And, in the rare case that you need it in 1 week, we will do whatever it takes. This is a 4 times price, but if we ship late, your order will be free.

This Mafia Offer guarantees a 4-week lead time on delivered products, but look what happens if they miss their delivery date. Imagine one of your suppliers deducting 10 percent per day off of your order, and if it is 10 days or later, then your order is free. In addition, this offer addresses changes caused by your customer. Yes, you pay more for an accelerated delivery, but again there is a provision for the order being late.

THE TEST: IS IT A MAFIA OFFER?

Dr. Lang advises us that "we should test the offer against our definition. Is the offer so good our customers can't refuse it?" [2]. Dr. Lang goes on to say that, "If we have done a good job with our analysis, it should be unrefusable to 80+ percent of the target market." She also advises us that no offer will be 100 percent accepted by any market. There will be some people, for whatever reason, that won't find your offer compelling. But imagine an 80 percent acceptance rate!

Dr. Lang tells us that "when we develop a Mafia Offer, we start by asking to whom the offer will be made [2]. We select a target market – a type of customer. The market we select can depend on a number of issues; for example:

- What market do we want to grow?
- What market has the best margins?

- Do we have too much business with one customer or in one market?
- Which customers or types of customers do we dread?
- What market has tons of room for us to grow?"

Let's look at one more good Mafia Offer from the consumer goods inventory. This offer is also from Dr. Lang's Chapter 22 of the *TOC Handbook* [2].

Mister Customer, we know that everyone promises sell-through and high gross margin, but places all the risk on you to forecast and manage the inventory. If the forecast is wrong, you miss an opportunity with fast movers and then end up discounting the slow movers. So, our offer is to manage our inventory on your shelf, and we guarantee we will meet or exceed your historical return on shelf-space or we will pay the difference.

SUMMARY

The Theory of Constraints tells us that in any business, there is always an internal or external (marketing) constraint that limits the performance of the system relative to the goal of your company. In other words, the constraint limits your company's profit margins. When you create a Mafia Offer, you are building a business proposal for customers and prospects that will guarantee the elimination of constraints and significantly increases their perception of the value of your products. The Mafia Offer is seen as unrefusable, and if it is written and delivered correctly, the acceptance rate by customers and prospects can be in the neighborhood of 80 percent!

In all three examples presented in this chapter, the companies involved were required to examine their processes to identify and exploit or remove their constraints which permits you to give your customers what they want, while at the same time creating a condition that your competition is either unable or unwilling to match.

VIABLE VISION: COMPLEXITY VERSUS SIMPLICITY

In Dr. Eli Goldratt's book, *It's Not Luck*, he explains that "within any complexity, there is an inherent simplicity that governs the throughput of the organization" [1]. Gerald Kendall tells us that "the fact is, you simply cannot break the system down into parts to find this simplicity. In fact, the opposite is true" [3]. In order to get a rapid and significant improvement in performance, it is imperative that we look at the entire organization as though it was a single system.

In many of my books, I have written how important it is that we find the system's leverage point (i.e. the system constraint) if we are to achieve huge jumps in system improvement. Likewise, to take advantage of this leverage point, all parts of the organization must focus on this leverage point. This is the essence of Kendall and Goldratt's Viable Vision. The fact is, if you don't have a Viable Vision for improvement, all you really have is a bunch of improvement projects.

Most companies address this idea of complexity by dividing the organization into small, bite-sized, and "manageable pieces," and then try to improve each individual piece. And since each of these pieces (i.e. different functions and departments) are typically cost centers, the order of the day is to focus on reducing costs in each function and this approach often leads to huge problems. Things like cost reductions in one part of the organization having a negative impact on another part of the organization is a common occurrence.

Creating a good Viable Vision typically results in major improvements in profitability. In fact, what Kendall tells us that "your future profits could and should equal your current sales dollars if your Viable Vision is constructed correctly" [3]. Kendall also explains that "in order to achieve the magnitude of results described by Eli Goldratt, we must establish a Viable Vision using a new frame of reference to manage the organization."

This new frame of reference deals with complexity by finding the inherent simplicity, the leverage point. As I've written about before, this guiding assumption is that improvement in the throughput of any system is governed by very few factors and it is these few factors are what drives the inherent simplicity. But the real question is, which factors must the management team focus their improvement efforts on to get the kind of results Kendall describes?

The guiding assumption behind Viable Vision is that improvement in the throughput of any system is governed by very few factors and it is these few factors that drive the inherent simplicity.

THE SILO APPROACH

As mentioned earlier, most organizations deal with complexity by breaking down their organization into functional areas and then demand that each area go figure out how to improve itself. Kendall refers to this approach as the "silo approach" for obvious reasons [3]. The important thing that we must understand is why this silo approach blocks the realization of a Viable Vision and fails to improve the system.

Kendall explains that "the cross-functional conflicts are driven by this silo approach where the organization measures each silo on improvement individually." If you are treated as an independent cost center (e.g., procurement, manufacturing), improvement typically means that you will focus on cost reduction and greater efficiency within your silo rather than improvement to the system as a whole.

In order to implement a Viable Vision successfully, it is clear that senior management must remove Cost Accounting distortions (e.g., how inventory is treated, make-buy decisions). Clearly, senior management must find a way to leverage its resources by identifying the "right place" to concentrate improvement efforts. This right place is, of course, the "system constraint" and nowhere else! Kendall explains that in order to improve the system [3], every senior manager (and lower-level managers) must overcome four major challenges as follows:

- Identify the biggest leverage point for improvement, not within your silo, but within the overall organization. Only such a leverage point can bring your organization to have net profits equal to total current sales within 4 years.
- Define what each part of the organization must do to exercise that leverage.
- Remove distortions by developing a deeper understanding and measurement system among all managers of the cause-effect ramifications of their decisions across the supply chain.
- Develop the logistical systems to alert the entire senior management team to the early warnings necessary to prevent disaster in their day-to-day operations. This will enable their major focus to remain on achieving the leverage.

DECISION-MAKERS SIMPLER FRAME OF REFERENCE

Kendall tells us that, "For the most part, top management teams use a holistic frame of reference (such as net profit or return on investment) to make decisions" [3]. The problem is that this does not mean that the lower levels of the organization do the same. The fact is, just as soon as the organization is segmented into isolated components and measured individually, non-holistic actions begin. It's clear that if we want to achieve our Viable Vision, according to Gerald Kendall [3], our new frame of reference must:

- Identify the huge leverage point.
- Connect every action and every decision at any local level to the impact on the remove the distortions.

Just to give you a feel for what has happened in other companies using this frame of reference, in a study conducted by Mabin and Balderstone of dozens of reported cases [4], the following mean improvements were noted:

- Lead time: 70 percent
- Due date performance: 44 percent
- Inventory reduction: 49 percent
- Revenue Improvement: 83 percent
- Profitability improvement: 116 percent

Based upon these results, Kendall tells us that "the first recommendation is: Move away from the super sophisticated, complex cost allocation system to a much simpler frame of reference" [3].

Kendall also tells us that "to be effective, the new frame of reference must act like a compass to guide managers, at any level, to make good decisions as indicated in the five major areas of judgement":

- *Judgement of the system as a whole.* We must be able to help managers at all levels, judge the impact of a decision in their local department on the company as a whole.

- *Investment.* In reality, an investment is only a tangible benefit to the business owners if additional products can be made and sold, or real costs can be eliminated.
- *Profit center.* Many organizations turn a part of their company into a profit center which is a mistake.
- *Make or buy.* If you are managing a plant that is under pressure to reduce costs, decisions like outsourcing to a "cheaper" source must be made based on system improvement.
- *Product cost/profit.* How is it possible for a company to cut a money-losing product and end up worse off than before? When a product is discontinued, many of the overhead costs don't go away, they're just reallocated.

So here is your roadmap for stimulating profit margins you probably haven't ever observed before. Mafia Offers and Viable Vision, two must-haves if you are to grow your company to new levels of profitability! Try them both and I truly believe you will be amazed at your final results!

REFERENCES

1. Eliyahu M. Goldratt, *It's Not Luck*, The North River Press, Great Barrington, MA, 1994.
2. Dr. Lisa Lang, Mafia Offers: Dealing With a Market Constraint, in *Theory of Constraints Handbook*, James F. Cox and John G. Schleier (Eds.), pp. 603–328, The McGraw-Hill Companies, 2010.
3. Gerald Kendall, *Viable Vision: Transforming Total Sales into Net Profits*, 2005 (self-published).
4. *International Journal of Operations and Production Management*, Spring 2003.

Index

Printed in the United States
by Baker & Taylor Publisher Services